About the editors

Ray Bush is professor of African studies and
development politics at the University of Leeds, UK.
He is deputy chair of the *Review of African Political Economy*. His most recent book is *Poverty and
Neoliberalism: Persistence and Reproduction in the
Global South* (2007). His work focuses on the political
economy of economic reform, resources, social and
rural transformation.

Habib Ayeb is a researcher at the Social Research
Center, American University in Cairo, Egypt.
His research focuses on agrarian change, water
resources, poverty and marginality. He has worked in
the Ministry of Agriculture in Tunisia, the University
of Paris 8-St Denis, CEDEJ (Centre d'Etudes et de
Documentation Juridiques et Sociales), IRD (Institute
of Research for Development) and the SRC.

Marginality and exclusion in Egypt

edited by Ray Bush and Habib Ayeb

Zed Books
LONDON | NEW YORK

Marginality and exclusion in Egypt was first published in 2012 by
Zed Books Ltd, 7 Cynthia Street, London N1 9JF, UK and Room 400,
175 Fifth Avenue, New York, NY 10010, USA

www.zedbooks.co.uk

Set in OurType Arnhem and Monotype Futura by Ewan Smith, London
Index: ed.emery@thefreeuniversity.net
Cover design: www.rawshock.co.uk
Printed and bound in Great Britain by the MPG Books Group, Bodmin
and King's Lynn

Mixed Sources
Product group from well-managed
forests and other controlled sources
www.fsc.org Cert no. SA-COC-1565
© 1996 Forest Stewardship Council

Distributed in the USA exclusively by Palgrave Macmillan, a division of
St Martin's Press, LLC, 175 Fifth Avenue, New York, NY 10010, USA

A catalogue record for this book is available from the British Library
Library of Congress Cataloging in Publication Data available

ISBN 978 1 78032 085 4 hb
ISBN 978 1 78032 084 7 pb

Contents

Tables and figures

Tables

Figures

Measures

1 feddan = 1.038 acres or 0.42 hectares

One US dollar = LE6.032 (Livres Egyptiennes, Egyptian pounds), January 2012

One UK pound sterling = LE9.361, January 2012

Acknowledgements

We are grateful to the Ford Foundation for helping to fund the workshop upon which many of these contributions are based. We are also happy to acknowledge their support and encouragement in the publication of this volume. Thanks are also due to Clare Smedley for editorial assistance. The usual caveats remain.

The book is dedicated to all those who lost their lives and who have been maimed and injured in Tunisia's and Egypt's 25 January revolution and the continuing struggle for political, economic and social justice.

PART ONE

Marginality, poverty and political economy

1 | Introduction: Marginality and exclusion in Egypt and the Middle East

RAY BUSH AND HABIB AYEB

Revolutionary upheaval in Egypt and Tunisia in 2011 has challenged many commentators to rethink their often limited interpretations of politics in the Middle East and North Africa (MENA). Ideas of an 'Arab mentality' or of Arab 'mice' content with 'political passivity' and of a region simply not ready for democratic deepening have been upset by momentous struggles to throw off the yoke of repression and struggle for new patterns of justice and equality (Fisk 2003; cf. Fisk 2011). Yet commentators have been reluctant to talk about *revolutionary* struggles. There has also been a reluctance to contemplate agendas set by, among others, independent trade unions and the Youth Coalition in Egypt which pushed beyond the initial framing of rising demands for political rights to advance root-and-branch social and economic transformation. Commentary and analysis on the revolutions have preferred to speak of an 'Arab spring' or at best 'awakening'. There was a 'season', it seems, of demands for citizenship, political and social rights and respect rather than permanent and persistent revolutionary challenges to transform exploitative political economies. Repressive political regimes in Egypt and Tunisia were built not only upon networks of local crony capitalist power but also Western, especially US and EU, collusion with dictators who promised guaranteed stability, prevented the ascendancy of radical Islam, especially after 9/11, and refused to challenge Israel's destabilization of the region with continued occupation of Palestinian territory and invasions of its Lebanese neighbour.

If one interpretation of the revolutions has been to view regional turbulence as the result of more or less spontaneous popular mobilization against repression and absence of the rule of law, another has been to see the uprisings in Egypt and Tunisia as the result of social media networking sites such as Facebook and Twitter. This narrative suggests that the revolutions were driven by new technology linking individuals to common causes of demands for improved human rights and the rule of law. Facebook helped mobilize protesters in Egypt sickened by the very public police murder of Khalid Said in Alexandria in June 2010. The role of social media sites in explaining the ousting of Mubarak was given credibility by an important icon in the Egyptian struggle. Google executive Wael Ghonim was imprisoned for twelve days at the start of the Cairo demonstrations in 2011, and he noted in an interview with the *Huffington Post*:

> I want to meet Mark Zuckerberg one day and thank him [...] I'm talking on behalf of Egypt. [...] This revolution started online. This revolution started on Facebook. This revolution started [...] in June 2010 when hundreds of thousands of Egyptians started collaborating content. We would post a video on Facebook that would be shared by 60,000 people on their walls within a few hours. I've always said that if you want to liberate a society just give them the Internet. [...] (Huffington Post 2011)

The uprisings, it seems, were now driven or facilitated by changes in communication technology. It helped network individuals and helped organize their mobilization, yet at the height of the revolution itself protesters were deprived of access to the internet. Mobile telephone companies, moreover, complied with dictators' requests to shut down communication networks.

Many interpretations of the revolutions and the role of Facebook share two immense flaws – something Rabab el Mahdi examines in more detail in Chapter 8. First, they fail to offer the historical context in which to understand the revolutions. By doing that they ignore more than a decade of resistance to autocracy. Secondly, they are reluctant to account for the social and class forces that created the revolutions. Working-class and peasant mobilization was the agent of change and remains a bulwark against counter-revolutionary challenges that have tried since the ousting of Mubarak and Ben Ali to impose the status quo ante. Failure to understand resistance as a product of social-class mobilization against dictatorship and political authoritarianism, as well as the power of many different marginalized groups, is a product of decades of neoliberal ideology. This is an ideology that focuses on individuals and their assumed 'free choices' and the sanctity of private property rights. Neoliberalism has deflected attention away from how social classes are constituted in conditions of capital accumulation and crony capitalism and how subaltern classes can mobilize to stop immiseration and challenge authority and dictatorship. None of this is surprising. Neoliberalism is a class project to reinstate capital accumulation after the capitalist crisis of the 1970s. In MENA reference to class has been erased from most of the academic landscape. Imperialism has promoted limited and partial economic reform, tied

4

dictatorships into programmes of aid and military assistance, softening demands for democracy by calling for (limited) political reform, governance and institutional change. The mechanism for promoting limited reform, and thus the sustainability of regimes that must remain stable, unless they can be replaced by direct military intervention, as in Iraq and Libya, was to fund and promote civil society advocacy. The irony is that the two MENA regimes that were closely monitored and received regular glowing reform reports from the international financial institutions (IFIs), and politicians in Washington and Brussels, were Tunisia and Egypt.

There has been a general refusal to understand the transformations that have taken place in Egypt and Tunisia as manifestations of resistance to wealth and power. Resistance has often been class based, from trade unions and farmers' associations and the autonomous actions of workers and peasants to challenge the reinstatement of a political economy that has promoted dispossession and increased inequality. After failing to recognize the strength of the revolutionary forces, after sticking with 'their dictators' for too long – until it was clear Mubarak and Ben Ali were being ejected from office – Washington and Brussels have tried to claim and co-opt the revolutions. Suddenly imperialism's erstwhile regional office-holders were dictators who blocked the people's claims for the universal rights of freedom and democracy. But as Marion Dixon has noted, the

> effort of claiming and co-opting is funneled squarely to prop up the neo-liberal agenda that has brought to the region much of what the movements have risen to reject – a revolving door between wealthy businessmen and ruling party members, monopolistic and oligopolistic economies, rising food and housing prices, slashed wages/prices and protections for workers and farmers, dropping standards of living with weakened public welfare programmes, heightened restriction of rights and liberties ... (Dixon 2011: 309)

The West has been active since the revolutions to bolster their interests, to contain revolution and re-create new stability for increased market access driven by the agencies of international capital, the World Bank and the International Monetary Fund (Bond 2011).

This volume of essays begins to uncover many of the underlying processes that inform why class and the mobilization of workers and peasants were so central to the revolutions in Egypt and Tunisia. The collection also examines groups of Egyptians who have existed on the margins of mainstream Egyptian society – street children, the disabled, women and farmers. Many of the essays were first drafted before the tumultuous events of 2011, for a workshop in Cairo in 2009. All contributions have been revised, however, and they offer a glimpse of Egypt's political economy that has been much neglected. The collection provides an important insight into how conditions for revolution in Egypt were partly structured by long-standing patterns of repression, economic inequality and social injustice. The volume provides an essential insight into how Egyptians who were marginal to the erstwhile ruling party's strategy of crony neoliberalism emerged to support the toppling of the regime.

The collection provides an important backcloth to the revolution, indicating why the depth of feeling against the Hosni Mubarak regime was so intense. The essays may help explain why and how the structures of the state were ultimately brittle when confronted by so much rage and anger. The level of opposition, its spread to the major cities and also rural Egypt, confronted an overwhelmed security apparatus that was initially, at least in January and February 2011, less openly supported by the military. The military actions since the revolution, especially through the coordination of the Supreme Council of the Armed Forces (SCAF) and its brutal attempts at quelling street protest, have frustrated, among other things, popular demands for the ending of military courts, summary arrests and routine detentions. The January revolution became not only a struggle against autocracy but also against the system that the dictatorship advanced: a neoliberal political economy wherein Egypt developed but Egyptians did not. The essays crucially expose why the struggles that toppled the thirty-three-year dictatorship of Hosni Mubarak and the twenty-three-year brutal rule of Ben Ali need to be understood not only in terms of the immediate and dramatic events of early 2011. They need as well to be set in a historical context of persistent and recurrent struggles of opposition to dictatorship and neoliberalism. And they have been struggles that have been driven by workers and peasants, organized and unorganized youth, the middle class and the dispossessed and marginalized.

The collection interrogates the concept of marginality. Some authors argue its importance as an analytical category and endeavour to show how the term can usefully describe a range of Egyptian empirical realities. It becomes clear that the concept of marginality is nevertheless ambiguous. It has often been used to account for the ways in which some people, usually seen as individuals, or parts of distinct social groups or categories of people, rather than as part of social classes, have been excluded or pushed to the periphery of economic growth or political development. The term marginal or marginality has a certain vagueness about it. It is used as a 'catch-all' phrase to encompass a range of very different situations. These may be situations of the most dramatic condition of poverty, or where individuals or groups of people experience merely a condition of less wealth or 'bad luck' compared with the 'average' person.

Significantly, the revolutions in Tunisia and Egypt were accelerated by young people without leaders or organizations or political party membership. The demonstrations in Tunisia and in Cairo's Tahrir Square quickly developed from protests against dictatorship, rigged elections and security-force violence to include agendas for radical transformation of the structures of political repression and economic power. Collectively the revolutionaries objected to the ways in which wealth was concentrated in the hands of a super-rich class of capitalists who benefited from close links with the state and the governing parties.

The essays in this collection begin to unpack a myriad set of perspectives on who in Egypt was seen to be marginal to national development and what the backcloth was to the revolution. Before the detailed case studies, Ali Kadri offers an important framework for understanding the regional dimensions of immiseration and an answer to the paradox of the region: why, when there is so much wealth, especially from oil revenue, is more than half the population condemned to a life of poverty? He convincingly argues that the people in the Arab Mashreq have not developed. There has in fact been a process of de-development of commodity production centred on the petroleum sector and repressive political apparatuses. And the region's autocratic rulers have been defended by the USA in its overall defence of energy supplies and Israel's sub-imperialist role as policeman for Washington, and the interests of capital in general. This has ensured a high level of militarization in the region and the social and economic costs that this entails. Thus the recurrence of war and the continual fear of it, and the occupations in Palestine and Iraq, create justifications for heightened militarization and the downward spiral of political repression. This series of consequences is not inevitable. Ali Kadri does not echo the 'resource curse' mantra of the inextricable link between resource abundance and underdevelopment. Instead he sees the repressive character of states in the region, and the marginalization of workers and peasants in them (including labour migrants), as a product of the epoch of contemporary capitalist development and the specific form that it has taken in the Middle East.

By locating the region of the Middle East in the context of global strategies of capital accumulation, Kadri's contribution raises questions about the efficacy of the term marginality. He exposes the idea that those on the margins may be more effectively incorporated into a declared policy of economic growth or political reform. This theme is extended by Ray Bush, who argues the importance of questioning the analytical veracity of marginality and exclusion. He argues instead that people's poverty in the region and in Egypt is the result of their exclusion not from government policy but from development. Capitalism is structured around class positions of wealth and power. The wealth of the capitalist class is based on their appropriation of surplus value from the exploitation of workers and peasants: if subaltern classes are excluded from wealth creation (marginalized) this is a systemic consequence of the capitalist organization of the political economy where this takes place. If marginalization is a direct and important dimension of capitalist development, the improved incorporation of the poor and those on the outskirts of the market economy will not reduce marginality or exploitation, it will merely sustain the reproduction of it. People are necessarily unevenly incorporated within capitalist relations of production and social reproduction, and this is clearly evidenced in Egypt. Improved incorporation of people who are poor, jobless and landless, without rights and much opportunity, will redress their 'marginality' only when commodity production is not organized for the private appropriation of *socially* created wealth.

If capitalist growth generates marginal people or the exclusion of workers and peasants, it also generates the promise and realization of opposition to the mechanisms that create impoverishment. Thus Asef Bayat offers a provocative account of how people's marginality may also 'provide space for alternative norms and lives, a place of respite and counter-power, by the very excluded and self-excluded'. The optimism and possibilities for struggle that exclusion creates is a theme that runs throughout this volume, making it unsurprising that revolutions succeed in ousting dictatorship. Reem Saad further problematizes the concept of marginality as referring to an individual or group of people situated on the 'margin' of 'society' or its global 'structure'. In everyday language, and also much academic literature, people's marginality or marginal status relates to extremely different and varied social categories and conditions. These definitions of marginality are various, multiple, contradictory and contested. Reem Saad argues that marginality can 'provide a greater impetus for change', and in some cases may have 'positive consequences'. She highlights her argument with two enthralling illustrations of women perceived to be marginal in Upper Egypt.

The centrality of struggle in the creation of opportunity for dramatic political transformation is captured in detail by Rabab el Mahdi. She shows in Chapter 8 how debates about marginality have tried to substitute for centrality of social class in understanding why and how Egypt's revolution emerged. She documents the ideological hold that neoliberalism has had in perspectives accounting for social transformation in Egypt, and the Arab world more generally. She demonstrates that 'the Egyptian revolution was the outcome of a historical process and not simply a momentary explosion'. In particular she highlights how labour protest dating back to 2006 created the conditions for the successful toppling of Hosni Mubarak.[1]

Part One of this collection locates debates about marginality in the context of poverty and political economy. Part Two explores how marginality and poverty are produced and reproduced with case studies of examples that have historically been somewhat neglected and obscured from focus. In addition to the global and regional context established by Ali Kadri in Part One, Habib Ayeb details the underdevelopment of agriculture in Tunisia and Egypt. He offers a comparative analysis of the revolutions by documenting their rural origins. He examines how immiseration of smallholding farmers is accelerated by neoliberal agrarian policy. He documents how and why the struggle to depose Ben Ali in Tunisia began in the countryside and what the policy failures for promising food security have been. He locates the reasons why rural struggles over access to land in Egypt fomented in the years leading up to 2011, and why and how legislation to reward large landholders increased rural poverty. In so doing he helps to explain why after 25 January rural struggles, land occupations and farmer demonstrations emerged, although they have still been underplayed, in trying to establish the debate about a future post-revolutionary agriculture.

Saker el Nour also focuses on rural impoverishment and the difficulties that were evident in the erstwhile Egyptian government policy of at least rhetorically geographically targeting the rural poor. The strategy employed by the government of Egypt was flawed, El Nour argues, and it failed to meet the targets of policy-makers. He argues that this was because of a weak understanding of who the rural poor are, that they were not identified effectively, that decisions about poverty targeting were determined by corruption and spoils politics, and that as a result the programme was ineffectual in reducing rural poverty and actually added to the wealth of the rich.

One of the key processes that combined and uneven capitalist development has promoted is a spatial dimension to the way in which

9

economic power and authority are maintained. In a fascinating account of spatial marginalization, Dalia Wahdan, in Chapter 7, traces how transport policy in the growth of a Cairo satellite city, Sitta October, captures 'the spatial dynamics of marginality'. She also accounts for government failures and corruption, institutional incompetence and individual venality in creating marginal residents who become dependent upon 'an ailing and overstretched transport network'. Crucially she contributes to an understanding of urban space (cf. Singerman and Amar 2006), highlighting how the Egyptian authoritarian regime used mechanisms to control the flow of labour into Cairo and how 'the driving motive of governing transport infrastructure and services in Sitta October sustained the economic power of the erstwhile Egyptian elite and its political stability'.

The case studies of how marginality has been reproduced under the erstwhile regime also include a compelling account of participatory action research with Cairo street children. Kamal Fahmi problematizes the difficult issues that confront workers with street children and also the tremendous dynamics and complexity of relations between children themselves as they deal with life on the street. The experiences of the dispossessed children and the attempt to assemble a strategy that engages with them, rather than alienating them further, will be an enormous challenge to a new Egyptian democratic government.

Two further case studies by Moushira Elgeziri and Heba Hagrass contribute to a discussion of two crucial issues in a period of possible democratic deepening in Egypt: its education system and the position of the country's disabled citizens. Elgeziri performs a crucial stocktaking exercise on the role of vocational training in Egypt. But she also goes farther than that. The country's education system has for decades been the source of fierce contestation about curriculum, teacher training, the delivery of teaching and learning and the widespread use of private tuition after school. She focuses on how young women from poor families seem to have internalized the historically changing socio-economic context of education and work. She shows how the women in her study make educational decisions and how the decisions may ultimately result in reinforcing their marginalization. This is because the decision-making about education and training for women is socially embedded within their families. She thus traces the ways in which technical education developed in Egypt from a strategy of promise to one which has served to marginalize those who take part in it. She also shows, therefore, how this marginalized dimension of education provision is synonymous with the poor.

10

Heba Hagrass examines the challenges facing Egypt's disabled people. She explores the scale of the difficulties that confront them, she situates their many different experiences in the context of local and international legislation that is meant to have met those challenges, and she highlights how the country's disabled identified with the 25 January revolution. The revolutionary slogan of 'change, liberty, social justice' was supported by Egypt's disabled. They also struggled to topple the government and the system that has undermined their livelihoods and they constitute an important element in the process of democratic deepening.

The case studies highlight how people labelled as being marginal have tried to oppose or struggle against the policies that have created their marginalization. The case studies provide an important summary of key dimensions of social policy in Egypt and the significance of the areas discussed for post-revolutionary reform. Rabab el Mahdi's argument about the centrality of the need to understand the role played by the working class in Egyptian politics and society is compelling. And as independent trade union struggles continue as part of Egypt's permanent revolution their significance will remain key to holding a new government to account.

The Tunisian and Egyptian revolutions are challenged by strong and deep-seated counter-revolutionary forces. They are forces of the old guard still entrenched in the state security apparatus and powerful business interests that remain central in the persistence of neoliberal economic policy driven by the IFIs and US geostrategic anxiety that a new Egypt may resist imperialist overtures. Struggles have continued since 25 January in Egypt between the military and demonstrators. The military were first thanked as guardians of the revolution but increasingly they are viewed as coup-makers and defenders of their own very considerable corporate interests. The SCAF has refused to open the books of the military, has declared that issues pertaining to the military's financial holdings will remain off limits, and it continues to argue that it, rather than the democratic popular will of the Egyptian people, will be the final arbitrator of the country's new political settlement. With this entrenched position the SCAF challenges political liberalization, unless it is very limited in scope or on its own terms as the generals advance the status quo ante. Anti-labour legislation banning strikes and demonstrations has challenged the key element of the revolution. The revolution had at its heart the aim to improve the living standards of the more than 40 per cent of Egyptians who eke out a meagre living on less than US$2 a day. It was also a revolution to legitimize the right of organized labour to strike, for Egyptians to demonstrate and organize democratically without fear of beatings and summary imprisonment, usually by military courts, and it was a struggle for openness and transparency in government: in short, it was a revolution to change the system that Mubarak and the ruling National Democratic Party (NDP) tried to orchestrate. The SCAF is obdurate in resisting calls for political liberalization but the revolution has made significant gains. It has deposed the brutal dictatorship of Mubarak, outlawed the erstwhile ruling NDP, identified and promoted the arrest of corrupt officials (although many court appearances of defendants have been frustratingly delayed). These gains and the continued struggle to prevent the redeployment of security agents, including the *baltagiya*, or thugs paid for by the interior ministry, will only be consolidated with permanent revolution and repeated occupation by revolutionaries of Tahrir Square. The human cost of the revolution has been immense: more than one thousand killed in the struggle to topple dictatorship and the structures that underpinned it, and many more people who have suffered terrible permanent injury, blindness and other disability. Those sacrifices are a spur to workers, peasants and the poor, who will continue an agenda of emancipation and social justice and ultimately confront the forces of law and (dis) order that want to persist with neoliberal orthodoxy in the face of its repeated failure. The new irony as Egypt's first election results after the revolution are confirmed is that the Muslim Brotherhood and more radical Wahhabi Islamist Salafi allies will form a government that will defend SCAF military interests and those of businessmen linked to previous crony activity, who were always the most vociferous, and brutal, critics of any Islamic trend. But this is only the beginning of Egypt's permanent revolution.

Note

1 For more detail on the historical account of labour unrest see El-Hamalawy (2008) and Solidarity Center (2010).

References

Bond, P. (2011) 'Neo liberal threat to North Africa', *Review of African Political Economy*, 38(129).

Bush, R. (2004) 'Poverty and neo-liberal bias in the Middle East and North Africa', *Development and Change*, 35(4): 673–95.

Dixon, M. (2011) 'An Arab spring', *Review of African Political Economy*, 38(128): 309–16.

El-Hamalawy, H. (2008) 'Egypt's tax collectors and the fight for independent trade unions', *Socialist Review*, December, www.socialistreview.org.uk/article.php?articlenumber=10654, accessed 18 March 2011.

Fisk, R. (2003) 'A million march in London, but faced with disaster the Arabs are like mice', *Independent*, 18 February.

— (2011) 'Revolution by Twitter as Egypt's corrupt regime clings to power', *Independent*, 28 January.

Huffington Post (2011) www.huffingtonpost.com/2011/02/11/egypt-facebook-revolution-wael-ghonim_n_822078.html, 11 February, accessed 13 July 2011.

Singerman, D. and P. Amar (eds) (2006) *Cairo Cosmopolitan. Politics, Culture, and Urban Space in the New Globalized Middle East*, Cairo and New York: American University in Cairo Press.

Solidarity Center (2010) *Justice for All: The struggle for worker rights in Egypt*, February, www.solidaritycenter.org/files/pubs_egypt_wr.pdf, accessed 18 March 2011.

2 | Marginality: curse or cure?

ASEF BAYAT

Introduction

In recent years there has been an explosion of interest in the notion of 'marginality'. Interest comes from fields of inquiry as diverse as psychology, literary critique, cultural studies, political economy, urban studies, and especially development studies. In most of these accounts, 'marginality' is treated largely in negative terms – as an undesirable state or process, or in terms of a positionality that places certain social groups and spaces, 'marginals', away from (or envisages them as excluded by) the 'centre' or the 'mainstream'. And the mainstream is perceived as the site of power. Thus, marginality is equated somewhat with a state of powerlessness or as characterized by life chances inferior to those in the world of the 'mainstream'. In this sense, the term signifies a structural process through which certain groups or entities become 'marginalized' from the 'centre' against their will.

There is certainly a great deal of plausibility in such negative conceptualization. After all, what name can one give to the substandard status and poor life chances of so many 'marginal' nations, classes, ethnic groups, age cohorts, gender groups and individuals with 'abnormal' lifestyles? For some, the state of marginality looks like an inescapable destiny; for others it is an encounter with which they have to cope. Yet 'marginality' may remain just a name, a mere designation, if it is not explored comprehensively as a meaningful social category. In other words, if we treat 'marginality' as a mere semantic, why not use the term 'exclusion' instead? 'Exclusion' usually signifies a structural process which condemns the subjects to an inferior status. 'Marginality' as a social category is more complex than just a name, and thus different from the reality of exclusion. I would like to suggest that marginality may not just be a curse; it can and does serve also as an opportunity – a space where those who cannot afford the cost of the 'normal' and the mainstream can survive and thrive. Thus, a marginal position may not be simply a state of powerlessness; it can provide a space for alternative norms and lives, a place of respite and counter-power, for the very excluded and self-excluded. In this

14

conceptualization, the term 'marginals' does not simply refer to the poor and working classes; the economically well off and people of prestige may also experience a state of marginality.

The term and its trajectory

It seems that the origin of the concept of 'marginality' in the field of development goes back to early twentieth-century urban studies in the USA. In fact, the discussion seemed originally to be (and in many ways continues to be) associated with the history of and debate over transition to modernity. And urban life and all that came with it became a concrete context, a laboratory, in which to observe and analyse how modernity was actually evolving. This is mainly a story of the late ninteteenth and early twentieth centuries in Europe.

The term appears to have been used first by Robert Park, one of the key scholars in the Chicago School of urban sociologists, in his 'Human Migration and the Marginal Man' (1928) (Perlman 1976: 98–9). For Robert Park, marginal man was a 'cultural type', a cultural hybrid – a 'man on the margin of two cultures and two societies which never completely interpenetrated and fused'. The marginal man is a migrant in the city, one who retains his original culture, and is not quite integrated in the new society. But this state is not all that negative. In fact, in contrast to the current prevailing perceptions, Park actually saw something positive in this marginal man, in that he is the one who could possibly initiate change and innovation in his society.

Following Robert Park, thinkers like Stonequist (1935) pushed this notion of marginality farther into the psychological domain, describing marginal man as displaying a 'double personality' and 'double consciousness' (Perlman 1976). Thus the rural migrant, as the archetype of 'marginal man', embodies a personality and consciousness that simultaneously carry both rural and urban attributes. And in this state of in-betweenness, he is perceived as someone who is confused and lost; he is imbued with anomie and alienation, acting as neither truly rural or urban.

Such conceptualization of the marginal character profoundly influenced the later understanding and studies of migration and poverty in both academia and social policy circles in the 1950s and 1960s. It became a principal model with which to examine rural–urban migration, migrants' behaviour and poor people's housing in the cities in transition. Marginality so understood moved later to inform the widespread debates about the issue of 'integration' – in terms of both the integration of rural migrants into the urban social fabric, and at the international level the integration of foreign immigrants into host national societies and cultures. Indeed, the current raging debate – and anxiety – in Europe over the presence of Muslim immigrants in today's Europe is deeply informed by such a depiction of marginality – a perception that postulates the Muslim community as refusing to become integrated into the 'European cultural fabric'.

An important legacy of this perspective in urban anthropology included Oscar Lewis's notion of the 'culture of poverty', which he formulated based upon ethnographies among the urban poor in Puerto Rico and Mexico. The culture of poverty perspective had a tremendous influence on the study of the urban poor and urban housing in academia. It also had a great impact on social policy, anti-poverty discourse and state policies on how to deal with ghettos, the urban poor neighbour-hoods and racial and ethnic minorities in the USA and Europe. For the most part, the 'culture of poverty' perspective equated the urban poor with 'marginal characters'. It attributed a number of cultural/psychologi-cal essentials to urban marginals and their 'culture of poverty' – such as fatalism, traditionalism, rootlessness, inadaptability, criminality, lack of ambition, hopelessness and so on (Lewis 1966, 1968).

The ideas of Park and Lewis, and those of later theorists travelled well beyond the USA and Europe into the academic and policy institutions of the developing world, in particular Latin America (Perlman 1976: 118–23). In the Middle East, the notion of 'marginality' – whose equivalents *hamishiya* (in Arabic), *hashiye-nishini* (in Persian) and *marjinalik* (in Turk-ish) are in fact the literal translation of the English term – structured the perceptions of mainstream researchers, planners, urban elites and policy-makers vis-à-vis the migrant poor. Indeed, there is little difference between the discourses of the European elites on Muslim migrants, Cairo elites on the *ashwaiyyat*, and Istanbul's privileged groups on the Anatolian migrants to the city. They all view their poor migrants as 'outsiders', as people who do not fit into the prevailing social fabric, but remain on the periphery of what they consider 'normal' life.

Marginality and modernity

Clearly Robert Park, Lewis and their co-thinkers had a great impact on our current thinking about the life of the urban subaltern. But Park himself had been influenced by an earlier generation of European observers, such as Georg Simmel and Ferdinand Tonnis. It seems that Simmel's idea of the 'stranger' as a social type is a precursor to the idea of the 'marginal man'. The 'stranger' is a 'social type' that navigates between 'detachment' and 'attachment', just as a trader wanders around in different social settings and communities to trade his merchandise. Even though Simmel does not attribute negative traits to the stranger/trader (in fact he perceives the 'stranger' as one who is objective and often receives intimate confessions from people precisely because of his neutral position), the stranger is still considered an abstract man, a social type, who remains remote from the norms of mainstream society and culture (Simmel 1950).

Principally, the formulation of marginality has been guided by a dichotomous paradigm whereby 'marginality' stands opposed to the 'mainstream'. In fact these writers on marginality were operating at a time when grand dichotomies and 'dualisms' had preoccupied the thinking of the major social theorists in Europe. Nineteenth-century industrialization had transformed Western societies. It had undermined certain established patterns of life, such as community, countryside, extended family and attachment, and had created new process and structures such as large cities, secondary associations, individuality, anonymity and national markets. Thus, Tonnis famously proposed *Gemeinschaft* (village or small town) in contrast to *Gesellschaft* or the metropolis. Emile Durkheim had formulated his 'mechanical solidarity' as opposed to 'organic solidarity'. Max Weber counterposed 'traditionalism' against 'rationality'; and Marx distinguished 'feudalism' from 'capitalism'. Probably the greatest of these dualities was that between 'tradition' and 'modernity', which in many ways reflected and encompassed all other dichotomies.

So it seems that the discussion of marginality in the context of urban sociology was closely tied to the question of modernity or its absence. Accordingly marginality was perceived as an attitude, behaviour and existence that stood against or aloof from modern conditions – modern institutions, rationality, the modern state and economy, modern behaviour and thinking. In this sense, 'marginal man' is a non-modern man – a perception that continues to underline the current thinking on marginality and the urban subaltern in diverse parts of the world. In this thinking, marginality is considered a social type or a positionality that derives either from the sociocultural traits of the poor themselves, from their supposedly 'essential' features, or from their particular ecology – the space in which they operate and subsist. At any rate, it is considered to be a fact.

Marginality and capitalism

Since the 1970s, however, such critical scholars as Janice Perlman, Manuel Castells and other scholars of Latin America insisted that marginality – understood as emanating from poor people's cultural traits – was a myth. For in reality the poor were not marginals, they argued, but rather integrated into urban society. To be precise, the poor are not marginal but 'marginal*ized*' – meaning that they are economically exploited, politically repressed, socially stigmatized and culturally excluded from a closed social system. Not only do the poor participate in party politics, elections and mainstream economic activities, more importantly they establish their own territorial social movements to advance their overlooked claims. Thus community associations, barrios, consumer organizations, soup kitchens, squatter support groups, church activities and the like were understood as manifesting organized and territorially based movements of the poor striving for 'social transformation' (according to Castells), 'emancipation' (in the view of Schuurmann and Van Naerssen), or an alternative to the tyranny of modernity, in the words of John Friedmann (Castells 1983; Friedmann 1992; Schuurman and Van Naerssen 1989). In their immediate day-to-day activities, the poor struggle for a share of urban services, 'collective consumption', and for the 'right to the city', as argued by De Certeau and others (De Certeau 1984).

Unlike the Chicago School sociologists, these authors worked broadly in the Marxian paradigm of structural and class conflict, even though they departed from Marx's own formulation of such subaltern groups in terms of the 'dangerous classes'. It is well known that, given the centrality of the working class as the agent of social transformation, Marxist theory did not pay much attention to the urban poor, or otherwise described them in terms of the 'lumpenproletariat'. However, in Marx's perception, 'lumpenproletariat' was not simply a misunderstood expression of anger or prejudice against a segment of the urban population. Rather, for Marx, 'lumpenproletariat' was a political economy concept; it referred to those poor people who (unlike the working classes) did not produce surplus or their own wages; they subsisted on the labour of others by resorting to begging, theft, bullying or criminal acts. Consequently, because of their peculiar position in capitalist class relations, these groups were susceptible to the 'politics of non-commitment', which in the end would work against the general interest of the working class. Hence the designations 'social scum', 'refuse of all classes' and 'dangerous classes' (Draper 1978).

The urban subalterns that Castells, Perlman and others like them had focused on were clearly different from the types of social subjects that Marx had in mind. The slum poor of Latin American cities were striving to earn a living; many of them did, but they were structurally placed in a more exploitative position – in terms of pay, conditions (work and life) and status. These subaltern groups had been excluded from the provisions of normal life chances by the very capitalist system in which they were operating. Some segments, such as the unemployed, the casual workers or the 'reserve army of labour' lacked even the chance to be exploited by capitalism! In short, in these critical treatments, the marginals were poor, and had been marginal*ized* by the larger structures of the political economy within a particular regional or national economy. Up to this point, the concept of marginality was applied largely to the local and national contexts.

Since the 1980s, with the rise and prevalence of debates about globalization, the marginality discussion moved from local and national situations into the global economies and the world market. The term 'marginalized' came to describe not only certain classes or social groups, but also poor nations and regions of the world, such as sub-Saharan Africa. This 'marginalized' characterization effectively replaced the earlier terms 'dependent' nations or the 'periphery'. This was not a merely semantic shift. It reflected a profound alteration of development discourse in the wake of the collapse of the communist or Eastern bloc and the end of the Cold War, when the designation 'Third World' was rendered obsolete. In the development discourse, this represented a shift towards the post-dependency paradigm. The new perspectives disclosed a radical paradigmatic shift, and indeed a discursive irony, when one thinks of the prevalent development discourse and debates of the 1960s and 1970s. In the dependency discourse of the 1960s and 1970s, poor countries were considered to be poor because they *were* integrated into global capitalism (i.e. they were exploited and subordinated by the centre, the metropolis of the global economy). But in the development discourse of the 1990s and 2000s, couched in terms of 'globalization', the poor countries were poor because they *were not* – that is, they were considered to be excluded or marginalized from the global economy and its developmental consequences (*inter alia*, Hoogvelt 1997).

In all of these deployments, the notion of 'marginality' – whether as a social group, class, region, nation or a group of nations and regions – refers primarily to a state of poverty, deprivation and subordination; and 'marginals' are invariably poor and stigmatized. But do they have to be so? In recent years there has been a significant shift on the question of who constitutes the 'marginals'. 'Marginality' has now been extended beyond the original status of the urban poor classes, or poor countries, to include also the economically well off – those who, nevertheless, are 'marginalized' in the political realm, or in the domain of lifestyles, or in their position as members of a particular gender, ethnicity, religion or sexual orientation. Thus, beyond the economic marginal, we can also speak of political and social marginals. In Egypt and Iran today, for instance, many people, including affluent individuals and social groups, may simply not be allowed to participate effectively in the decision-making processes concerning major domains of public life. Many are deprived of the right to run for parliamentary or presidential elections. In addition, most religious minorities in Iran are deprived of equal rights with Muslims. Coptic Christians in Egypt speak about their marginal position in the political system, even if they may be doing well in economic domains. Demands for a free choice of lifestyle – for instance, the choice over sexual orientation – remain as serious as those related to religious and ethnic rights, if not more so. Discrimination against and thus marginalization of homosexual individuals remains probably more widespread than that against other 'minority' groups.

In these domains, marginality does not necessarily signify, as it did in the classical case of 'urban marginals', a social location between two societies/cultures and being part of none. It rather means a social position of inferiority – one that is caused not by the actors' essential features, but by the dominant discourse, law and institutions. Thus defined broadly, marginality comes to mean distance or exclusion from the mainstream as the site of power. It means being away from or excluded from power; or being on the opposite side of hegemony. It means 'hegemony in reverse'. If this understanding is of any value, then a solution to marginal status would be to bring the marginals to the mainstream, to empower them.

Curse or cure?

But is marginality all curse, a condition of powerlessness and sub-ordination? Can marginality be a site of liberation, a locus of alternative power? Is it possible to see marginality as fostering practices of alternative lives – norms and behaviour, places of survival, respite and even flourishing for the very people who feel excluded or self-excluded?

We saw how Marxian urban theorists like Castells, Perlman or more recently Mike Davis viewed the shanty towns as spaces of exclusion where inhabitants were pushed by the structural workings of capitalism to undertake a life and work not of their choice but of necessity for survival (Perlman 1976; Castells 1983; Davis 2006). In contrast to such a prevailing position, a number of post-development scholars such as Arturo Escobar, Majid Rahnema, John Friedmann and others have recently looked at the Latin American *favelas* not from the perspective of poverty and misery but as domains of alternative social arrangement and life-worlds, where people subsist at a relative distance from the diktat of capitalist modernity. In the *favelas*, they argue, inhabitants are possibly in a position to practise principles of reciprocity, negotiation, flexibility and producing use value rather than market value – qualities that are downplayed and rejected by the capitalist mainstream (Escobar 1995; Friedmann 1992; Rahnema and Bawtree 1997).

There is certainly some truth in these latter arguments. However, the question is raised as to why only certain specific groups tend, or are put in a position, to practise such a 'marginal' life – one that invites such diametrically opposing interpretations. I tend to think that marginal domains are not all torment and subordination; they can also be seen as the realms of opportunity for the exertion of power. Marginal sites may foster survival, growth and alternative social arrangements for people who cannot afford to bear the cost of the 'normal' and the 'mainstream'. For marginal spaces (while they are deprived of the opportunities offered by the mainstream) are by definition free from the costs and constraints of mainstream economic and social life. Creative actors can turn the marginal locus into a terrain of vitality and invention, a possible place of counter-power. If, in Foucault's words, 'to govern is to structure the possible fields of action of others' (Foucault 1982: 220), then marginal life-worlds would subvert mainstream power, because they constantly cause anxiety by threatening to pollute the mainstream and disrupt its governmentality (Douglas 1966: 112–13). This may be true both in the context of the world system, and at the local neighbourhood level; it is pertinent to developmental/economic domains as well as social and cultural processes.

In the context of the world system, the argument for socialist revolutions in 'backward or marginal capitalist societies' was precisely based on the latter's 'weak links' with world capitalism, less capitalist resistance, and greater potential for change. Thus 'revolutionary socialist development in the Third World', as in Mozambique, Vietnam, Cuba, China, not to mention the classic case of Russia, seems to confirm the key role of the 'weak links', the marginal position, in transcending capitalism (White et al. 1983). Writing on colonia Africa, Albert Memmi in fact advocated that the colonized remain marginal, or maintain their independence from the centre, because the colonized were more privileged (Memmi 1991). How much these non-capitalist models succeeded in offering a viable life to the majority of their peoples is, of course, a different question – after all, most of them reverted back to market economies through the policies of the IMF and the World Bank. Yet, as some might suggest, the status of marginality may force certain nations to be, by default, more independent and innovative. Japan is said to have become stronger after its defeat in the Second World War than it had been previously because of this marginality by default (Davis 1997). But clearly Japan enjoyed a developmental infrastructure that most of the Third World non-capitalist countries lacked. Indeed, its story and destiny may arguably give credence to Marx's original idea, and indeed dilemma, that socialism may flourish not in the backward capitalist societies, but in advanced capitalism. The Marxian dilemma is that socialism might thrive in (advanced capitalist) societies and economies which display most resistance to radical change.

The dynamics of marginal spaces may perhaps be better explored at the micro, local or neighbourhood scales. A close look at the activities of the so-called urban marginals (such as squatters, street vendors, etc.), as I have shown elsewhere, would reveal that they pursue two major goals (Bayat 1997). The first is the *redistribution of social goods* and opportunities in the form of often unlawful and direct acquisition of collective assets (e.g. land, shelter, piped water, electricity, roads), public space (street pavements, intersections, street parking places), opportunities (favourable business conditions, locations, labels, licences), and other life chances essential for survival and acceptable standards of living. The other goal is *attaining autonomy*, both cultural and political, from the regulations, institutions and discipline imposed by the state and modern institutions.

In a quest for an informal life, the marginals tend to function as much as possible outside the boundaries of the state and modern bureaucratic institutions, basing their relationships on reciprocity, trust and negotiation rather than on the modern notions of individual self-interest, fixed rules and contracts. So they may opt for self-employed activities rather than accept the discipline of the modern workplace; resort to informal dispute resolution rather than the police; get married through local informal procedures (in the Muslim Middle East under local sheikhs) rather than by governmental offices; borrow money from informal credit associations rather than modern banks. This is so not because these people are essentially non- or anti-modern, but because the conditions of their existence compel them to seek an informal mode of life. Because modernity is a costly existence, not everyone can afford to be modern. It requires the capacity to conform to the types of behaviour and mode of life (adherence to strict time discipline, space, contracts, and so on) that most vulnerable people simply cannot afford. So while the disenfranchised wish to watch colour TV, enjoy clean tap water and possess security of tenure, they are weary of paying taxes and bills or reporting to work at specified times.[1]

The argument is especially pertinent in debates on the 'integration' of poor migrant communities – whether rural migrants to cities or (especially) those residing in foreign countries – in the mainstream society, economy and culture. For instance, in the current debate on migration to Europe, a central concern pertains to the 'marginality' of Muslim communities, their seeming failure to 'integrate into the mainstream life-world'. Migrants congregating in mosques or Muslim community centres, attending Islamic schools, wearing headscarves and exotic 'traditional' clothes and turning to non-European television programmes are seen as an anomaly in the social body of European societies. If 'integration' means a two-way process of give and take between different cultural collectives, then any real integration would involve movement from both minority and mainstream communities. The minorities are expected to interact with the mainstream, and engage in the economy, civil society and state institutions, while the mainstream is expected to facilitate such exchange and engagement, recognizing 'minorities' as a part of the national citizenry.

It is, however, crucial to realize that for the most part 'integration' is not simply a voluntary 'matter of will' process whereby individuals 'choose' or 'refuse' to integrate; nor are 'cultural groups' uniform collectives whose members supposedly hold the same aspirations, orientations and capacities. Rather, 'minority groups', whether Muslim or non-Muslim, each possess differential capacities for mixing and exchanging with the mainstream; they hold varied resources to cope with the exigencies of integration. While segments of migrant populations (such as the well off, educated and socially skilled) may succeed on this path, others (such as the first generation with low skills and education) are often engaged in a protracted struggle to cope with the reality of mainstream life.[2]

To illustrate, a significant group of Muslim migrants to Europe includes to a large extent the first-generation immigrants who, while struggling to speak the European languages, striving to hold regular jobs and establishing the props of a normal life, are still oriented to practise many aspects of their home culture – food, fashion, rituals, or private religious practices. Most of them struggle to survive and to live in peace and with dignity, and rely on their children to get by in the societal settings they often find too complex to operate. So they tend to resort and revert to their immediate circles, the language and religious groups, informal economic networks and communities of friends and status groups built in the neighbourhoods or prayer halls. They feel at home on the margin of the mainstream.

As such, this 'feeling at home on the margin' is hardly an Islamic feature, or a sign of resentment against the mainstream, or a primordial desire for 'tradition'. Rather, it represents a familiar trend – a typical coping strategy that lower-class immigrants often pursue when they encounter complex foreign life-worlds. It reflects the paradoxical reality of peripheral communalism that enables the members to get around the costs, to endure the hardship, and to negotiate with the mainstream in an attempt to be part of it. Because to immerse fully in the mainstream requires certain material, cultural and knowledge capabilities that most plebeian migrants, Muslim or non-Muslim, do not possess, which in turn compels them to seek alternative venues. Thus, being part of an organized economy demands regular payment of various dues and taxes; if you cannot afford them, then you go informal. When a migrant cannot afford to pay to fix his kitchen through regular firms, then he or she will look for, or generate, a network of friends, relatives and locals to mobilize support. If he cannot afford to shop in the mainstream modern supermarkets, or to borrow money from regular banks (because he does not have the credit and credentials), then he resorts to ethnic street bazaars to get his/her affordable supplies, and to informal credit associations to secure loans. When he lacks the necessary information and skill to function within the modern bureaucratic organizations – which do not accommodate flexibility, negotiation and interpersonal relations – he relies on the locals with whom he establishes flexible transactions based upon mutual trust and reciprocity. If people cannot operate within cultural settings that are perceived to be inhospitable, too formal and strict, then they are likely to become involved with those that allow them to fit.

An unintended consequence of these economic and cultural processes is the likely revitalization of 'negative integration', in parallel and peripheral communities where ethnic networks or religious rituals are revived and reinforced to serve as structures of support and survival. It is no surprise that 'ghettoization' is more pronounced among lower-class British Muslims for whom unemployment remains three times higher than for other minority groups. This process of 'feeling at home on the margin' represents a way of coping with the imperatives of modernity embodied in bureaucratic arrangements, the discipline of time, space, fixed and formal contract, and the like. As such this process is not specific to Muslims, but includes all comparable migrant communities. Nor is it limited to international migration.

Rural migrants in Cairo, Tehran, Istanbul or Casablanca undergo more or less similar experiences (and receive similar levels of hostility from their national elites), as do many residents of Turkish or Moroccan origin in Germany or the Netherlands.

The argument about 'marginal space as opportunity' pertains equally to social and cultural realms. In the mainstream societies where the expression of difference, 'abnormal' lifestyles and sexual orientations are shunned, marginal domains often facilitate opportunities for respite, realization and vitality among social marginals. The tendency among certain 'social misfits' – groups of intellectuals, artists and individuals with unconventional lifestyles – to undertake a peripheral subsistence testifies to the potential of these sites for self-realization. Many hippy communities of the late 1960s in California or the 'artist village' in today's Egyptian Fayyoum represent a 'choice' of what looks like a bohemian lifestyle.

The discussion is not meant to romanticize marginal spaces. For beyond the realities of misery and insecurity, these 'free zones' and socio-escapes can also nurture control, crime and repression. Historically, bohemian arrangements aimed to facilitate communal living for those 'moderately deviant' members of Western societies in order to structure their 'integration', albeit on the margins of mainstream life (Mirzuchi 1983). Historical bohemianism, just like monasticism, emerged as a mechanism of social control and regulation, a process quite distinct from the trajectories of the modern social 'misfits'. Many members of the current bohemian subcultures are more or less privileged groups who appropriate and develop peripheral, untainted physical and social spaces to advance their own taste, style and mode of life. The elite gated communities in cities of the global North and South may be said to follow a similar logic – self-isolation in a quest to maintain purity. These groups can usually afford to navigate between the marginal and the mainstream, rather than having little choice but to seek a marginal life – a feature which distinguishes them from gays, the migrant poor or the cultural underdog, who find mainstream existence too costly, and are thus compelled to pursue a life on the edge.

It is true that the peripheral communities of the poor migrants certainly serve as 'home' for many people who are unable to bear the multiple costs of the mainstream. But these peripheral free zones and escapes can also be exploited by criminals, drug lords, gangs and warlords whose self-interest and greed can cause immense misery, violence and insecurity for the ordinary people. Observing such unfortunate trends in some Brazilian *favelas*, Janice Perlman is compelled to acknowledge that the 'myth of marginality' has now turned into the 'reality of violence' (Perlman 2009). The same can be said about the marginal regions or nations of the world. The experiences of North Korea, Burma, Taliban Afghanistan and to some extent the Islamic Republic of Iran suggest that the national states whose authoritarian ideology and governance cannot withstand the global practices of democratic governance and pluralism may resort to isolation and peripheral existence in the name of cultural 'authenticity' and 'independence'.

In sum, the key to understanding the dynamics of marginal space is the fact that the domains of the 'mainstream', the 'normal', the 'integrated' and the 'modern' each have both benefits and costs. Their benefits include being in the centre, enjoying the position of power, comfort, respect, security, protection and recognition. And their costs consist of, for instance, compulsion to abide by the norms of society, social obligations, the rules of the game, having to be like others rather than being different, having to pay taxes and dues, and enduring risk and insecurity. But people have different degrees of capacities – capitals – to operate within the mainstream, the normal, the modern. Not everyone possesses the necessary material, social, cultural and knowledge capital to operate successfully within the mainstream. In order to be part of it and enjoy its benefits, a group needs to have certain resources and abilities to manoeuvre within it, and afford its costs. If someone lacks those capacities, or wants to escape the costs, then he may go marginal (just as the migrant poor go informal, poor countries choose autarchy, authoritarian regimes seek isolation, or sexual minorities form peripheral escapes). Here marginal domains can facilitate respite, an opportunity to develop alternative social arrangements, economic organizations, modes of life and governmentality; primarily because these spaces are relatively free of the costs, obligations and constraints of 'the normal'. In this sense, marginal sites become domains of liberation, alternative norms and practices and thus domains of counter-power – and at the same time the realms of possible risk insecurity and even repression. Thus marginality is not simply a state of mind, attitude or a culture. It is very much tied to the material and non-material capacity of people who are thrown into life-worlds not of their making. Marginality becomes a mechanism to tackle troubling encounters with the 'normal'.

Notes

1 The preceding two paragraphs are adapted from Bayat (2010: 59).

2 These paragraphs have been adapted from Bayat (2008).

References

Bayat, A. (1997) *Street Politics: Poor People's Movements in Iran*, New York: Columbia University Press.

— (2008) 'Feeling at home on the margin', *ISIM Review*, 21, March.

— (2010) *Life as Politics: How Ordinary People Change the Middle East*, Stanford, CA: Stanford University Press.

Castells, M. (1983) *Cities and the Grassroots*, Berkeley: University of California Press.

Davis, B. (1997) 'Marginality in a pluralistic society', *Eye on Psi Chi*, 2(1), Autumn.

Davis, M. (2006) *Planet of Slums*, London: Verso.

De Certeau, M. (1984) *The Practice of Everyday Life*, Berkeley: University of California Press.

Douglas, M. (1966) *Purity and Danger: An Analysis of the Concepts of Pollution and Taboo*, New York: Praeger.

Draper, H. (1978) *Karl Marx's Theory of Revolution*, vol. 2, New York: Monthly Review Press.

Escobar, A. (1995) *Encountering Development: The Making and Unmaking of the Third World*, Princeton, NJ: Princeton University Press.

Foucault, M. (1982) 'The subject and power', in H. Dreyfus and P. Rabinow (eds), *Michel Foucault: Beyond Structuralism and Hermeneutics*, Chicago, IL: University of Chicago Press.

Friedmann, J. (1992) *Empowerment: The Politics of Alternative Development*, Oxford: Blackwell.

Hoogvelt, A. (1997) *Globalization and the Postcolonial World: The New Political Economy of Development*, Baltimore, MD: Johns Hopkins University Press.

Lewis, O. (1966) 'The culture of poverty', *Scientific American*, 215(4): 19–25.

— (1968) *The Children of Sanchez: Autobiography of a Mexican Family*, New York: Vintage.

Memmi, A. (1991) *The Colonizer and the Colonized*, New York: Beacon Press.

Mirzuchi, E. (1983) *Regulating Society: Marginality and Social Control in Historical Perspective*, New York: Free Press.

Park, R. (1928) 'Human migration and the marginal man', *American Journal of Sociology*, 33: 881–93.

Perlman, J. (1976) *The Myth of Marginality: Urban Poverty and Politics in Rio de Janeiro*, Berkeley: University of California Press.

— (2009) 'Megacity's violence and its consequences in Rio de Janeiro', in K. Konings and D. Kruijt (eds), *Megacities: The Politics of Urban Exclusion and Violence in the Global South*, London: Zed Books.

Rahnema, M. and V. Bawtree (eds) (1997) *The Post-Development Reader*, London: Zed Books.

Schuurman, F. and T. van Naerssen (1989) *Urban Social Movements in the Third World*, London: Croom Helm.

Simmel, G. (1950) 'The stranger', in K. Wolff (trans.), *The Sociology of Georg Simmel*, New York: Free Press, pp. 402–8.

Stonequist, E. (1935) 'The problem of the marginal man', *American Journal of Sociology*, 41: 1–12.

White, G., R. Murray and C. White (eds) (1983) *Revolutionary Socialist Development in the Third World*, Brighton: Wheatsheaf Books.

3 | Accumulation by encroachment in the Arab Mashreq

ALI KADRI

For more than two decades before the uprisings of 2011, economic supply-side policies dominated the development landscape in the Arab world.[1] For every five entrants into the labour market, little more than two jobs were created, and the policy advice from the international financial institutions (IFIs) was that the region's educational systems produced people who were unqualified for the existing jobs (ESCWA 2004a). When wages and incomes were steadily falling, led by the compression of public sector incomes, the policy advice was that the labour market was too rigid (Kadri 2008). With declining productivity, rising inequality, an absence of autonomous civil society institutions, and incomes derived principally from rents, wealth was generated by absolute (as distinct from relative) measures, e.g. by paying working people less than they needed to maintain their living conditions. Working people were being systematically impoverished, and the siphoned-off wealth was being sent abroad.[2] It was a marriage of neoliberal ideology: brutal Arab dictatorships were backed by various NATO military fleets, several US military ground bases and the state of Israel, which has been dubbed an immobile US aircraft carrier.

At any one point in this historical process, it was plain to see that the trend of driving people into abject poverty was unsustainable. In retrospect, it might have taken a few more civil liberties and small inputs of financial resources to partly redress the inequitable political and distributional arrangements and, presumably, delay the revolutionary conditions of 2011, but these were neither considered nor undertaken. Failure to undertake these measures was not short-sightedness on the part of the institutions, which have mediated capital and ensured its resilience so far: global capital accumulation is reinforced by neoliberal ideology and proceeds by encroachment and dispossession. Nowhere is this truer than in the Mashreq. In this region, wars have served to dispossess the working people of their political and social rights as well as of their resources, leaving the security of the labouring classes and national security both exposed and vulnerable.

US and Western aggression, when couched under the rubric of international law and humanitarianism and stripped bare of falsification, is made to appear more costly to imperialism than the gains that it is set to expropriate. Economic prices and the sums of financial resources that they add up to are brokered by a structure of power from which Arab people have been discarded. After the Arab elites and foreign capitalists have appropriated the larger share of the national wealth, the remaining resources are insufficient for the Arab labouring classes to maintain a historically determined decent standard of living. A dispossessed and disempowered working population cannot negotiate the conditions for its survival. People in the Arab world are thus continually denied any possibility for development, with the result that the security of working people and national security are laid wide open – indeed insecure – and the terms of power, which underlie the process of reproduction of global accumulation, remain calibrated in favour of the USA. The deepening crisis of capital implies a further escalation of the process of dispossession of the Arab working people, and a devaluing of Arab human and material resources. Although enforced public-to-private transfers take place under liberalization, it is still wars which act as the ultimate instrument of encroachment, dispossession and dislocation. Wars on an Arab world that is already substantially defeated have served to maintain US control of oil supplies through direct military presence; they have stabilized a financial order in which the US dollar remains the world reserve currency and medium for holding wealth; they have reinforced militaristic, religious and ultra-nationalist ideologies globally; and they have devalued resources to levels that impoverish the local population, helping to drive global wages down. Ultimately, US capital has held ascendant and competing imperialist powers at bay (Chossudovsky 2006).

Thus, in the Arab Near East, war is not the continuation of politics by other means; it is rather the continuation of war by means of politics. War, or the enduring prospect of war, in the Near East is the epochal constant in a system of global accumulation and international relations, and it is just the policy which varies. A growing crisis of capital implies the further dissolution of Arab social formations. From the wars of decolonization, the colonization of Palestine and the regional conflicts that flared up as manifestations of the Cold War, to the war on Iraq and selective NATO bombings, there is one common denominator: military aggression has been intended to aggravate and further incite conflict. 'Militarism is not only in itself a province of accumulation,' it also serves through encroachment and dispossession to offset the inherent crisis of accumulation on the realization side through simple market expansion (Luxemburg 1973 [1913]).[3] Lenin emphasized that militarism represented a determining moment in a process under imperialism. For him, war became 'the principal means by which capitalism could overcome the disparity between the development of productive forces and the accumulation of capital on the one side, and the division of colonies and spheres of influence for finance capital on the other' (Lenin 1966 [1916]). There is little evidence that any of the main players have tried to defuse regional tensions.[4] Wars on the Arab world mediate inter-imperialist rivalries, which were not written off by the financialization phase of imperialism and which relate to the discord between the USA and other rising powers over US imperial rent acquisition that endangers the dollar as the world's medium of holding wealth.

When Gunder-Frank's tripod of capital accumulation embodied in oil, militarism and the dollar comes together in a single territory, every Arab state swings closer to the potential for failure (Gunder-Frank 1991). Arab states are ineffectual in promoting sovereignty over their own territory, including, of course, the legitimacy drawn from popular constituency and control over natural resources. These countries appear to fall at the tail end of a system of international relations that *necessitates* a state of being that oscillates between fully fledged conflict and a high degree of tension. The highlighting of the verb 'necessitate' is of particular value for our argument. The high frequency of regional conflicts is self-evident, and the aggravating crisis of global capital destroys any possibility for the peoples of this region to exercise the right to self-determination. War in the Near East is the mediation and subordinate outcome of the crisis of capital accumulation on a global scale. There is an immediate *social link*, coming before economics, between the maintenance of capital's rate of profit and the dislocation and immiseration of Arab people. Arab development is denied by encroachment and dispossession. This ensures that the reproduction of global capital, in social, physical and ideological terms and attendant upon the extraction of absolute value, fails to deliver even a humanizing development that could give Arab people individual and communal security.

The argument in this chapter has five key themes. The first is to highlight why the Mashreq is different from other regions of the world. The second is why the failings of the national bourgeoisie in the region have deep historical roots, while the third explores why the fomentation of instability and the control of oil are interrelated causes of war.

Fourthly, in the absence of an alternative humanist ideology, wars create a sustainable downward social impact, further fragmenting the working class along ethnic and sectarian lines. Finally, with capitalism and nationalism hand in hand, the chapter asks why certain aspects of inter-imperialist rivalry have moved away from the entente of the Cold War and remain relevant in the context of the Near East.

The Arab Near East

The Mashreq is characterized by acute inequality of incomes and tremendous wealth in some individual cases. This inequality undermines social cohesiveness and ties the governing elites to the West. When the business cycle is dictated by rents and conflicts, merchants and rentiers are unlikely to presumptively share nationally or regionally in what could become a game where both lose out. Regional oil rents flow abroad in US treasury bills or through affluent consumption and weapons purchases. Simple calculation reveals that in the Gulf Cooperation Council (GCC) states alone, in over thirty-five years there has been nearly four trillion dollars more saved than the amount invested (World Bank 2009). The intra-regional disparities are also glaring: the average monthly salary in Qatar stands at more than US$6,000, while that in Yemen is less than US$100, with nearly 40 per cent of Yemen's children suffering from malnutrition. Many governing patriarchal oligarchies are militarily covered by the USA and Israel. In one historical incident illustrative of cross-border class alliances, Syrian troops moved towards Jordan in 1970 to assist in halting the Jordanian offensive against Palestinian refugees, and the Israeli air force intervened to stop them.

As rents from oil permeated the circuit of capital in the early 1970s, the nascent industries of non-oil-producing Arab countries went through a process of deindustrialization as a result of worker remittances from the Gulf and geopolitical rents. It was impossible for heavily protected and autarkic economies to sustain the assault of huge petrodollar flows and the oil-exporting social model of non-labour-based earning (ESCWA 2008). The economies of the region progressively lost all significant productive activity. The non-oil economic cycle of the region hence became increasingly determined by oil rents and war (ESCWA 2003). The Gulf States generated the oil rents, while the few neighbouring Arab economies, by reasons of propinquity and being diversified, became more dependent on geopolitical rents. Egypt is second only to Israel in the amounts of US direct aid received, while Jordan is an 'American protectorate' and used as a showcase for the benefits of Official Development Assistance. Rents promote an idle way of earning without mobilizing any resources or labour, and oligarchs distribute the rent on the basis of patronage and political loyalty. By reducing the space available for industrial expansion, rents and merchant capital militate against the possibility of socializing across the sects or across ethnic groups. In this context, the Gulf model of development is a model of oil wells: these states consist of a very small resident indigenous population, serviced by millions of indentured Asian labourers. In the main, the expatriate labourers receive poverty wages of around US$200 a month and are deprived of rights. In absolute numbers, the expatriates exceed the national workforce in most Gulf countries (ESCWA 2007b). Productivity in key sectors becomes negative. This is not just as a result of the substitution effect, but more that the chronic dependence of the merchant class on cheaply remunerated, exploited foreign labour may be seen as a case of more workers per physical capital stock.

The way in which the reproduction of capital through rent determines the ranks devolved to each of the social classes is related to the class rapport of the nationals to the social means of production or oil. It is also related to the function of each class in material and social reproduction, and in the distribution of social wealth, with the form and the amount of revenue to each class determined by its share in the state power structure. The Asian expatriates are denied all political rights and, consequently, the basic living conditions of the members of this class are abysmal (ESCWA 2009a). One may add that the salary or wage of each worker is determinedly social; it is the salary/wage of a social class, and *not* that of an individual, aggregated and redistributed to workers (in contrast to the neoclassical paradigm). Thus, although the nationals are the least productive in the economic sense, their hold on power forms the basis of their revenues. It is this rent-based labour process which led to the internal institutional arrangements of the Gulf States being devolved. The more relevant institutions relating to oil and defence, such as the GCC Council, are, in view of the insubstantial sovereignty of these states, formed and dictated by the USA.

Although the share of the non-oil sector in the Gulf economy has risen, leading some to argue that Saudi Arabia has traits of a developmental state (Niblock and Malik 2007; Hertog 2010), the Saudi supply chain remains shallow. There are no extensive backward and forward linkages in the national economy to point to an industrialization process. Some industrial plants were imported along with their skilled labour and know-how, tapping into cheaply paid Asian labour and energy, implying few linkages to the national economy and little indigenous technology imparted upon the industrial process (ESCWA 2007a). Far from signifying development, the inhumane conditions of work in these establishments point in the opposite direction. The share of industry appears to have risen slightly only because the capital-intensive, labour-saving petrochemical mega-projects, which represent a further increment on the chain of value addition, come under the heading of 'industry' in the national accounts. In any case, the share of industry as a source of the national income remains low.[5] With the rise in oil prices from 2002, the contribution of oil has also risen as a proportion of national incomes (ESCWA 2009a).

Gulf States imports constitute as much as 90 per cent of national consumption. As a result, the predominant economic activity centres on imports and commerce, with a specific social class monopolizing trade in imported consumables.[6]

Trading among the Gulf States is minimal compared to trade with the rest of the globe (ESCWA 2009b): disconnected commercial enclaves that are experiencing a thriving desert construction boom, founded on cheapened Asian labour, produce little to trade with one another. All of the Gulf States price their oil in dollars, peg their currency to the dollar and hold dollar reserves, despite the fact that most of their trade takes place outside the dollar zone, and the impact of a falling dollar on the domestic price level and holdings of wealth has been significant. The ruling oligarchs hold tremendous sovereignty over the repression of labour nationally, yet they fail to exercise autonomy over their monetary policy, which would ultimately connect to the very sensitive area of pricing their oil in dollars.

Oil and geopolitical rents dichotomized the regional states and created an economic and social divide. For those states with oil, labour and remuneration were characterized by a number of common features. A highly capitalized oil sector creates few jobs relative to the capital invested in it, and creation of jobs occurs principally by patronage in the public sector (Ayubi 1995). Sectors linked to oil, including the public sector, offer high wages and employ nationals, while sectors not linked to oil, i.e. much of the private sector, pay relatively low wages and mostly employ expatriates. In the presence of weak financial intermediation between financial resources and physical capital, and a healthy rise in income associated with rising productivity and organized labour action, the rest of the economy leans more heavily towards the service and informal sectors and, in the main, these sectors pay out poverty wages far below the decent living standards to which nationals aspire. Deepening differentiation between different sections of the working class raises profit margins and enhances short-term rents in all the economic sectors. High short-term rents make the present more valuable than the future. But inter-temporal preferences are above all underpinned by geopolitical risk factors related conjointly to institutional vulnerability, an already inherent uneven developmental state, and a possible spillover of regional tensions and conflicts. Presumptive redistribution that would allow for a lower concentration of private wealth, with greater interest in regional development in the shape of improved wage levels, is unlikely to take place, in view of the circuit of petrodollar capital that is underwritten by the US-commandeered regional security arrangement.

The oil price hike, which began in 2002, has given greater leverage to the rentier system, but still with very unequal distribution of the gains. When oil prices receded after the first oil boom, which ended around 1980, economic growth rates plummeted. In Saudi Arabia in 2001, per capita income was at a third of the level it had reached at the height of the boom in 1979. The combination of shrinking public sector revenues and employment meant that the unemployment rate

TABLE 3.1 Growth in real GDP per capita in the Arab Near East (%)

Country	1971–80	1981–90	1991–2000	1971–2000
Bahrain	9.25	(3.51)	0.97	0.48
Kuwait	(8.60)	(4.81)	9.43	(3.36)
Oman	1.05	2.81	0.83	2.07
Qatar	(4.75)	(5.22)	4.33	(2.61)
Saudi Arabia	3.69	(9.44)	(1.11)	(3.37)
United Arab Emirates	16.93	(8.29)	0.07	(0.10)
GDC countries	1.85	(7.67)	0.50	(2.78)
Egypt	3.81	3.26	2.52	2.73
Iraq	7.84	(1.87)	(5.23)	(4.95)
Jordan	2.84	(1.27)	0.00	0.88
Lebanon	(4.63)	(8.39)	3.41	(2.45)
Syrian Arab Republic	6.16	(2.96)	2.92	1.27
Yemen	3.96	12.23	0.70	7.87
More diversified economies	5.87	(0.16)	0.35	0.02
Total Near East	4.99	(3.43)	0.34	(0.85)

Note: ( ) indicates negative growth
Source: United Nations statistics database

soared, as average total fertility rates were at seven to eight children per woman. Despite the economic growth and increase in GDP in some countries, such as Egypt, albeit with massive inequality in incomes and rising unemployment, the collapse in the Saudi income – showing its significance within the region – compressed the income of the whole region. In the two decades between the first and second oil boom, the Mashreq region exhibited the highest unemployment rates, the lowest average real per capita growth rates and the widest gap in income distribution globally, compared to other developing regions in the world (ESCWA 2004b). With lower oil rents and neoliberal policies, investment in the social infrastructure fell. In 2002, investment in economic infrastructure was the lowest of all developing regions, at 16 per cent, and productivity per worker was on average negative (ILO 2003). Intra-regional trade remained as low as ever, at around 10 per cent, with much of the Gulf's excess saving being channelled abroad, instead of being used to mobilize real national resources for development. The economies of the region are underdeveloped and lack productive capacity, and the economic policies deployed channel financial resources not towards building capacity, but towards increasing capital flight.

These acute quantitative anomalies qualify and differentiate the way the region is articulated with international capital. They inform the way in which the balance of powers, tilted against the Arab people, deprives them of the right to exercise their civil and national rights. Western capital and, more specifically, US capital are reliant on complete suppression of the Arab state to the extent that the suppression is an indispensable condition for them. Arab regimes are tied by cross-border class alliances to the USA, and have been almost fully deprived of any relevant sovereignty, specifically over their national resources, when shared ownership and privatization of oil in the Gulf States and Iraq are major points on the US agenda. The region is thus subjected to the full force of a colonial anti-development agenda, with little remaining to prop up the national living standards of the working classes when imperialists and rentiers appropriate their shares.

The contemporary mechanism for resource allocation is markedly different from that in the mid-1970s when the first oil boom occurred. Oil wealth then, through the state, funded the social and physical infrastructures. However, with the recent neoliberal ideological grip of policy, the state has been retrenched. One remarkable symptom of this shift was the bubble in real estate assets and the leveraging of speculative activities on poorly regulated stock markets. The most visible case of this was the Dubai financial crash in 2009 (Yamamoto 2009). Unlike in the previous oil boom, which generated employment opportunities, growth in the contemporary crisis has involved virtually no new jobs. The region as a whole has grown by a cumulative 17 per cent since 2009, but the unemployment rate has declined by 1–2 per cent and remains the highest in the world (ESCWA 2009b). The onset of neoliberal policies also transformed the quality of investment, as less was invested in plant and equipment, and more took the form of low-productivity capital requiring a short gestation period. The actual productive base of industry underlying the national or regional economy shrank to a point where it became impossible to absorb new entrants into the labour market on the basis of an efficiency criterion in production. There was a further squeeze on the share of labour as a proportion of both the national income and that of the region, which meant that it had to remain as low as a quarter of total income (regional estimate). The same share for more advanced countries represents nearly three-quarters of income (ILO 2003). The principal alteration, which occurred as a result of neoliberal policies and exposing working-class security, was evident in the receding role of national agents of development. There is an absence of any commitment to lock in resources, and there has emerged a national class with extra-national aspirations and ties that is predisposed to shifting resources abroad. This has been accompanied by a shift in social relations and the devolution of divide and rule among classes, as well as a dogmatic acceptance of market liberalism and of a set of institutions that is geared to tailoring development to the requirements of global financial capital.

An inherently comprador ruling class

The social crisis characterizing the region and the defeat of national forces mediating the position of the Arab working classes left the social and political terrain open to deepening divisions. Imperialism, reinforcing these divisions via client regimes, devolved the region's own resources to pre-capitalist forms of social organization and institutions. The pre-capitalist or old social relations continue, however, to hold a symbiotic relationship with the new, more modern relations, with the despotic side of the old acting as a support mechanism for modern capitalism. This instils repression within the labour process, while the communal and more relevant side of the Arab world represents a ready platform for resistance. Social disarticulation in the newly formed Arab states was deepened under colonialism (Lutsky 1969). The social discord that forms along the politically instituted cultural lines grows by linking it to rent appropriation and by relegating to it a redistributive capacity. It is highly improbable that any of the ruling classes will be legitimized or draw sovereignty from nationally mediated working-class positions while this process of disarticulation continues. This disarticulation, with the frail structure of the institutions – including the state and the judiciary, implying the absence of social and legal rights – alongside a precarious rent cycle, extends into the formation of identity and consciousness. Identity politics, serving to differentiate and divide the labour force in conditions of crisis, militates against the development of conscious activity opposing the machination of capitalist exploitation. In a developing context of Third World development, exploitation occurs for the most part by effecting absolute extraction of surplus value, a process in which an unemployed and impoverished population acts to drag down wages and to ideologically support the formation of race-based and racist nationalist movements.

The decisive role of imperialist forces in the Arab Near East calls into question the usual characterization of the relationship between a post-colonial formation and the West. The frail cohesion of the Arab state, the precariousness of human and social development and the devastation of war manifest themselves in the utter dependency of the Arab state on the more advanced economies. In East Asia, certain welfare gains were able to be drawn from steady capital flows, as the Japanese capital had no military backing. In the Arab region, by contrast, the highly distorted balance of force resulting from the US–Israeli alliance holds back any progressive social and political development. As the East Asian case illustrates, no simple and quantitative logic can explain the complex relationships between conflicts and political and economic outcomes. Nevertheless, East Asian economies have performed well, in dynamic terms, in the last five decades.

There are various articulations that have to be investigated before a real and concrete understanding can be achieved of the processes of war, security, state formation and sovereignty, in relation to their impact on development. In other words, it is necessary to comprehend how violence and security arrangements were deployed in East Asia in ways that did not form an obstacle to economic development, and yet how their specific articulation in the Middle East turned out to be an obstacle to sovereignty, state formation and economic development. The difficulty of this exercise lies in exposing the 'productive' impacts of war: war acting as a form of primitive accumulation can impact on the pattern of economic mobilization, technological innovation, control of the population, management of military forces, and, specifically, the alignment of national security and development goals. This last point of reconciling Arab national security and development in a global context is the main reason for the differences between the Arab world and the East Asian experiences.

Capitalism in the Arab Mashreq – unlike in Europe, where it was associated with the restructuring of the 'old' – was accelerated as a result of a relationship imposed from outside by colonialism. Many of the archaic social relationships characterizing a pre-capitalist social order, in particular the labour process, remained unreformed, merely accommodating the new relationship with 'capitalism' by becoming legally institutionalized. The structure of the extended family, and many forms of pre-capitalist social bonding, did not run counter to the new capitalist economic relationship, because it disciplined and regimented the working classes. At one end of the spectrum, the pre-capitalist institution acts as a redistributive repository that assists the perennially disengaged labour force under a process of enforced proletarianization. At the other end, the patriarchal hold over national resources bestows reified legitimacy and inalienable property rights on the ruling patriarchs. There were periodic exceptions to this process: these occurred in short-lived periods following national liberation movements during the Cold War. But that said, the exceptions did not last long enough, nor were they serious about changing the core despotic relationships of the social process. This was because working-class participation in the political process was curtailed by despotic militarism. With the political agency of the working class commandeered by the military populist cliques, when reversions to comprador positions occurred – as in Egypt under Anwar Sadat, for instance – workers were denied the right to struggle to safeguard their post-independence achievements.

Much of the 'Third World' can be classified under the generic heading of geostrategic significance. The Arab Mashreq is evidently strategic, as it is the location of more than half of the world's known oil reserves and a third of global supply. In these circumstances the concept of 'primacy of politics' assumes new dimensions. The Mashreq matters far more in terms of how imperialist interests can secure outright control of its resources than in terms of what growth there may be in the meagre value-added of the Arab market that might accrue to investment capital. There is a lack of national autonomy over the policy space in the states of the region which is the result of frail sovereignty. National economic relations and policies are not given the chance to mature into a politically conducive domestic setting, and political and economic relations rarely run in tandem. Politics appears as *force majeure*, with economic relations of any sort struggling to keep pace or not given the space to grow. The degree of political coercion in the region is not an accident of history, unrelated to the necessities of world capital and to the fundamentally different characteristic of a region carved up and reshaped by the continued practice of direct or proxy colonialism. It is because oil, in its raw form and especially in the value-adding contributions of its derivatives, represents an extraordinarily relevant prerequisite for the accumulation process, and a means of control in order to maintain the stature of the US empire.

The *casus belli*

Development remains poor in the Mashreq, and capitalism has brought very little progress in the region. A more fitting concept that would capture the recent historical phase of this part of the Arab world would be that of 'reverse development' or 'de-development'. De-development represents a combination of retrogression in the build-up of physical capital and a denial, by the exercise of absolute authoritarianism, of the right of people to struggle to build a better life. On the basis of the highly inequitable growth that has persistently undermined the well-being of the majority of the population, it has been suggested that de-development has already taken place in this region.

De-development could also describe small developing countries, where working-class security is exposed to higher risks and uncertainties, co-determined by their precarious national security. This is both a conduit and an outcome of the mode of integration with global capital. Although lack of capacity, capital scarcity and technological progress are significant, much of development, or the lack of it, can be explained by the right to security and to sovereignty based on working-class security and geopolitical considerations. The countries that are developing least – mainly in African and Islamic states where the extraction of raw materials is vital to global capital accumulation and the *rapport de force* favours imperialism – represent areas defined by de-development and abjection. In so far as the concept of de-development is manifested in the Mashreq region, the drive, belligerence and domination of US capital in the Arab Near East expand in direct proportion to the relevance of oil as a strategic commodity and, equally, as a result of the dependency of US capital on oil, not solely for energy use and its technological derivatives, but considerably more for its role as an instrument for control and geostrategic positioning. US seignorage and imperial rent acquisition require other colonialist and competing imperial partners to be held at bay.

The argument for oil – both in itself and as a means of furthering control – as a cause of war is inextricably linked. Oil is the most traded commodity, and the dollarization of oil ensures that the demand for oil implies a demand for dollars (UNCTAD 2001). The demand for oil from China and India especially, and from the developing world more generally, is twice that of the OECD, and this makes the 'oil-hungry' economies vulnerable to whoever controls the resource. Only a few months before the invasion of Iraq, 'it [had] been hoped that the fight for oil would be carried out in cash and not with missiles' (Deffeyes 2002). Notwithstanding the scaremongering argument of resource depletion, oil is important in its own right and in how it figures centrally and strategically in the web of economic relations that underlies capital accumulation. This is why serious discussions on the cause of Near Eastern wars cannot avoid the oil issue. There are views that assess US intervention as an effort to replicate its own democratic model in the Middle East, but, as the Iraqi case has shown, organizing elections at the end of the colonial gun barrel resulted in, among other things, more than one million abandoned children roaming the streets of Baghdad (Arraf 2011). It is not necessary to dwell on the idea that the USA is spreading democracy: as Wolfowitz noted, Iraq's war was about oil (Wright 2003). Strengthening control over oil resources provides the USA with more than adequate leverage over most oil-dependent countries and imperialist partners. Even when discussion centres on the principal contradiction in the US economy – that American hegemony is positively correlated to the health of the US economy or that a stronger, more expansive US power implies a stronger US economy – the underlying premise remains oil (Petras and Morley 1994; Patnaik 2005). Oil price fluctuations matter less to the USA than to other countries when this strategic commodity remains priced in dollars, which is another morsel of imperial rent.

Viewed as one part of a broader imperial totality, the oil–dollar nexus, and in particular the dollar-priced barrel element of modern accumulation, represents a necessary mediation of declining US power. In terms of dwindling shares of world industry income and trade, the USA is no longer the global competitive economic force it used to be (Wallerstein 2000). Its chronic trade deficit, of nearly a trillion dollars a year, has recently incorporated characteristics of declining competitiveness in the areas where the USA had been a leader, such as the high-tech industries. Despite a sizeable depreciation of the dollar vis-à-vis the euro and other principal currencies over the last ten years, the trade deficit persists for reasons related to outsourcing and loss of capacity resulting from long-standing degradation of industry. Since the late 1970s, when Paul Volker as chairman of the US Federal Reserve raised US interest rates in order to redress indebtedness by foreign savings, US imports have steadily outstripped US exports. Dwindling US industrial performance was propped up by the USA, using its political and military weight. Although for Petras and Morley (1994) the empire had to save the republic, the USA's retreat in domestic social reforms and the rising levels of poverty within the country implied greater public tolerance in the USA of the fierceness of aggression and dislocation in places such as Iraq and Afghanistan. In standard terminology, a higher rate of exploitation in the USA further alienated the working class from its own humanity. There also surfaced more evidence of the old equation of interrelatedness of domestic and foreign policy. As US domestic reforms worsened, foreign policy mimicked, although at a steeper rate, the brutality of slum poverty cum incarceration within the USA. Calibrating the level of instability in the Near East to a degree at which the USA would ensure for itself the circular flow of petrodollars for treasury bills or weapons represented only one minor aspect of its imperial aggression (Kohler 1999). The more relevant component lay in the direct control of an oil region whose governments, as well as states, could be remoulded by US imperial design, held as collateral against issued US debt, have their resources cheapened at will, and play a principal role in the lingering undercurrent of inter-imperialist rivalry.

The severe crisis under globalization reduced the scope and scale of accumulation by commodity realization as a result of deflationary policies (lower wages and demand) and, inversely, boosted the role of development by encroachment and aggressive ventures of capital through war to maintain profit rates. Direct or proxy wars weakened social formations and became the leading practice by which the mounting difficulties arising from maintaining profit rates and balancing production and distribution of commodities are resolved. There is insufficient momentum in continuing deflationary conditions to lift investment and consumption simultaneously even in the developed world, and conditions are far more severe in the developing world (Brenner 2003).

The crude counter-argument to what I am proposing is that if most trade and capital flows occur within the OECD (already at around

three-quarters of world income) (World Bank 2009), there is consequently no need for imperial powers to invade or recolonize, as it
is not worth the effort. In the context of global accumulation, when
the USA seizes the jugular of the oil in the Gulf, it also achieves a
stranglehold over imperial contenders. What double-entry accounting conceals, however, is that an empire that enjoys imperial rents
and seignorage gains can afford a war or two, so that it does not
miss out on the benefit of borrowing indefinitely in its own currency.
The apologist stance assumes that the USA and Europe invade out
of ignorance or benevolence, and that they end up footing the bill.
Colonialism may have been more costly to Britain than to the USA,
but the returns to both empires were immense (Patnaik 1997). There
is more to colonialism than the simple argument of accounts and
money flows. The real reason for colonizing is to strip the people
of the Third World of sovereignty over their natural resources. It is
to allow the balance of forces behind the scenes to set the price of
their primary commodities far below the social value necessary to
reproduce the living standards of their own populations. In addition
to this, the acquisition of Third World labour, which gets engaged in
capitalist production areas that have not initially borne the reproduction cost of the labour force, generates immense value. In this, as in
many other resources, imperialism gets something for nothing, thus
keeping buoyant the rate of profit. Although in the financialization
phase of imperialism capital has diluted much of its national identity,
inter-imperialist rivalry lingers on as a result of the growing voracious-
ness of the US rentier mode and capital imbalances, which destabilize
the universal wealth-holding medium or dollar. In any case, whether
Western powers colonize together or separately, Western capital must
expand by destroying and re-engaging old peripheral assets. It also
turns the reconstruction to its own benefit by commandeering the
monetary policies of developing formations because of the crisis of
realization. What the façade of pricing in the dollar conceals is that
values from the Third World create massive profits for the First World.
Capital in the Third World, and particularly in the Arab world, has
literally to make a killing before it makes a profit.

Evolving conditions

Oil prices began to rise in 2003. As a result, oil revenues and economic growth in oil-exporting countries also rose. But in a neoliberal
US–Arab regime-determined macro structure, along with mounting
conflicts or risks, the positive developmental impact was far from

TABLE 3.2 List of selected conflicts and wars in the Mashreq region

Year	Countries	Description
1948	Israel, Iraq, Egypt, Jordan, Lebanon, Syria	Arab–Israeli war
1956	Israel, Egypt, France, UK	Suez war
1958	Lebanon	Civil war
1962–67	Yemen	North Yemen civil war
1967	Israel, Egypt, Jordan, Syria	Arab–Israeli war
1973	Israel, Egypt, Syria	Arab–Israeli war
1975–90	Lebanon	Civil war
1980–88	Iran, Iraq	War
1982–2000	Israel, Lebanon	Invasion
1990	Iraq, Kuwait	Invasion
1990–91	International coalition, Iraq	Gulf War I
1994	Yemen	Civil war
2003–present	US, UK, Iraq	Gulf War II
2006	Israel, Lebanon	War

Note: This list excludes the ongoing Israeli–Palestinian conflict, the US embargo on Iraq in the 1990s, and the various waves of civil unrest, such as in Jordan in 1970, Syria in 1982 and Iraq in 1988

evident. Short-term gains or windfall oil revenues are continuously undermined and lost as a result of persistent tensions and the alleged pretext that a small oil state lacks absorptive capacity. The argument that an underdeveloped Gulf formation also lacks investment opportunities is too absurd and ludicrous to entertain: underdevelopment is synonymous with lack of capacity. As conflict continues to rage across the region, it is difficult to estimate the losses to the region associated with wars, but these are huge in human, social and economic terms. Even if oil revenues increase under conditions of instability, the savings retained for investment in the region grow proportionately smaller, and the effect afterwards on the saving rate is negative. The trend in the rate of investment in this region as a proportion of total GDP fluctuates between 16 and 20 per cent, which is one of the lowest levels globally (World Bank 2009). A high proportion of the oil funds end up as unrequited transfers in US treasuries (Yang 2006).

The destruction to life and infrastructure, the loss in forgone income and the exodus of the labour force, skilled or otherwise, represent a process of development by encroachment. In a circularly reinforcing fashion, the de-developmental process shrank the socializing space in which universal, as opposed to narrower, social values could grow.

TABLE 3.3 Military spending as a percentage of GDP for selected Arab countries, 1988–2005

	1988	1989	1990	1991	1992	1993	1994	1995	1996	1997	1998	1999	2000	2001	2002	2003	2004	2005
Bahrain	5	5.1	5.1	5.4	5.2	5	4.6	4.7	4.7	4.6	4.8	4.9	4	4.2	4	4.9	4.4	3.6
UAR	8.6	7.8	6.2	6.3	6.1	6.1	5.9	5.5	5.1	4.8	5.1	4.3	3.4	3.4	3.3	2.8	2.3	2
Oman	18.3	16.7	16.5	14.8	16.2	15.4	15.7	14.6	12.5	12.5	12.5	11.4	10.6	12.2	12.3	12.1	12	11.9
Saudi Arabia	15.2	13.4	14	12.5	11.3	12.5	10.6	9.3	8.5	11	14.3	11.4	10.6	11.5	9.8	8.7	8.4	8.2
Kuwait	8.2	8.5	48.5	117	31.8	12.4	13.3	13.6	10.3	8.1	8.8	7.6	7.2	7.7	7.4	6.5	5.9	4.8
Egypt	6.9	5.8	4.7	4.6	4.5	4.3	4.2	3.9	3.5	3.3	3.3	3.2	3.2	3.3	3.4	3.3	3	2.8
Jordan	8.3	8	6.9	8.9	6.1	6.2	5.9	5.8	5.4	6.3	5.6	5.6	5.5	5.2	6	6.7	5.7	5.3
Lebanon	1.2	–	7.6	5.2	8	6	7	6.7	5.7	4.3	4.1	4.9	4.4	5.6	4.9	4.6	4.4	4.5
Syrian Arab Republic	6.9	7	6	9.1	7.9	6.4	6.5	6.2	5.2	5	5.1	4.8	5.5	5	4.7	5.6	6.4	5.1

Source: SIPRI (2009)

The process further facilitated the divisiveness that results from rent capture being devolved by the state. There is also a scramble by foreign powers to obtain a foothold in the region, and subsequently geopolitical rents pour in, increasing the brittleness of the social structure. The rentier social model of earning without effort is deepened in the process. It is a mode, nonetheless, which is responsible for a form of social organization that underpins a gravely uneven and lopsided process of development, which in turn makes a more fertile breeding ground for future conflict. An endless spiral downwards lies in store for an Arab social formation: the people, with the resources formerly available to them taken away by imperialism, are endangered, as they are rendered incapable of reproducing their social formation under the same conditions in time and space.

Peripheralization in the Arab Near East

Development is partly the result of internalizing working-class aspirations in the political process or, more fully, the outcome of successful working-class struggle. A reversal of de-development lies in the unity and the struggle of the Arab people to retain and deploy their own resources for their own development. The principal contradiction therefore rests between the Arab people and the US–Arab regime alliance, which usurps the people's social product, appropriating what the people needed to galvanize their own development. However, as the differences grow between the US elite and popular opposition forces in the Arab world over issues of controlling Arab resources, the greater becomes the political scare and the call for a military aggressor and occupier such as Israel, which is capable of providing additional security to any threatened interests of world capital. Thus the flows of Israeli capital have been led by the USA, calibrated to serve their interests, so that Israel does not ever lean towards integrating commercially or politically with the rest of the Arab Near East. As a partner in international capital, Israel has to continue to belong geographically to the Near East, but not economically or socially. Its trade-heavy economic structure is geared to servicing more developed nations, and not the low-value-added, low-demand Arab markets. After years of 'peace' with Egypt and Jordan, there is only insignificant trade among those Arab countries (ESCWA 2009b). The litany of literature in the Arab world emphasizing Israel's role in exposing the national security of Arab nations also stresses its pivotal anti-developmental role (Abou Anaml 2006). An immiserized Arab working population imparts much of its insecurity at the national level, as insecurity and hunger render people unable to fight. Arab development becomes not just a betterment of living conditions, but is rather about redressing the regional balance of forces. On its own, the Israeli factor partly explains the deconstruction and dissolution of the Arab social formation and the prohibition of an Arab developmental project.

Israel's practices alone may be insufficient to fully substantiate the issue of the de-development that has already taken place in the Arab Mashreq. The overdetermined assault on the Arab people differentiates the practice of imperialism there from that which is conducted elsewhere in the developing world. The determinants of the Arab Near Eastern situation hinge broadly on the degree of inter-imperialist tensions or, more generally, on two interrelated issues: the relationship of US capital to itself, and the relationship of US capital to world capital.

The final brokering position of this equation holds to the extent that US capital equates with, or differentiates itself from, world capital. The Near East had already tested the limits of inter-imperialist collusion when, by occupying Iraq in 2003, the USA explicitly – acting almost alone – breached the outstanding covenants of international security enacted in the Security Council, implying that there were ceilings on diluting the national identity of capital in the age of financialization (Koechlin 1999). One may project into this conceptual image rising powers, such as those of the Brazil, Russia, India and China (BRIC) economies, and the potential ascendancy of the euro, to buttress the argument for inter-imperialist rivalry, but that would be a static picture that would not correspond fully to a historical process in which rifts between insatiable US appetites for imperial rents jeopardize the global financial order. For a fluid historical process to be solidly explained, a counter-process has to run alongside it. Hence, conflict – or the persisting possibility of conflict – in the Near East, in the presence of vast US military powers, infuses enough unease into the global accumulation structure to ensure that the USA is able to stay in control. The very perception of war or the possibility of conflict in the Arab Mashreq is in itself a pillar of the present global accumulation order.

The degree of tensions in the Mashreq region will depend on the degree to which the present dependent growth of US capital becomes a liability to world capital and warrants its parting with it – a liability not only in terms of simple economic cost–benefit analysis of the two closed systems, but in terms of how vital the USA and its arch-ally Israel are militarily as a security blanket for the interests of occidental capital in the Near East. The pauperization of the Third World is necessary for the profits of multinational bodies, and much will obtain to capital from fomenting fanatical ideologies around the Arab/Israeli question, doctrines of a 'clash of civilizations' and a culture of militarism. These factors will implicate most of the periphery of poor countries whose national security is exposed, enabling the dominant powers to cheapen the resources of Third World countries and usher in a commodification of human life, effectively a process by which labour power is priced in part against the death toll in devastated regions. But this imperial booty has to be set against the unequal share in imperial rent that the USA takes for itself, the global imbalances, and the unsteadiness of the US dollar endangering holdings of wealth. Although US debt is held by non-US citizens and sooner or later this would infringe on the ownership of US national resources, a destabilized Near East that is policed by the USA will delay the point at which the lenders would want to turn fictitious into real capital. Calculations of losses or gains made will be contingent primarily on the economic benefits of international capital as a whole from the region, including the safeguarding of the dollar as a stable medium of holding wealth, and particularly on the partial role that Israel plays, potentially or actually, in ensuring the control of oil at the behest of the USA.

Inasmuch as the accumulation of US capital is dependent on the growth of regional tensions, the pricing of oil in dollars and resource inflows to the US economy, it is also independent of them. Independence manifests itself as the differences within the circle of world capital over financialization and fiat wealth. This latter relates to the US ability to print dollars in excess of the collateral to support or underpin their value, something which jeopardizes the dollar as a medium of world savings. US control over the Gulf region, however, represents a premium collateral and a leveraging mechanism over the circle of capital. The recent financial crisis has revealed excesses in which the transfer of value cannot perpetually be underwritten in dollar-money form in the future. Hence US presence and capability of control and destabilization in the Gulf become a form of racketeering that the USA deploys to ensure imperial rents, and against people who hold their wealth in US dollars. The precariousness of this international security arrangement cum financial order was itself a reason for the rise of the dollar after the financial crisis. The resettling of the financial order into the low-intensity currency war and the calls for a change away from the dollar system indicate a resentment and a lack of trust in the mechanism underlying mediation of value in money form. US capital reaches at this point a threshold requiring further adjustment, either in the imperial collateral it holds or a devaluing of global wealth holdings in the dollar. In the light of the astronomical amounts of debt revealed by the contemporary financial crisis, the adjustment required will be set by more than just a devaluation exercise, and might require structural concessions on the status of empire.[7] It is at this juncture as well that the crisis of capital, by dragging the Arab world deeper into war and conflict, implicates the Mashreq in the historical process and poses a setback for the US aggression, meaning that the control of the eastern flank of the Persian Gulf may represent an ephemeral way out of the crisis of capital.

A post-revolutionary age?

The social conditions of the Mashreq in the post-revolutionary period following the 2011 uprisings have not improved. Income inequality, private sector hold over resources and low-productivity private investment all remain in place. The official rate of unemployment remains the highest in the world, more than half the labour force is employed in informal activities remunerated at poverty wage rates, more than half the population lives below the two-dollars-a-day threshold in the highest per capita food-importing region, and productivity is negative (AMF 2009). The statistics of this economic crisis reflect a social process that creates disaster.

The cross-border social class alliance of occidental, principally US, capital with Arab regimes has deliberately failed to promote development in the Mashreq. When development is gauged in terms of unleashing human potentialities and broadening the choices of people, with a fair and balanced outcome combining the right to decent living standards and the right to participate in the political process, the Arab Mashreq clearly has not developed. And when development is considered to represent the infusion of knowledge in production, incremental growth in capital stock and progressive institutional change, then it is also safe to declare that the Arab Mashreq has not developed. These factors, capturing the recent historical phase of this part of the Arab world, enable one to conclude that the region has been de-developed, as discussed above.

Although capital accumulation entails a blend of expansion by commodity realization and development by encroachment and dispossession, in this corner of the world it is the latter pattern of accumulation which predominantly determined the pace of development. Oil in its raw form – both in the way it is priced in the dollar, and in the multiplicity of technological permutations to its derivatives to create value-added – represents a decisive constituent of global accumulation, the control of which is central to maintaining the stature of US empire, the present global financial order and its associated rents. The articulation of the 'Arab formation' with US and world capital is conducted, in cahoots with Arab regimes, by maintaining outright military superiority, hegemony and repression over Arab working masses, hand in hand with maintaining Israel's military supremacy. However, as the US's room to manoeuvre in the international economy narrows as a result of the deepening crisis of capital and the recent financial crisis, its relation to the Arab Mashreq assumes more belliger-ent forms. The persistence of war in the region mediates unweathered inter-imperialist rivalries relating to the discord between the USA and other rising powers over the acquisition of US imperial rent, which endangers the global financial structure and the dollar as the world's medium of wealth-holding. Development supports and strengthens both the security of Arab working populations and national security, and would certainly distort the balance of forces in favour of the Arab people, thus undermining current imperial control over a geostrategic region. The immiserization of the Arab people is both an outcome of an entente and a complex articulation of global powers necessitating the de-development of the Arab world in the present phase of the crisis of capital. Power can be couched under various symbolic constructs. However, the escalation of aggression in the counter-revolutionary phase, the continued direct occupations in Iraq and Palestine, and the growing number of potentially and already 'failed' states make it clearer that the concept of power that is being unleashed against the Arab people amounts to firepower, i.e. the capacity to overkill by military force.

The difference between the Mashreq and the West is not quantitative. Neither is it cultural, in the sense of reducing culture to tradition. There is of course the cultural, *ad hominem* argument found in contemporary literature, in which Arabs are to be blamed for their underdevelopment because they are corrupt (Yamamoto 2009; United Nations 2007). The difference between the Mashreq and the West is, rather, socially quali-tative. The working people of the Mashreq are at the mercy of a joint assault by their regimes and Western powers led by the USA. They are, as a social group, in a subordinate rank, and their development and security run counter to the power structure holding together global capital accumulation. No macro policy is going to bear fruit unless the state begins to mediate the aspirations of working people. The ongoing political revolts are yet to restructure the configuration of the social classes, so have not yet become social revolutions. The policies that are being put forth shy away from radical ideas of land reforms, controlled capital accounts, selective protection of national industry, progressive taxation, egalitarian income distribution, needs-based social policies, and macro policies that nationally lock in the circuit of capital. For these policies to emerge, working people across the globe need to engage in the struggle of the Arab people for civil liberties, working-class security and sovereignty based on the well-being of the people. The Mashreq is central to a global process of accumulation based on finance, militarism and oil. Each of these three principal constituent elements of capital is present in the Mashreq. In order to begin to deconstruct capital and reorganize society and nature in people-friendly ways, working people know well that the Arab revolutionary process can win only with international solidarity.

Notes

1 This contribution focuses on the Arab Near East, or Mashreq, which includes Bahrain, Kuwait, Oman, Qatar, Saudi Arabia, the United Arab Emirates, Jordan, Lebanon, the Syrian Arab Republic, Yemen, Iraq and Palestine.

2 Nearly five trillion dollars have been exported from the Gulf region since 1970. The portion of outflows related to political tension in the form of capital flight is calculated at about one quarter of Saudi Arabia's GDP (ESCWA 2008).

3 The commodity realizes its cycle by being sold on the market and, subsequently, profits are derived from its sales, given a sufficient level of wage income.

4 According to the Stockholm International Peace Research Institute (SIPRI) database, the region has exhibited the highest frequency of conflicts worldwide (see Table 3.3).

5 SAMA Annual Report, various years for time-series data.

6 AMF's Joint Arab Economic Report, various years for time-series data.

7 In 1985, at the request of the United States, France, Germany, Japan and the United Kingdom agreed to deliberately weaken the dollar's exchange rate. The weakening of the dollar recently was accompanied by calls to move towards a multi-currency trading system, implying that the political structure has to shift, eroding the stature of the USA.

References

Abou Anaml, H. (2006) *Alikstad al Israeli*, Beirut: Markaz Dirasat al-Wahda al-'Arabiya (in Arabic).

AMF (Arab Monetary Fund) (various years) *Joint Arab Economic Report*, Abu Dhabi: AMF.

Arraf, J. (2011) 'Iraq's abandoned children', Al Jazeera documentary, 10 May, English. aljazeera.net/video/middleeast/2011/05/201151041017174884.html.

Ayubi, N. (1995) *Over-Stating the Arab State: Politics and Society in the Middle East*, London: I. B. Tauris.

Brenner, R. (2003) 'Towards the precipice: the continuing collapse of the US economy', *London Review of Books*, 5: 18–23.

Chossudovsky, M. (2006) *The Globalization of Poverty and*

the New World Order, 2006, Pincourt, Quebec, Canada: Global Research, Center for Research on Globalization.

Deffeyes, K. (2002) *Hubbert's Peak: The Impending World Oil Shortage*, Princeton, NJ: Princeton University Press.

ESCWA (UN Economic and Social Commission for Western Asia) (2003) *Analysis of Performance and Assessment of Growth and Productivity in the ESCWA Region*, 1, New York: United Nations.

— (2004a) *Analysis of Performance and Assessment of Growth and Productivity in the ESCWA Region*, 2, New York: United Nations.

— (2004b) *Summary of the Survey of Economic and Social Developments in the ESCWA Region 2008–2009*, New York: United Nations.

— (2007a) *Survey of Economic and Social Developments in the ESCWA Region 2006–2007*, New York: United Nations.

— (2007b) *Population and Development Report: International Migration and Development in the Arab Region: Challenges and Opportunities*, New York: United Nations.

— (2008) *Survey of Economic and Social Developments in the ESCWA Region 2007–2008*, New York: United Nations.

— (2009a) *Summary of the Survey of Economic and Social Developments in the ESCWA Region 2008–2009*, New York: United Nations.

— (2009b) *Statistical Abstract of the ESCWA Region*, New York: United Nations.

Gunder-Frank, A. (1991) *Third World War: A Political Economy of the Gulf War and New World Order*, www.rrojasdatabank.info/agfrank/gulf_war.html.

Hertog, S. (2010) 'Defying the resource curse: explaining successful state-owned enterprises in rentier states', *World Politics*, 62: 261–301.

ILO (International Labour Organization) (2003) *Key Indicators of the Labour Market* (KILM), Geneva: International Labour Organization.

Kadri, A. (2008) 'A regional unemployment strategy', Qatar: Arab Labour Organization.

Koechlin, T. (1999) 'The limits of globalization: an assessment of the extent and consequences of the mobility of productive capital', in S. Dev Gupta (ed.), *The Political Economy of Globalization*, London: Kluwer Academic Publishers.

Kohler, G. (1999) 'Global Keynesianism and beyond', *Journal of World Systems*, 2: 253–74.

Lenin, V. (1966 [1916]) *Imperialism, the Highest Stage of Capitalism*, Moscow: Progress Publishers.

Lutsky, V. B. (1969) *Modern History of the Arab Countries*, Moscow: Progress Publishers.

Luxemburg, R. (1973 [1913]) *The Accumulation of Capital*, New York: Monthly Review Press.

Niblock, T. and M. Malik (2007) *The Political Economy of Saudi Arabia*, London: Routledge.

Patnaik, P. (1997) *Accumulation and Stability under Capitalism*, Oxford: Oxford University Press.

— (2005) 'The economics of the new phase of imperialism', *IDEAs* featured articles, www.networkideas.org/featart/aug2005/Economics_New_Phase.pdf.

Petras, J. and M. Morley (1994) *Empire or Republic: Global Power or Domestic Decay in the US*, London: Routledge.

SAMA (Saudi Arabian Monetary Authority) (various years) *Annual Report*, Saudi Arabia: SAMA.

SIPRI (Stockholm International Peace Research Institute) (2009) *SIPRI Military Expenditure Database*, Stockholm: Stockholm International Peace Research Institute.

UNCTAD (2001) *Trade and Development Report*, Geneva: UNCTAD.

United Nations (2007) *The Millennium Development Goals Report*, New York: United Nations, www.un.org/millenniumgoals/pdf/mdg2007.pdf.

Wallerstein, I. (2000) 'Globalization or the age of transition?: a long-term view of the trajectory of the world system', *International Sociology*, 15: 249–65.

World Bank (2009) *World Development Indicators, WDI 2009*, Washington, DC: World Bank, databank.worldbank.org/ddp/home.do?Step=12&id=4&CNO=2.

Wright, G. (2003) 'Wolfowitz: Iraq war was about oil', *Guardian*, 4 June.

Yamamoto, Y. (2009) 'The Dubai crisis', Internal paper prepared for the Economic Analysis Division, Beirut: ESCWA (unpublished).

Yang, C. (2006) 'The downside of cheaper oil', *Business Week*, 4004: 50.

PART TWO

Creating and reproducing marginality

4 | Marginality or abjection? The political economy of poverty production in Egypt

RAY BUSH

It is indeed shameful that in a resource rich region, Arab countries as a whole have not witnessed any noticeable reduction in either malnutrition or food deprivation since 1990. For the Arab region to achieve this target in the coming years, it is required that hunger becomes a pronounced priority in the region's development plans and policies. (UNDP/League of Arab States, 2008)

The first lesson is that contrary to mainstream thinking, the market does not have a self-corrective mechanism. (Yash Tandon, Director of South Centre)

Introduction

This chapter questions the usefulness of the terms 'exclusion' and 'marginality' for understanding Egypt's political economy and the continuous and worsening conditions of poverty.[1] It explores the importance of understanding how poverty is (re)produced, arguing that poverty is the result of people being actively dispossessed rather than being simply left on the margins or being excluded from the creation of wealth. Marginality and exclusion are thus not incidental to capitalist society but are systemically part of it. Poverty is the outcome of capitalist modernization and the process may better be understood as abjection (Ferguson 1999). Abjection refers to people being excluded from development. It refers to their debasement and humiliation. Abjection might also refer, as Duffield (2007) has documented when talking about the character of post-Second World War development, to a process of creating a surplus population which has been a continuous feature of capitalist modernity. Egypt's reserve army of labour also became a force for revolution and change as the unemployed joined the youth and new independent trade unions in Tahrir Square in January 2011. Many of Egypt's poor have also continued to be an important component in the country's struggles for democratic deepening.

This chapter also asks why strategies to alleviate poverty fail to deliver their aims and objectives – an issue taken up by, among others in this volume, Saker el Nour and Moushira Elgeziri. I argue for the need to be cautious in the use of terms like 'exclusion' and 'marginality'. This is partly because there is a tendency to assume that if economic growth creates poverty this will only be a temporary phenomenon. Mainstream economic theory assumes that marginalization and poverty are temporary as overall economic growth eventually incorporates the poor into work. Thus economic growth within a neoliberal narrative advances the benefits of 'trickle-down' growth: tax breaks for the rich and for companies to provide economic stimulus for the economy as a whole and ultimately poverty reduction. But this has not been evident in Egypt. Since 1980 Egypt's economy has grown by 5 per cent per annum – a level of growth that is the envy of any developing country. But while Egypt developed Egyptians did not. Real wages stagnated during Mubarak's dictatorship, unemployment grew and international financial institutions (IFIs) pressured the regime to cut subsidies and liberalize the economy.

Egypt's pattern of capitalist development created winners and losers. The struggles between the broadly defined groups of those who benefited from growth – the political elite, crony capitalists and the military on one hand and workers and peasants on the other – shaped the revolutionary forces that toppled Mubarak. Reconstruction for a democratic and more equal Egyptian political economy after the revolution of 25 January 2011 will depend upon the economic militancy, political strength and continued mobilization of workers and peasants. Any democratic deepening that has taken place after the revolution has been won only by the continuous, permanent revolution of protesters in Tahrir Square and those workers and peasants who have continued with strikes, sit-ins and occupations of workplaces, streets and government buildings. The permanent revolution has impeded the military's mobilization of counter-revolutionary forces, promoting a status quo ante. The Supreme Council of the Armed Forces (SCAF) has aggressively advanced a strategy of promoting sectarian violence to justify a position as ultimate arbitrator and guarantor of 'law and (dis)order'. This strategy was evidenced at its worst in the slaughter of twenty-seven protesters with more than 330 injured outside the state broadcasting centre in Maspero on 9 October 2011. And in December 2011 the military and security forces violently attacked protesters outside the cabinet office and parliament building in Cairo, killing more than twenty and injuring hundreds. The SCAF has announced that it will not open the military's financial accounts to public or parliamentary scrutiny. The generals have said the SCAF will retain the final decision about how parliamentary elections will translate into the formation of a government and the timing of presidential elections. And the generals thumbed their nose at the USA in December 2011 when finally Secretary of State Hillary Clinton said she was appalled at the mistreatment of women protesters in Tahrir Square.

Poverty in the Middle East

The World Bank's *Global Monitoring Report* (2008) indicated that the region of the Middle East and North Africa (MENA) will reduce by half the number of those living on less than $2 a day in the years between 1990 and 2015. Progress is shown to be slow, with still more than 59 million people living on less than $2 a day, and there is particularly slow progress on gender equality in education – worse in Yemen and Djibouti – low female labour participation rates and more than half of the region's countries failing to meet millennium development goal (MDG) nutrition targets. There are persistently high under-five mortality rates but reasonable progress in meeting targets on numbers entering primary education, especially in Egypt, Morocco and Syria – the quality of education in schools, however, remains questionable. There have also been significant advances in health provision, but the regional starting point was low.

Poverty is seen by the UN agencies as a huge developmental problem and something that can be solved by appropriate policy intervention. In contrast I am suggesting that poverty is the outcome of systemic unequal global and local relations of production between capital and labour in the process of capital accumulation (Bush 2007; Bond 2006). The figures used by the international agencies to indicate the scale of the development 'problem' also need to be regarded with caution. Their accuracy and reliability are problematic and often seem to be contrived by autocracies to demonstrate improvements in living standards when none has taken place (Bush 2004; Sabry 2010). Twenty per cent of people in MENA are recorded as living in extreme poverty – on less than $1 per person per day. But MENA also remains, next to Europe, the region in the world with the second-lowest poverty incidence – but with tremendous regional variation: extreme poverty increased in Egypt between 2000 and 2005 by 3.3 per cent; 22 per cent live on less than $1 a day (perhaps as many as 80 per cent on less than $1 a day in rural Egypt). In Iraq more than 50 per cent live in absolute poverty with more than two million internal displacements and refugees; in Palestine 80 per cent of the 1.5 million in Gaza are dependent on food aid; 70 per cent live on less than $1 a day, with inadequate fuel, energy, water, health and education. And even in high-middle-income Lebanon poverty affects 35 per cent of the population and there is a 40 per cent overall poverty rate. And this has led to struggles relating to accessing minimum food and non-food requirements.

The persistent and uneven presence of poverty in MENA suggests we need to exercise care in agreeing with the often touted view that poverty in the region is relatively low in relation to international comparators. The *Arab Human Development Report*, in 2002 and 2009, emphasized the relative absence of poverty in the Arab world.[2] This absence was accounted for by historical patterns of egalitarian income distribution and the ways in which the poor benefited from periods of relative prosperity, for example in 1970–85. But the contemporary crisis of international capitalism is exacerbating poverty in the region. Although there was economic growth in the last quarter of 2008 it was dramatically affected by the global financial implosion. The impact is likely to be significant in four areas: the fall in financial and real estate prices; the fall in commodity prices, including not only energy sources but also metals and food (although food price *rises* triggered political and social unrest in Yemen and North Africa in general, and foregrounded the Egyptian revolution); shortages of financial liquidity in local markets; and dramatic falls in export earnings (ESCWA 2009). Socially the implications of the contemporary crisis have been equally dramatic. Food riots across the Middle East were sparked by food price rises in 2007/08 (Schneider 2009). The price of wheat, for instance, rose by 130 per cent, and rice more than doubled in price in the first three months of 2008 – Egypt is the world's second-largest importer of wheat. The direct impact of food price rises brings into question the efficacy of the one- or two-dollar-a-day measurement of poverty: an increase in food price inflation directly and immediately has life-and-death implications. The increase in staple food prices makes poor families particularly vulnerable to falling into acute hardship. As the World Bank noted,

> Poor households in the Middle East and North Africa region were disproportionately impacted by the 2008 food crisis because: (i) they spend a larger share of income on food, which accounts for more than 50 per cent of poor households' spending in Morocco, Yemen, Egypt, and Djibouti and (ii) most rural poor in the MENA region are net food consumers. (World Bank 2010)

As the crisis of global capitalism deepens poor people's income will fall, unemployment will rise as falls in domestic employment will be exaggerated, and remittances will plummet. If state responses to the crisis, as is likely, are to reduce fiscal stimulus, unlike the strategy adopted by the G8, any possible cushion for the poor that results from social spending will be reduced.

Egypt

Egypt's economic growth performance prior to the revolution was exemplary, although it was moot how growth would deliver poverty reduction (Ministry of Agriculture and Land Reclamation 2009). USAID noted that Egypt's growth and investment performance from 2002 was strong; growth more than doubled between 2002/03 and 2006/07 from 3.2 per cent to 7.1 per cent. Economic growth has outstripped increases in population, but per capita GDP of PPP$5,272[3] in 2006/07 is less than that of regional comparators like Jordan at PPP$5,964 and Turkey at PPP$9,816. A range of other macroeconomic indicators were used by USAID and the erstwhile government of Egypt (GoE) to demonstrate the vibrancy of the Egyptian economy: a gross fixed investment rate of more than 20 per cent; increased private investment and improved amounts of foreign direct investment.

There is also optimism that the improvements in Egypt's national economy have been due to increases in trade – and on the surface this looked encouraging. Between 2002/03 and 2006/07 trade increased from 46.1 to 65.1 per cent of GDP – USAID actually use the word 'surge'. But these figures need close scrutiny, and they do not promise the launch into self-sustained growth the IFIs promise. Export volumes have increased but so too have imports – imports grew by an average of 24.7 per cent in 2004–07 compared with an increase of 18.8 per cent in average growth of exports. Of course, this increased level of imports may suggest that investment has increased in productivity-generating activities. Fuels and consumer goods, for instance, may have accounted for less than 20 per cent of the increased imports. During Egypt's 25 January revolution an IMF visit to Egypt reported that 'Egypt's economy has been resilient to the [financial] crisis' and 'Economic performance was better than expected' (IMF 2010).

There is nevertheless a continuing frailty to Egypt's economy that the evidence summoned by the IFIs and the GoE cannot easily hide. This is characterized by the continued dominance of rent as a proportion of national income. Almost 50 per cent of Egypt's exports in 2006/07 were accounted for by hydrocarbons. This, together with the continuing dominance of rent from the Suez Canal and labour remittances, make the economy, and the security of poor people within it, very difficult to sustain.[4] The vulnerability of Egypt's economy to external factors has been a persistent feature of different regimes since 1952. Abdel Nasser's regime may have had most success in reducing dependence upon the vagaries of the world economy, perhaps ultimately undone by its regional ambition. In promoting de-Nasserization, President Sadat and Mubarak rhetorically followed *infitah* and the idea of market reform. Since 1991 and stronger foreign policy ties with the USA, the GoE has trodden a fine line between delivering enough macroeconomic reform and state retrenchment to appease the IFIs while never fully embracing reform. And how Egypt manages its poor remains a persistent and continuing feature of GoE negotiations and its relationship with the IFIs. The IFIs have become concerned that too much poverty may lead to heightened political unrest, whether in the context of post-2000 economic growth or the more recent economic 'downturn' and post-25 January revolution. And just how the GoE deals with 'the poor' or 'poverty' has been very unidirectional: growth leads to poverty reduction and greater tax and other financial incentives (benefits) for the already wealthy, which will ultimately reduce poverty more quickly than strategies of redistribution of existing wealth. Such a view was exemplified in GoE budgetary statements. In 2007, for instance, it was noted that: 'The wealthier classes are even more fortunate because they are linked to the market mechanisms, and better informed and therefore more likely to react within the system to generate more income' (cited in Hussein and Hussein 2007).

USAID concedes that 'poverty remains a significant problem', although it says little about the impact on poor people of twenty years of economic reform. It notes that the number of Egyptians living on less than PPP$1 a day was 0.9 per cent in 2004, a figure that clearly ignores other data. And while this is seen as a decline from 3.1 per cent in 2000, there are enormous contrasts between Upper and Lower, and rural and urban, Egypt (UNDP 2008). Moreover, if the figures for extreme poverty are accurate they seem to be overtaken by very high levels of poverty defined as those living on less than PPP$2 a day. In 2000 43.9 per cent of Egyptians lived on less than PPP$2 a day. This compares with 7 per cent in Jordan and 18.7 per cent in Turkey. A recent document has indicated that the proportion of Egyptians still living on less than $2 a day remains at about 43 per cent, up from 39 per cent in 1990. In 2007 almost 20 per cent of Egyptians had consumption expenditures below the national poverty line, an increase over the last fifteen years (ibid.). And if the measures for poverty go beyond income and expenditure levels, as they should, in 2004 UNDP placed Egypt 48th out of 108 developing countries on its human poverty index, and in 2006 73rd out of 135 developing countries. Egypt's human development index (HDI) has remained stuck at 20.0, not despite but because of the country's particular pattern of economic growth.

Egypt's Human Development Report (ibid.) noted that the country would not meet the first MDG, to eradicate extreme poverty and hunger by reducing by half the proportion of people living on less than $1 a day by 2015. There is likely to be an increase in the numbers of poor living in Cairo, and rural poverty continues unchecked, especially but not exclusively in Upper Egypt. The continued and worsening rural–urban divide, the biggest in the region for lower-middle-income MENA countries, is especially noticeable, with relatively high Egyptian infant mortality and appallingly low access to sanitation – in the latter case, 52 per cent in rural Egypt compared with 85 per cent for urban residents. Uneven development in Egypt is confirmed by the evidence that six out of the eight governorates that will not meet the MDG related to poverty are in Upper Egypt. And neither will the governorates in Cairo and Ismailia meet the poverty MDGs.

The (re)production of poverty

Egypt's macroeconomic and poverty profile raise three interlinked questions. The first is why is there such a divergence between policy announcements and promises with regard to poverty reduction and actual reduction in the numbers of poor. Secondly, why, if there has been such a historically high and sustained period of economic growth, has it not reduced poverty?[5] And thirdly, to what extent will a new democratic Egyptian government, after the 25 January revolution, seek to reverse the failures of the previous Mubarak era? The early indications from the Muslim Brotherhood, the clear victors in the December 2011 and January 2012 parliamentary elections, are that they will do little to rock the boat of business and international capitalist interests. Indeed, as early as the summer of 2010 the Muslim Brotherhood's number two, Khariat el-Shater, told a group of international fund managers that the private sector and foreign investment were very welcome in Egypt (Fam and Reed 2011). It would seem that there is little enthusiasm to challenge IFI pressure to accept foreign borrowing, continue the downward pressure on wages and persist with anti-strike legislation. The challenge to this policy of the status quo ante seems to come exclusively from the revolutionary socialists and the April 6 movement (Socialist Worker 2011). These groups, along with some smaller groupings, have expressed alarm that little has changed since the revolution to redress high levels of poverty. And there has been reluctance by most newly formed political parties to understand why poverty in Egypt increased alongside high levels of economic growth. Those increases emerged during the period of neoliberal reform after 1991, and especially after the government of 2004 of Prime Minister Atef Ebeid. This is looked at in more detail later in this volume by Rabab el Mahdi.

The *Arab Human Development Report* (AHDR) (UNDP 2009) was clear why MENA may do less well in the face of the global financial crisis: it was because of policy failure. The persistence of regional poverty was the result of a strategy that focused 'more on the security of the state than on the security of the people' (ibid.: v). This led to 'an all too-common sense of limited opportunities and personal insecurity, witnessed in the world's highest levels of unemployment, deep and contentious patterns of exclusion, and ultimately strong calls from within for reform [...] the pursuit of state security without attention to human security has brought on sub-optimal outcomes for the state and citizen' (ibid.: v–vi).

The AHDR (ibid.) argued instead for the need to promote human security. Development in the region had stalled and with it human development. This is because, the report asserts, the region has fragile 'political, social, economic and environmental structures', an absence of people-centred development and vulnerability to outside intervention. Human security is now elevated to a key strategy, defined as 'the liberation of human beings from those intense, extensive, prolonged, and comprehensive threats to which their lives and freedom are vulnerable' (ibid.: 2). It is not clear when exactly the missed opportunities for human development emerged. And it is also unclear how an emphasis on the traditional conception of security 'ensured the continuity of the state', leading 'to missed opportunities to ensure the security of the human person' (ibid.: v). What is clear from the detailed report, however, is that 'Despite moderate levels of income inequality, in most Arab countries social *exclusion* [my emphasis] has increased over the past two decades.' There has also been a greater worsening of inequalities in wealth than of income inequality, although that has got worse too. It is important that the report highlights a concentration on asset wealth and access to land as measures that have worsened exclusion (ibid.: 12), but the conclusions drawn from these observations do not grasp the reasons why abjection, rather than exclusion, has intensified, and neither does the use of the term exclusion adequately explain deterioration in the living conditions of more than 65 million Arabs living in poverty in MENA.[6]

It is important that human security is given such a steer by the AHDR, but it is important too that the other forms of security, national and democratic, are not eclipsed. ESCWA, for example, has stressed the significance of rights-based economic development as the overall driving force for reform (ESCWA 2009). But the positions taken by IFIs and advocacy groups remain wedded to a neoliberal formulation (Bush 2004). Neoliberals may (reluctantly) accept that the system may be faulty in that poverty continues to be a concern, but this is usually seen only as a temporary and short-term problem of exclusion, which can be fixed. Fixing the problem entails incorporating 'the poor' (undifferentiated) into work, but where and in what sectors, with what levels of welfare provision and improvements in education curriculum and delivery?

The issue of inclusion as a remedy for poverty has been ultimately at the core of human development initiatives (UNDP), rights-based approaches (UNICEF) and livelihoods (DfID) and human security (UN). The issue that underpins all these approaches is that if the exclusion of the poor can be reduced then so too will their poverty. And this approach (the need for greater inclusion) goes beyond a strategy for poverty reduction within poor countries.[7] It extends to relations between the global North and global South. Thus the dominant position regarding international debt is that if only poor countries were included more fully in globalization, poverty would fall (World Bank 1995, 2008; DfID 2000, 2009), and so too would incentives for terrorism.

There are a number of problems with this approach of exclusion as the cause of poverty. The most significant is that the focus on exclusion avoids understanding how poverty is produced and reproduced. Focus on exclusion prevents analysis of the differential way in which poor people are incorporated into economic and political practices (Bracking 2003). And ultimately, the social policy focus on inclusion/exclusion avoids discussion and analysis of capital, power and politics, the real parameters that determine poverty. Put simply, preoccupation with the language of inclusion and exclusion avoids the realities of the struggles between winners and losers in the process of development: in the struggles between capital and labour. This chapter has argued that poverty can only meaningfully be analysed if it is grasped in its 'structural and relational sense'. This is because it is necessary to understand the specificity of different poor peoples' experiences (Francis and Murray 2002: 486). We need therefore to ask, among other things, who benefits from existing economic and political strategy, as well as who does not. We cannot simply support the policies of donors, aid agencies and others who assert that the only really necessary reform to promote poverty alleviation is the promotion of asset-building (for the most simplistic position on this, see De Soto 2003). Reducing poverty is neither an issue of throwing money at the poor – although many would benefit greatly from that – nor is it simply a question of asset-building. Access to resources helps produce wealth *and* poverty, and understanding the processes linked to the relationship between wealth creation and the reproduction of poverty means that discussions about assets must be seen in the relational context in which they are used.

The mushrooming of rural poverty after 1992, for example, can clearly be attributed to, among other things, the reform of tenancy, which became fully effective in 1997. Very few analyses of that process have dissented from the positive hype of the erstwhile GoE, USAID and EU that market-driven rural transformation was beneficial for Egypt. There is little evidence, however, to support the view that market reform in the agricultural sector has reduced poverty, or indeed generated the promised level of growth. What is clear, however, is that the beneficiaries of tenancy reform and market deregulation were landowners and business interests. This is evidenced by accelerated rural social differentiation since 1992 and shifts in landholding categories, on which there is a need for more research. There has been, for instance, an increase in the landholding category of 'fully owned' compared with 'fully cash paid' tenancies. The proportion of fully owned rose from 68 per cent in 1990 to 88 per cent in 2000. And the proportion in the category of fully cash paid rental fell from 14 per cent in 1990 to 5 per cent in 2000. But just which households have been thrown out of agricultural production and how have they been reintegrated into productive work, if at all? This is a key area for research, but it is not clear that there are any agencies interested in more fully understanding what the consequences of market liberalization have been for the rural poor. And it remains unclear whether the new government of Egypt will prioritize an investigation into the causes of poverty, especially in the countryside. The early signs are that the pressures for establishing economic stability will preoccupy the new Egyptian government and parliament. This will in all likelihood mean a prioritization of economic growth, bolstered by foreign lending rather than policies of effective and deliverable mechanisms of redistribution, a comprehensive and progressive taxation regime and a boost for the incomes of the rural and urban poor.

Egypt's strategy of agrarian market reform was most significantly introduced in 1987. Although it has at different times been hailed as the leading reform that can drive poverty reduction, it has instead politicized land, rewarded landowners, especially those that are absentee, and served to throw many in the countryside into poverty. The failures to renew contracts for female-headed families have been documented (Bush 2002), the abjection of the rural poor lamented (Fergany 2002) and the consolidation of landowning interests acknowledged (Saad 2002). We know too that budgets for agriculture have fallen, apart from the enormous financial drain of the irrigated Toshka agricultural scheme (Farag 2003). Moreover, Egypt has promoted the idea of itself as a regional market player, but there is little evidence for this other than its subordinate agrarian capitalism, which confirms the abjection of the country's poor farmers while Egyptian elites have profited and purchased land in sub-Saharan Africa (Bush 2011).

Conclusion

Inequality results from contemporary capitalism and the way in which power is distributed. This singular truth is avoided by mainstream analysts intent instead on, at best, incorporating (some) poor people into the existing social structures of inequality. This strategy, however, merely perpetuates the system of inequality. And this reproduction of poverty creates further differential incorporation. The strategies that follow from the characterization of the poor (usually undifferentiated) as being those people who are on the margins of wealth creation and thus just need to be brought more fully into a capitalist market economy are twofold. The first is to increase the production of wealth and the second is to ensure greater efficiency in the production of that wealth. The policy that follows from the preoccupation with growth under existing conditions of relations between capital and labour usually involves a moderate improvement in welfare spending – ensuring that there remains an incentive to get into employment (irrespective of the type of work) – downsizing the public sector and providing incentives for wealth creation – tax breaks for the wealthy. A shopping list of measures then emerges which has dominated the neoliberal period since the early 1970s, and which alludes to concerns over income distribution and poverty reduction but fails to consult 'the poor' about their poverty. As one commentator noted in the mid-1990s the problem with the social policy strategy in the UK was that men and women were not seen as agents of social change, only as victims of exclusion (Jordan 1996). This has a strong resonance in the Middle East.

The dominance of neoliberal ideology has ensured that where there has been any discussion of poverty it has tended to ignore debate about who the poor are. In the Middle East, as Joel Beinin has noted, this has served the purpose of eliminating 'workers and peasants as social categories altogether' (2001: 148), and the reason for that is the reluctance to recall the era of social compacts between the working class and peasantry and authoritarian populist regimes. That era of the late 1950s and 1960s, especially in Egypt, is reflected upon now in the media only negatively or to reify the dignity of Nasser without exploring what his agenda of action was, whether flawed or not. Thus even within the prevailing neoliberal framework of economic adjustment (and despite or rather because of the global financial crisis) there is failure to debate the value of increased social expenditure as a strategy to increase the inclusion of the poor. And there is a failure to understand that it is the system of wealth creation which creates poverty.

In this context it is not surprising that public spending on health, education and social security fell in Egypt in 2003–07. It fell by 25 per cent in health. Public expenditure in education also fell as a proportion of total government expenditure, from 16.2 per cent to 12.6 per cent. In contrast there was an increase in spending on defence and national security – one of the measures of which the AHDR (UNDP 2009) was so critical. As a recent *Egypt's Human Development Report* noted (UNDP 2008), there was a sharp contradiction between the declared rhetoric of the GoE to 'improve the quality of life and standard of living' of Egyptians, as declared in Egypt's five-year national plan of 2002–07, and the actual level of spending allocated to social measures and defence. As Egypt's per capita GDP rose from US$4,361 in 2003 to US$5,052 in 2007, state spending on defence and security rose by 85 per cent. The transitional post-25 January GoE did begin to plan for an increase in selected social expenditures. However, it became increasingly clear that it was unable to initiate any policy without agreement from the SCAF, which defended both the corporate interests of the military and those of Egypt's most powerful economic elites. And the military backed up its sclerotic hold on government by imprisoning, between February and July 2011, via the deplored military courts, more than ten thousand young activists who were found 'guilty' of defending the aims of the revolution – among other things the promotion of human dignity (Soueif 2011).

There has long been a view that foreign assistance can help reduce exclusion by targeting the poor, but there has been little success from this strategy. In 2004 about $134 million in international aid was directed to programmes that were intended to erase hunger and poverty. That was about 18 per cent of total foreign assistance, with agriculture receiving 34 per cent of that. But the poorest governorates, Assiut, Beni Suef, Suhag, Menia and Qena, received only between 5.6 and 2.2 per cent of that assistance. Governorates with less poverty, Al Behaira and Damietta, received proportionately more foreign assistance intended to help with poverty alleviation (UNDP 2008: 46).

The GoE, like all governments, is accountable for its public expenditure, and if it is not, political mobilization and popular protest are likely to result to address the grievances of the poor. Popular protest, as discussed in the chapter by Rabab el Mahdi, preceded the revolution of 25 January 2011. Many of the political struggles centred on wage and working conditions, with a tremendous mobilization of working-class activism. Political demonstrations in the build-up to the revolution were promoted by intolerably poor living conditions and escalating food prices. The GoE conceded many workers' demands before the occupation of Tahrir Square. And what was perhaps most significant of all in terms of the worker unrest was that much of it was led from outside the state-run trade unions. The growth of new labour and farmer syndicates before the revolution and throughout 2011 gave Egyptians who had been thrown out of the processes of development an arena in which to voice demands for a new Egypt.

This chapter began with some observations about the region, and it is important to note that while the focus on Egypt's poor is central to this collection of essays, the continued successful struggles for social and economic transformation may be more effective if they become part of a broader regional protest. This is because it is unlikely that anything meaningful will be done about poverty reduction, and the continuing creation of poor people in Egypt, without a regional strategy. It needs to be remembered that the combined national income of twenty-two Arab countries is less than that of Spain, and just under twice the national income of Belgium at $771.2 billion, and the region exemplifies tremendous unevenness in growth. Wealth is concentrated in oil-rich states, yet more than 40 per cent in the region live on less than $2 a day, with an unemployment average of more than 13 per cent – the highest of any region in the world – with youth unemployment of 26 per cent, again the highest in the world.

The regional disparities are significant and may be a block or a spur to greater regional collaboration to reduce poverty. Oil wealth has generated a regional divide – between the countries of the Gulf Cooperation Council (GCC) and the more diversified economies and the non-resource-rich states. But rather than wealth in the region being retained it has been sent overseas or used to purchase weapons. The Arab region can boast twice the world share of GDP on military expenditure, and it is the region with the highest volume of US military aid. Yet it is also the region with excess savings over investment, skewed especially towards the GCC states.

The failure of Arab elites to invest locally or regionally is the biggest obstacle to sustained levels of economic growth. It is a failure explained by security worries, and there are clearly many of those – Israel's occupation of Palestine, the USA's continued large presence, despite troop withdrawal in Iraq, the fuelling of sectarianism and fears of an attack against Iran, as well as the other concerns of food import dependency, water constraints, poor infrastructure limiting delivery of contracts and the persistent regional divisions aggravated by US and EU geostrategic interests.

As Ali Kadri demonstrated earlier in this volume, the context of war, occupation and regional uncertainty sustains the opportunity for US and EU leverage to continue the promotion of a neoliberal agenda. While that agenda has been discredited following the global financial crisis and the inability of the IFIs to sustain economic growth, the ideology of neoliberalism prevails. Given resource-led growth and the rents that accrue from it, whether in the form of revenue from ships transiting the Suez or oil and gas, and the imperative to sell to Israel, one of the actors undermining the possibility of regional poverty reduction, it is not surprising to see Arab merchant classes, the political elites and crony capitalists attached to the various regional states seeking fast returns on their limited investment. Opportunity for industrial development and regional organization that does not systemically create and reproduce poverty for the majority of people in the region still seems very distant, but there have been significant political challenges to the status quo, and Egypt's 25 January revolution has led the way.

Notes

1 Many thanks to Ali Kadri for comments on a draft of this chapter.

2 The *Arab Human Development Report* refers to the Arab world and not MENA.

3 Purchasing Power Parity refers to the idea that an amount of money is assumed to have the same purchasing power in different countries.

4 The GoE *Economic and Social Indicators Bulletin* of June 2009 operates a 'sleight of hand' with its overview summary of the state of Egypt's economy. It draws attention to the fact that receipts from the

Suez Canal, at US$346.9 billion in April 2009, were 5.8 per cent more than in the previous month – they were, however, 22.7 per cent down compared with twelve months previously.

5 There is another important issue, touched on only briefly here. This is that the data for growth and poverty are not accurate – there are certainly divergences on growth and other macro data between the IFIs, the GoE, advocacy groups and academic commentators. And on understanding what constitutes poverty the Arab League and the UNDP have tried to distance themselves from what might be seen as stylized facts on income poverty. Income measures alone are criticized for not recognizing different consumption patterns across regions; those data often ignore different basic needs for different categories of household members and may also ignore economies of scale in households that may share food and utilities. Remember too that there is an absence of timeline data for more than nine Arab countries for household income and expenditure.

6 Many in the Arab world would find it difficult to comprehend that they are alongside sub-Saharan Africa as one of only two regions in the world where the number of undernourished has risen since the beginning of the 1990s – from 19.8 million in 1990–92 to 25.5 million in 2002–04 (UNDP 2009: 12).

7 This is also the strategy in developed capitalist economies. Look at recent US, UK and French domestic social policy initiatives, for instance.

References

Beinin, J. (2001) *Workers and Peasants in the Modern Middle East*, Cambridge: Cambridge University Press.

Bond, P. (2006) *Looting Africa: The Economics of Exploitation*, London: Zed Books.

Bracking, S. (2003) 'The political economy of chronic poverty', Working paper for the Chronic Poverty Research Centre, Institute for Development Policy and Management, University of Manchester, February.

Bush, R. (ed.) (2002) *Counter Revolution in the Egyptian Countryside*, London: Zed Books.

— (2004) 'Poverty and neo liberal bias in the Middle East and North Africa', *Development and Change*, 35(4): 673–95.

— (2007) *Poverty and Neo Liberalism*, London: Pluto.

— (2011) 'Coalitions for dispossession and resistance? Land, politics and agrarian reform in Egypt', Special issue, 'The dynamics of reform coalitions in the Arab world', *Journal of Middle Eastern Studies*, 38(3).

De Soto, H. (2003) *The Mystery of Capital*, New York: Basic Books.

DfID (Department for International Development) (2000) *Eliminating World Poverty: Making Globalisation Work for the Poor*, London, HMSO.

— (2009) *Eliminating World Poverty: Building Our Common Future*, www.dfid.gov.uk/Documents/whitepaper/building-our-common-future-print.pdf.

Duffield, M. (2007) *Development, Security and Unending War. Governing the World of Peoples*, Cambridge: Polity Press.

Egypt's Revolutionary Socialists (2011) 'Statement by Egypt's Revolutionary Socialists', socialistworker.org/blog/critical-reading/2011/12/27/statement-revolutionary-social, accessed 2 January 2012.

ESCWA (2009) *Economic and Social Developments in the ESCWA Region 2008–2009*, Beirut.

Fam, M. and S. Reed (2011) 'Egypt Brotherhood courts investors with pro-business stance', Bloomberg, 8 July, www.bloomberg.com/news/2011-07-07/egypt-s-brotherhood-courts-investors-with-pro-business-stance.html, accessed 2 January 2012.

Farag, F. (2003) 'Green desert – at what cost?', *Al Ahram Weekly*, 622, 23–29 January.

Fergany, N. (2002) 'Poverty and unemployment in rural Egypt', in Ray Bush (ed.), *Counter Revolution in the Egyptian Countryside*, London: Zed Books.

Ferguson, J. (1999) *Expectations of Modernity: Myths and Meanings of Urban Life on the Zambian Copperbelt*, Berkeley: University of California Press.

Francis, E. and C. Murray (2002) 'Introduction', Special issue, 'Changing livelihoods', *Journal of Southern African Studies*, 28(3): 485–7.

Hussein, S. and M. Hussein (2007) 'Créateur de disparités', www.hebdo.ahram.org.eg/arab/ahram/2007/5/16/evep1.htm.

IMF (International Monetary Fund) (2010) *Arab Republic of Egypt – 2010 Article IV Consultation Mission, Concluding Statement*, February, Cairo, www.imf.org/external/np/ms/2010/021610.htm, accessed 23 December 2011.

Jordan, B. (1996) *A Theory of Poverty and Social Exclusion*, Oxford: Polity Press.

Maher, S. (2011) 'The political economy of the Egyptian up-rising', *Monthly Review*, monthlyreview.org/2011/11/01/the-political-economy-of-the-egyptian-uprising, accessed 2 January 2012.

Ministry of Agriculture and Land Reclamation (2009) *Sustainable Agricultural Development Strategy towards 2030*, Cairo: Agricultural Research and Development Council.

Saad, R. (2002) 'Egyptian politics and the Tenancy Law', in R. Bush (ed.), *Counter Revolution in the Egyptian Countryside*, London: Zed Books.

Sabry, S. (2010) 'Could urban poverty in Egypt be grossly underestimated?', London: Centre for Development Policy and Research, www.soas.ac.uk/cdpr/publications/dv/file58993.pdf, accessed 2 January 2012.

Schneider, M. (2009) '"We are hungry!" A summary report of food riots, government responses, and states of democracy in 2008', December, www.scribd.com/doc/9021751/We-Are-Hungry-A-Summary-Report-of-Food-Riots-and-More-in-2008.

Socialist Worker (2011) 'Statement by Egypt's Revolutionary Socialists', socialistworker.org/blog/critical-reading/2011/12/27/statement-revolutionary-social, accessed 3 January 2012.

Soueif, A. (2011) 'Egypt's revolution is stuck in a rut, but we still have the spirit to see it through', *Guardian*, 13 July, p. 29.

UNDP (2008) *Egypt's Human Development Report*, Cairo.

— (2009) *Arab Human Development Report*, Regional Bureau for Arab States, www.undp.org/rbas.

World Bank (1995) *Claiming the Future: Choosing Prosperity in the Middle East and North Africa*, Washington, DC: World Bank.

— (2008) *Global Monitoring Report*, Washington, DC, web. worlbank.org/WBSITE/EXTERNAL/ EXTDEC/EXTGLOBALMONITOR/ EXTGLOMON REP2008/0,,menuPK: 4738069~pagePK:64168427~piPK: 64168435~theSitePK:4738 057,00. html.

— (2010) *Project Information Document (PID)*, Concept stage, Report no. AB6559, www-wds. worldbank.org/external/default/ WDSContentServer/WDSP/IB/2011 /05/27/000001843_20110601143246/ Rendered/INDEX/P126506000 AW IFS000PID000ConceptoStage.txt.

— (2011) 'Concept Arab world initiative for financing food security', Project Information Document (PID), www-wds.worldbank.org/ external/default/WDSContent Server/WDSP/IB/2011/05/27/000 001843_20110601143246/Rendered/ PDF/P126506000AWIFS000PID-000ConceptoStage.pdf, accessed 3 January 2012.

5 | The marginalization of the small peasantry: Egypt and Tunisia

HABIB AYEB

Introduction

Late in 2010 and early in 2011 unexpected political events took place in the southern Mediterranean. Popular uprisings ended two particularly tough and inflexible dictatorships. The first of these was in Tunisia, where Ben Ali escaped after his regime collapsed on 14 January 2011 after twenty-three years of exclusive power. The second was the Egyptian dictatorship, which ended one month later with the resignation of its head, Hosni Mubarak. He had been in power since 1981. In both cases, the end of dictatorship was a real political surprise as observers did not expect it. With hindsight we can see a relationship between these great political upheavals and broader political struggles in both countries in the preceding three years. These included the two most important protests in the mining region of Gafsa in south-west Tunisia, from January to June 2008, and those of Mahalla Al-Kobra in the Nile Delta in Egypt, in April 2008. There was in both countries a history of other significant demonstrations, but on previous occasions the ruling powers had managed to put them down.

Despite many evident differences there are similarities in the revolutionary processes that led to political transformation in Tunisia and Egypt. The most obvious similarities are that no leaders and no political movements organized the protests; the outbreak of demonstrations and strikes was initiated by populations and social groups that were politically, economically and socially marginalized: poor people, labourers, underpaid employees, non-qualified and unemployed people, and unemployed graduates. And the protests started first in geographically marginal and economically, sociologically and politically marginalized areas, such as mining areas, regions suffering from a serious lack of public services, areas bordering major towns, poor urban cities, villages and neighbourhoods and, more generally, the south and the centre of each country.

The revolutions in Tunisia and Egypt were initiated by people struggling on the margins of their respective societies and from often peripheralized geographical regions, and against social groups, political institutions and central areas and power. This is a source of the originality of the Tunisian and Egyptian revolutions, as well as those in progress in other Arab countries, including Yemen, Syria and Libya – despite the militarization and external intervention that may have transformed a revolution into a civil war – and also conflict in Morocco and Algeria. It is through the process of marginalization and of social, economic and political exclusion that we can find some key factors which particularly affected the revolutionary processes in the so-called 'Arab spring'.

This chapter[1] looks at the socio-economic marginalization of the small peasantry of the Nile valley in Egypt and the oases of Gabes in the south-east of Tunisia. It explores how processes of marginality created the conditions for widespread support for revolutionary transformation in Egypt and Tunisia. In Egypt this was demonstrated before the revolution by struggles over Law 96/1992, and subsequent land occupations, and a range of conflict and protest. In Tunisia it is demonstrated by struggles driving the revolution that culminated in Tunis after a series of events after January 2008, beginning with the strikes and protests in the south-west mining region of Gafsa, and their spread across the country.

The marginalization of farmers and landless workers in rural Tunisia and Egypt resulted from and has been reproduced by unequal competition over agricultural resources (land and water) and by the dispossession imposed on small farmers in the two countries. After examining the dynamics and mechanisms of marginalization in Egypt, the chapter addresses similar processes that have occurred in and around the Tunisian oases. The intention here is not to present a comparison of the two regions but to show that despite significantly different local contexts, the global processes of marginalization have been similar.

Since the 1950s peasant agriculture and smallholder farming have been central to the agricultural sector in Egypt and Tunisia. Irrigation is central to production in Egypt and important in Tunisia, and in both cases smallholders provide the bulk of production, jobs and incomes. According to the 2002 Egyptian National Agriculture census,[2] the Nile valley and delta consist of about three million hectares of irrigated land, and there were about 3.6 million farmers in 2000 (MALR 2002). Two or three crops a year are harvested on the same plots, giving among the highest yields per hectare in the world. This ancient and traditional farming area was until the 1970s and 1980s the centre of agricultural production, and it continues to provide the bulk of production in terms of overall volume. Paradoxically, this rich agriculture, among the most productive and intensive in the world – 100 quintals of wheat per hectare (Ayeb 2010) – has been undertaken, since the agrarian reforms of the 1950s, by one of the poorest peasantries in the world (ibid.). However, despite their obvious poverty, small farmers – those with less than three feddans[3] – have mostly maintained a minimum level of family food security. That has been the result of generalized multi-activity at least until the early 1990s. Since 1990 a new agricultural policy was developed based on an agrarian counter-reform that was embodied by Law 96/1992, adopted by parliament in 1992 and effective after a five-year transition from October 1997. Law 96/1992 liberalized the land market (selling and renting prices) and the relationship between owners and tenants. Since October 1997 owners have been free to reoccupy 'their' land or rent it with a new contract to former tenants or to somebody else at the price and for the period at their discretion.

In the irrigated oases of Gabes (in the south-east of Tunisia), there are three 'green' levels (sustaining date palms, fruit trees and seasonal crops) and a complex 'oasis system', combining irrigated plots within the irrigated oasis and a much larger surface in the steppe, where peasants raise livestock and engage in rain-fed agriculture. Around the oasis the steppe is extensively cultivable with low rainfall of between 100 and 200 millimetres per year. Here farmers are engaged in arboriculture, cultivating olive, fig and almond trees, grow some cereals and rear sheep using pasture. Within the irrigated oasis they cultivate vegetables (two or three crops a year on the same plot, as in the Egyptian Nile valley), fruit trees and date palms. The irrigated oases of Gabes and large parts of south-east Tunisia including Djerba Island and the plain of Jeffara had always guaranteed food, including fruit and vegetables, for thousands of smallholders and their families. The couscous of the region of Gabes is made using olive oil, lamb and semolina, from the steppe, and vegetables from the irrigated oasis.

Irrigated agriculture in Tunisia and Egypt suffered from the damaging consequences of economic reforms and the process of economic liberalization launched in the 1980s and, more specifically, the structural adjustment programmes (SAPs) implemented from 1991 in Egypt and 1986 in Tunisia. Economic reform accelerated a process of impoverishment of the small peasantry. Yet the peasantry of Egypt and Tunisia remain important in terms of their numbers, the size of the area they cultivate, their 'contribution' to total agricultural production and their productivity per hectare. They thus occupy a central position in the agricultural sector. However, despite this incontestable central economic role and contribution to the national economies, the processes of social, economic, political and even environmental marginalization experienced by the peasantry are extensive. It has been a 'qualitative' marginalization of the centre; a progressive exclusion in favour of new, highly mechanized and export-oriented agribusiness projects, undertaken mainly in new reclaimed lands in the desert and/or steppe areas.

In the oasis of Gabes, social marginalization went hand in hand with a considerable loss of 'traditional' agricultural lands, a decline in the number of peasants and a drop in productivity per hectare. Unable to ensure a minimum income from their agricultural activity in the oasis, a lot of small farmers left their farms and looked to other activities and sources of income from commerce, services and labour migration. Some small farmers were forced to sell their plots of land to families and speculators looking for land on which to build. The combination of these processes has reduced the traditionally irrigated area of Gabes by 50 per cent. 'Abandoned' areas have been built on or have projects under construction. A process of urbanization of the oasis or of the emergence of peri-urban oases is in progress, and important parts of the oasis have been urbanized. The most visible example is the new informal neighbourhood of Zrig in the south of the city.

The processes of marginalization of small farmers in Egypt are similar to those in Tunisia, particularly in and around the oases in the southern part of the country. In both cases there has been furious competition between the small peasantry and agribusiness for land and resources. This competition is supervised by the state, which sets the rules and the objectives of the game, exercises judgement and chooses, in advance, the winner that best reflects the state's own projects and political and economic goal of rewarding political patrons (Ayeb 2010; Ayeb and Saad 2006).

While there are significant differences between the two countries, the global economic context and pressure on both states has been similar. This context consists of one internal and one external dimension: the early 1980s structural adjustment (1991 in Egypt and 1986 in Tunisia), and the ongoing economic liberalization and globalization processes. These are the mechanisms that marginalize the small peasantry and subsistence agriculture at the same time.

One of the principal differences between the countries lies in the nature and volume of the available water resources for irrigation: the Nile waters in Egypt and the rains and underground waters in southern

Tunisia. In Egypt, along the Nile, agriculture is possible only through irrigation, and all crops are irrigated, mainly by water from the Nile. The lands enclosing both sides of the Nile valley and the delta are deserts and unable to sustain any agriculture without an underground or a river water supply. In contrast with the oasis system of Gabes, in the Nile valley in Egypt farmers have only irrigated plots. When they cultivate the nearby desert lands, it is also through irrigation. The reclaimed desert lands are the 'new lands' as opposed to the silty 'old' lands of the valley.

The small farmers' dispossession in the steppe-lands, through the rapid and large-scale development of intensive agribusiness and export-oriented crops and products, and related intensive use of underground water, deprives them and the oasis system of the extensive rain-fed production land.

Moreover, in Egypt, as in the area around the oases of Gabes, the emergence of new irrigated schemes outside the Nile valley deprives traditional agriculture of a considerable part of its water resources. This has led to competition over natural agricultural resources (especially water and land), in addition to the inequalities of access to other 'man-made' agricultural resources, such as subventions, credit and markets. Disproportionate competition has resulted in both cases for three reasons: peasants' limited access to different crucial agricultural resources; secondly, the reduction in subsidies and aid to small farmers in favour of investors in the new lands; and thirdly, the impoverishment of small farmers whose incomes have been reduced by the loss of the areas of production and by the excessive increase in production costs. This competition has led to the spatial and social marginalization of the processes of traditional agriculture and of the small farmers whose work and function were devalued and the benefit derived from their efforts reduced.

Despite many similarities, the Egyptian and Tunisian agricultural situations are also fundamentally different. It is therefore important to consider separately and in detail both cases to see in what way the global processes of marginalization are similar despite the distinct local contexts.

Social marginalization in Egypt

Geographically, the Nile valley and delta occupy about 5 per cent of national territory. Yet 96 per cent of the population – about eighty-two million people – live there. The Nile valley and delta host almost all the rural and urban agglomerations, including Cairo and Giza with fifteen to twenty million people. They are also the location of essential infrastructure, economic activity and nearly all of the agricultural area and farmers, who number about 3.6 million, cultivating a total surface area of about seven million feddans. That is about three million hectares, irrigated by the Nile, which is the backbone of this geographic, demographic and economic centre of Egypt.

The paradox of rural Egypt is extensive poverty and inequality alongside intensive irrigated agriculture and one of the highest agricultural productivities in the world: more than one hundred quintals per hectare for wheat. In addition, Egyptian agriculture boasts one of the greatest cropping intensities, with an average of two and sometimes three crops a year on the same plot. Finding one abandoned irrigable square metre of land in this agricultural area is a real challenge. Yet Egyptian small farmers are intensely poor.

One of the reasons for farmer poverty is inequality in landholdings. In 2010, 43.5 per cent of farmers were able to access one feddan or less of agriculture land; 67.5 per cent of farms accessed less than two feddans and 93 per cent less than five feddans. Half of the cultivated lands are held by almost 90 per cent of the small farmers, with an average farm size of less than five feddans. The remaining 10 per cent exploit the remaining agricultural lands with an average of more than five feddans. Finally, only 3 per cent of farmers control 33.5 per cent of agricultural lands with an average of more than ten feddans each[4] (Ayeb 2010). However, it is perhaps not the arithmetical differences in landholding size that are most striking. Rather, it is that there is a gap between a minority of rich farmers (3 per cent) and a mass of small farmers (90 per cent). According to a range of studies and surveys, including official surveys, more than half of the small farmers live below the poverty line (2 USD/day). This evidence reveals what is meant by the marginalization of Egyptian small peasantry.

According to the International Food Policy Research Institute (IFPRI), 'there is a negative correlation between the indexes of poverty and the size of the cultivable land moving from 35.28 per cent for small farms (say less than 0.07 feddan per capita) to 23.82 per cent for the "medium" farmers (between 0.07 and 0.24 feddans per capita) and 7.08 per cent for the "large" farmers (more than 0.25 feddans per capita). The difference of indexes between the "big" and the small farmers is statistically significant' (Saad and Nagi 2001: 62, 63). If we calculate these indexes by taking the total cultivated land at the level of household and not per capita, the results are the following: 32.63 per cent of small farmers, 22.81 per cent of intermediate and 13.9 per cent of big farmers are poor (ibid.: 64). Even if we know that not all small farmers are poor (some of them have alternative sources of income), the large majority of poor farmers are near landless or cultivating relatively small surfaces with a maximum of 5 feddans. 'In any case, both results (based on either per capita or total area cultivated) indicate that access to land and the opportunities to undertake agricultural cultivation [have] an important bearing on the well-being of the rural Egyptian household' (ibid.: 64).

Perhaps as much as 80 per cent of peasants work part or full time away from their lands, either for 'bigger' farmers or in services and commerce, or even migrate to the city or abroad. Labour migration is a mechanism for attempting to escape from social marginalization. Some migrants manage to raise small amounts of capital to enable them to enlarge their farms or to get out of farming altogether and move into commerce – small supermarkets, for example, or other activities such as petty commodity production, brickmaking or taxi-driving. When small farmers want to work away from their plots and to diversify their activities, it is mainly because the land they work no longer provides them with a sufficient livelihood. When asked about his own strategy for facing economic difficulties, a farmer replied that 'small farmers were obliged to have one or many other activities to defray their necessary family needs [...] Otherwise, we will end up begging' (Ayeb and Archambeau 2003).

There are many political and social processes at work upstream from this marginalization process. First of all, the Egyptian peasantry has never been very rich. Moreover, until the 1950s the agricultural system was not very different to what was conventionally called a feudal system. Peasants, the majority of which were landless, were first of all at the service of big owners on whom they almost totally depended. They had to wait until the takeover by the 'Free Officers' with Gamal Abdel Nasser to benefit from considerable change, with the agrarian reform that redistributed some land held by large owners.

The land reforms of the 1950s and 1960s for the first time gave security of access to tenants and smallholders (Ayeb 2010).[5] Although Nasser's land reforms redistributed only one seventh of landholdings, they guaranteed an important level of access to agricultural resources which allowed hundreds of thousands of rural families to live partially or totally on their agricultural incomes. Many problems persisted, and the value of the land redistribution has been questioned since Nasser's death in 1970. The counter-revolution to Nasser's reforms was initiated by Anwar Sadat in 1974 and culminated with deposed

President Mubarak's Law 96 of 1992. This law liberalized the agricultural land market, including the contractual relations between owners and tenants. It promoted an acceleration of the impoverishment and processes of marginalization of the small peasantry. As an example of the counter-reform's effects, an estimated 700,000 jobs in the agricultural sector were lost between 1990 and 1995 (Bush 2002: 16).

Economic liberalization and the marginalization of Egypt's peasants

One of the main governmental justifications for the new agrarian policies and reforms like Law 96/1992 was the necessity to reverse the decline in agricultural growth. The fall was estimated by the IMF at around 17 per cent per year in 1989–90. Reform was seen as necessary to stop the deterioration in the agricultural trade balance and, more generally, to develop crops for export.

The government of Egypt (GoE) and its landowning members of parliament argued that small farmers were not in a position to fulfil new objectives. The agrarian counter-reform was considered an economic tool to transfer agricultural land from small farmers to bigger farmers and investors financially able to operate a progressive regrouping of land, to reconstitute large agricultural domains and 'modernize' a sector considered too archaic and 'traditional', despite the very high productivity per hectare.

The strategy adopted to reach the objectives was an irreversible process that could be executed over two or three decades. It was to marginalize progressively and continuously small farmers and to reduce their number by dispossessing them of their principal means of production: land and water. The small and medium farms had to 'disappear' to promote larger capitalist farms that Nasser's agrarian reforms had abolished in the 1950s. The construction of new capitalist agricultural holdings was part of a neoliberal policy to facilitate increased integration of the Egyptian agricultural sector into world markets.

The former National Democratic Party (NDP) deputy Shari Imam Aground, elected as a farmer,[6] had strongly supported Law 96/1992 during its discussion in parliament. Surprised, five years later, by the opposition of peasants and civil society mobilization, he argued that 'the small ownerships' were over and that larger landholdings would allow an increase in agricultural production. He asked rhetorically, 'What will those who have half a feddan do?' before replying: 'When the owner possesses 500 feddans, he is required to utilize scientific mechanization in order to ameliorate his production. Nowadays is really different from the old epoch where we could watch, while walking in the road, the fellah lying by his plot side. What is required now is that all those people work for the large investors'[7] (Saad 1999).

In addition to the low prices of new reclaimed lands, new investors benefit from numerous aid subsidies, subventions and tax exemptions, and especially from the absence of any ceiling on the size of farms. In the mega-projects already created or being created in the desert, the only stipulation concerns the minimum of the acquired land needed to become eligible for state assistance: 500 feddans. Moreover, in contradiction to what is usually argued, what is considered as the state's disengagement from the agricultural sector, and the broader economy, has instead represented a transfer of competences, means and tools – particularly financial and administrative – from subsistence family agriculture to agribusiness interests and from small peasantry to large-scale investors. The Egyptian state has always played the leading role in the agricultural sector, often under the rhetoric of seeking to maintain economic efficiency. The welfare function of supporting small farmers during Nasser's period was increasingly replaced by a neoliberal view of export-led growth through the development of a large agribusiness sector.

Law 96/1992 was the final step in the liberalization of the agricultural sector and therefore of the state's abandonment of the small peasantry. According to Ray Bush, the modernization of Egyptian agriculture has been designed to create scaled economic conditions and technical efficacy. This led political decision-makers to favour the standardization of 'farm units by reducing the viability of small holdings and changing tenancy rights' (Bush 1998: 94).

Law 96 of 1992: the revenge of large landowners and the marginalization of small farmers and tenants

Law 96/1992 established that tenant farming, sharecropping and land markets (sales, purchases and rentals) would be completely liberalized in October 1997. It also stipulated that the price of rent for the period 1992–97 would immediately increase from seven to twenty-two times the land tax, leaving no breathing space for tenants, who felt the full brunt of this reform. On 6 October 1997, all tenancy contracts ended and all rented lands returned to the owners. Law 96/1992 ended rental contracts for life and rights of inheritance for families of tenants. The legal duration of the new contracts was limited to five years but without fixing a minimum period. Previous rental agreements were replaced with informal contracts for a maximum period of one agricultural year and more often for just one season or even for a single crop. Contracts are not registered, leaving tenants in a very precarious situation, unable to benefit from any legal security.

The consequences of Law 96 of 1992 are evident from the two last agricultural censuses undertaken in Egypt, in 1990 (two years before the adoption of Law 96/1992) and 2000 (three years after it came into force in 1997) (see Figures 5.1–5.5). The contrast between the results of the two censuses is stark. Evidence suggests that the categories of peasants that have been mostly affected by the reform are tenant farmers (Figures 5.4, 5.5). As a direct consequence of Law 96/1992, tenant farmers suddenly and totally disappeared from the statistics. As a consequence of the absence of any registration of these short-lived tenancies, the statistical category of tenants does not exist any more. Field investigations that were held in Fayoum, in Minya (Middle Egypt) and in Behera (Delta), and an examination of one village land register of numerous cooperatives, show the erosion of tenancies and mixed tenures (ownership + tenancy).

The registers of agricultural cooperatives indicate that the column of tenant farmers almost disappeared after 1997. Owners usually refuse to sign a contract with the tenant and the tenant can no longer register in the cooperative and loses identity and any possible support (Ayeb and Saad 2006). However, this disappearance is misleading. Landless peasants and those not having enough land continue to rent but for very short periods of time and without contracts. As a consequence, tenants' lives have become more vulnerable.

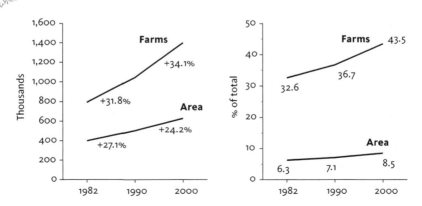

5.1 Evolution of the number and area (in feddans) of farms in Egypt of less than one feddan, 1982, 1990, 2000

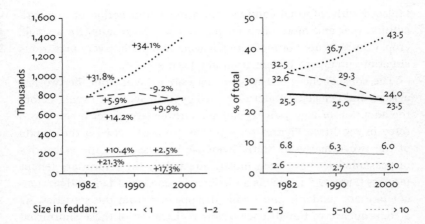

5.2 Evolution of the number of farms in Egypt classified into area categories, 1982, 1990, 2000

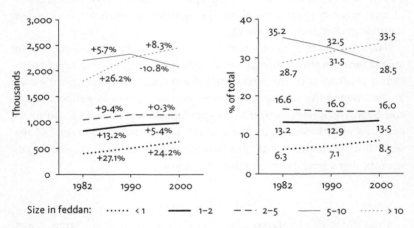

5.3 Evolution of the area (in feddans) of farms in Egypt classified into area categories, 1982, 1990, 2000

GoE figures indicate that about 904,000 farmers (almost 25 per cent) were affected by Law 96 of 1992. Most of those tenant farmers became landless peasants. Indeed, during the same period (1997–2000), the annual rent per feddan of agricultural land rose from LE500 to more than LE2,000, and in some areas of the delta exceeded LE3,000 or LE3,500. Rents of LE4,000 or LE4,500 were not uncommon. In 2011, the annual rental rates were between LE4,000 and LE6,000 per feddan.

For pre-1992 tenants, the most obvious impact of the full implementation of the law was their abrupt impoverishment resulting from the

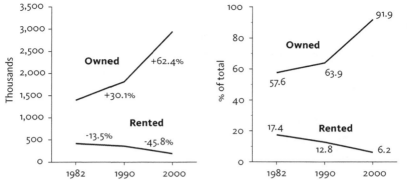

5.4 Evolution of the number of owned and rented farms in Egypt, 1982, 1990, 2000

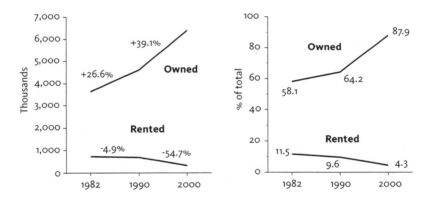

5.5 Evolution of the area (in feddans) of owned and rented farms in Egypt, 1982, 1990, 2000

loss of the main asset on which tenants' households relied for their livelihood (Saad 2004: 2). A widow mentioned that she had to let her son leave school after receiving a warning from the school for not paying his fees. She noted how 'other families were not able to supply their children with the daily pocket money. This applies especially to preparatory and secondary school students who need the money for transport to schools far from their villages' (ibid.: 6). In several villages of the governorate of Minya, where detailed fieldwork was conducted over many years, families withdrew both girls and boys from schools owing to financial hardship that resulted from loss of tenancies. It may not be uncommon for young girls in conservative rural communities to stay at home rather than attend school, but the withdrawal of boys undoubtedly reflected an additional and painful choice for household heads to make.

During the first year after the loss of their lands, the ex-tenants liquidated their remaining assets to survive. Women sold their jewellery, which caused them to lose their savings and had implications for family interpersonal relations. Men, usually the breadwinner of the family, felt humiliated relying on money from their wives and their savings. In these processes of collective impoverishment of hundreds of thousands of small farmers and their families, a group of tenants has been particularly affected by the deteriorating living conditions: 'women who headed households and worked tenancies registered in their late husband's name. These women were expelled from the land in October 1997. They either could not pay the new, higher rents, or were victims of prejudiced landlords who did not want to rent to women' (Bush 2004: 21).

Land fragmentation and peasant marginalization in Egypt

An indisputable sign of the permanence of agricultural land fragmentation, which also signified accelerated peasant impoverishment, was the increase in the total number of farms from 2,845,952 to 3,213,827 between 1990 and 2000.[8] There was a total increase of almost 13 per cent in the number of farms while, during this same period of time, the total under agricultural cultivation increased by only 1.6 per cent. The total number of farms of less than one feddan might logically have been expected to decrease, because about 45 per cent of tenant farmers abandoned their lands between 1992 and 1997. Since 1997 many others have followed. Nevertheless, the two categories that register the biggest increases in their numbers are respectively those of less than one feddan and those of between one and two feddans. This is explained by land fragmentation – more and more farmers became near-landless or had (through ownership or tenancy) holdings often of less than one feddan. There was also an increase in the landholdings of more than ten feddans.

Here, the effect of Law 96/1992 is obvious. An assessment of the last three agricultural censuses of 1982, 1990 and 2000 indicates a continuous process combining two dynamics. The first is an increase in the fragmentation of farms of less than two feddans. The second is a regrouping of agricultural lands, particularly in favour of the ten-feddan farm category and at a lower level of those from five to ten feddans. Those two dynamics are detrimental to the category of holdings of two to five feddans, whose number and total area farmed continue to fall regularly.

Near-landless – less than two feddans: the losers

The number of farms of less than one feddan increased from 1,044,897 in 1990 to 1,401,295 in 2000. This was an increase of 34.1 per cent. This acceleration probably happened during the short period 1997–2000, following the application of Law 96/1992. Between 1980 and 1990, the rate of growth in the number of farms of less than one feddan was 31.81 per cent (Figure 5.1). The growth in the number of farms was greater than the increase in the total area of farmed land. This confirms and defines agricultural land fragmentation as promoted by the GoE and the resulting increased social differentiation. Between 1990 and 2000, the category of less than one feddan increased from 36.7 per cent to 43.5 per cent of the number of farms. The fact that 43.5 per cent of farmers control only 8.5 per cent of the country's total agricultural surface confirms the inequality of landholdings. In 1990, 36.7 per cent of farmers shared 7.1 per cent of agricultural lands. In 1982, 32.6 per cent of farmers controlled 6.3 per cent of the agricultural lands. The average size of holdings of less than one feddan fell from 0.48 feddans in 1990 to 0.44 feddans in 2000. These data highlight how this borderline of 'micro-peasants' has been affected by impoverishment and processes of marginalization (Figures 5.2, 5.3).

The category of less than one feddan was considerably enlarged with a total surface area growth rate of 27 per cent between 1982 and 1990 and 24.19 per cent between 1990 and 2000. The total surface area occupied by farms of less than one feddan increased from 397,597 feddans in 1982 to 505,285 feddans in 1990 and 627,555 in 2000. This category (less than one feddan) was mostly enlarged by the division of farms in the category of two to five feddans.

The poorest farmers in Egypt are those with less than two feddans. These farmers and their households often depend upon income derived from working as agricultural labourers or in work outside the agriculture sector. Given the economic crisis, however, these sources have diminished, and rural poverty has increased. In these circumstances access to even very limited landholdings provides a lifeline for self-provisioning. The category of farms of one to two feddans is also subject to fragmentation, thus continuously transferring part of these lands to the category of less than one feddan. These farms represented 24.8 per cent of farms in 1990 but only 24 per cent in

2000. The proportion in terms of total surface area increased from 12.9 per cent in 1990 to 13.5 per cent in 2000. The total surface area occupied by the one-to-two-feddan category keeps enlarging. It increased by 5.4 per cent between 1990 and 2000. Despite boosting the less-than-one-feddan category, the one-to-two-feddan category seems to compensate for its own 'losses' through transfers from the two-to-five-feddan category, whose number and surface area fell quite suddenly (Figures 5.2, 5.3).

Landholdings of two to five feddans: dispossession and accumulation

It is particularly interesting to observe the dynamics that shape the farms in the category of landholdings of 2–5 feddans. The total number of farms of all categories rises more or less consistently except for those of 2–5 feddans. Their number increased by 5.85 per cent between 1982 and 1990 before falling by 9.2 per cent between 1990 and 2000. In the period 1990–2000, the number of farms of 2–5 feddans fell from 834,153 to 757,059. This shift shows the fragility of that category, aggravated by the new agrarian reform Law 96 of 1992, and confirms its fragmentation. There was a sharp decline at all levels, including the number of farms and the total area occupied, which fell from 2,330,864 to 2,078,282 feddans, a drop of 10.8 per cent (Figures 5.2, 5.3).

Holdings between two and five feddans represented 32.5 per cent of all farms in 1982, falling to 29.3 per cent in 1990 and to 23.5 per cent in 2000 (Figures 5.2, 5.3). It seems that the category of farming households occupying 2–5 feddans 'feeds' other categories of landholding because of its division and fragmentation as landholdings become more concentrated into larger units. There is a process of social differentiation between those who are becoming impoverished and marginalized (small farmers and the landless) and those who consolidate their economic and social position by gaining from the liberalization of the agricultural sector.

The Tunisian south-east: social and spatial marginalization

The dominant arid climate in the south-east of Tunisia, and especially the limited water resources, has drawn a very particular 'cartography'. It reveals a sharp contrast between the resources, the agricultural potentialities and the settlement system. Human settlement is relatively dense in the irrigated areas and rather scattered in the 'desert' and steppe zones. Nevertheless, the region of Gabes is mainly composed of two distinct areas with different yet complementary agricultural potential. The first of these is the wadi – seasonal rivers or small streams with a weak rate of flow, generally fed by the water table and the springs that helped form the ancient irrigated areas of oases, or what locals call 'ghabas' or forests. The irrigated agriculture used the ground water from numerous springs and wadis. The second area of agricultural potential is the steppe, in which the exploration of very deep underground water has recently become possible. Until the early 1990s, extensive and semi-pastoral rain-fed agriculture was almost the only agriculture activity in the steppe. The structural complementarity of both agriculture areas (developed by the same oasis peasantry) constitutes the 'oasis system', which is not limited to the irrigated areas. In this oasis system, it is the small farmer who has at his or her disposal (either by possessing or, rarely, by renting) the land and the irrigation water. His or her agricultural activities extend beyond the oasis (Abdedaym 2009a: 116).

In the traditional oasis or *ghabas*, sustainable irrigation has permitted the development of an intensive and diversified agriculture with high yields per hectare. The agricultural system has three distinct levels: the date palm, which always keeps its head high and its roots deep in water, fruit trees, which are smaller, and finally vegetables and green fodder. In the steppe, the rain-fed and extensive agriculture occupies more extended areas, with two main levels: arboricultural, mainly olive and fig trees, and occasionally cereals, mainly barley and wheat. Associated with these two levels, the pasture (dry natural grazing land) occupies relatively important areas. Generally, sheep and goat flocks belong to several families, who entrust them to a herder (usually a landless or near-landless peasant) for production of milk, meat or newborn animals. The functioning of such complex livestock farming systems, largely devoted to self-provisioning, 'is regulated by seasonal cycles of movements and activities, highly dependent on the rainfall frequency and on its spatial repartition' (Romagny and Cudennec 2008: 5).

Women traditionally play an important role and participate in most aspects of agricultural labour, in the oasis as well as in the steppe. They hoe and weed irrigated cultivation, reaping green fodder (clover), harvesting fresh fruit in the oasis (except dates) and olives in the steppe. Caring for and milking animals, making cheese or butter, curd cheese (*rayeb*) or whey (*lben*) are exclusively done by women. With all these outdoor and indoor activities, peasant women in Gabes have always played an important role in preserving biodiversity in the oasis – in the irrigated areas as well as in the surrounding steppe. Moreover, male migration and sometimes the breaking off of traditional family relations (which have increased the number of female-headed households) have boosted the agricultural activities performed by women.

Women have responsibility for preparing household food, and in Gabes they have therefore also become involved in selecting which vegetables to cultivate, in livestock farming (goats and sheep) and, if necessary, in choosing the varieties and the seeds that are needed to maintain food quality. Women may use the by-products of agricultural activities to make handcraft objects, including the famous palm hats. In the region, women devote up to sixteen hours a day to producing, transforming, commercializing and preparing food, collecting firewood and accomplishing other housework.[9] Since the 1960s, oasis agriculture has experienced serious challenges to its system of production. It has first of all felt the effects of water shortage as the city of Gabes has increased its consumption and petrochemical industries established in the 1970s grew. More recently, since the 1990s, oasis agriculture has felt the impact of the development of a new intensive agriculture in the steppe areas.

Since the creation of the first wells (the first was dug in 1890 in Oudhref to the north-west of the city of Gabes), there has been a gradual drying up of springs that are close to wells, and a reduction in the flow of those located at greater distances. Especially since 1965 (the date of the foundation of the industrial compound of Gabes and the creation of the first wells that supply it with water), this phenomenon of drying up of water sources has become serious and dangerous. Two wells drilled in the 1970s, downstream of the oasis, delivered the *coup de grâce*. By 1990, all the sources in the oasis had dried up.

The diminution of water resources was accompanied by serious industrial, urban and agricultural pollution of soils and water tables. This was caused by the seepage of chemical products and by manure-spreading that directly attacked crops and trees. Since 1990 the oasis has stopped relying on its own water resources and its irrigation water has been exclusively managed by the local agricultural authority, the Regional Commissionership of Agricultural Development (RCAD). Water now comes from deep wells dug in the nearby steppe. This transformation of access to water helps explain the aggravation of competition for rural resources and the exacerbation of conflict over gaining access to land, water and rural income. Small farmers were the first to suffer the dramatic consequences of falling agricultural production caused by lack of irrigation water, particularly in summer. Some farmers had to wait more than thirty days to secure their place in the queue for water; irrigation had previously taken place once every three weeks, or even more than three weeks during July and August, the hottest months of the year (Abdedaym 2009a: 3).

Oasis in danger: from palms to concrete

With up to 170,000 inhabitants in the city and its environs, Gabes is the biggest city in south-east Tunisia. It is considered the capital of the south-east by virtue of the concentration of public services, industries, universities, infrastructure and specialized medical equipment. In 1970, major industry, particularly chemical and petrochemical industry, began to be established. Gabes has a large phosphate processing plant, built in an industrial port zone near the oasis city of Ghannouche, and the infrastructure for offshore oil. In terms of traffic and sales, Gabes is the fourth most important commercial port in Tunisia. It is the first point of convergence and the main hub for the inhabitants of the south-east. This city is also the last stop on the unique railway line that links Tunis to the south-east and a place of convergence for permanent or temporary migrants: civil servants, students, industrial workers, engineers and workers in commerce.

The municipal area of the city of Gabes has been greatly enlarged since the 1970s, to the detriment of the oasis and the peasantry, who were the first to be affected by this expansion. The oasis is suffering from a process of 'gardening' – the conversion of farmland into comfortable villas with gardens. At the same time, the oasis attracts a very large number of families who come from Gabes and from other southern regions, and who create 'spontaneous' (informal/'illegal') neighbourhoods, built on land that had previously been irrigated, which the authorities invariably end up legalizing. Urban growth, the need for jobs and incomes, the impossibility for many families of settling in 'legal' quarters and increased corruption led to the emergence of these spontaneous neighbourhoods. Moreover, many of the illegal houses were built by people who worked in public administration – the very people who were meant to have prevented the construction. Other residents in the new settlements were from branches of the security services and the army.

The competition for land between the subsistence agriculture of the oasis and the concrete of the city includes a struggle over water. This competition between small-scale subsistence farming and the other consumption sectors (industry and the city itself) is not new, and the relationship between the drilling of new wells outside the oasis and the groundwater level has been known for a long time (Veyrac 2005: 53; Abdedaym 2009a: 147). In 1965, however, when the Gabes industrial zone was established and wells were drilled to supply it with water, the situation worsened, until by the 1990s all the oasis springs were completely dry. There has also been serious pollution of both urban and industrial water caused by chemical products running into watercourses.

Shortage of water: dried springs

The entire supply of irrigation water comes from outside the oasis, and is managed exclusively by the local agricultural authorities. This has intensified the competition and conflict over water. It has led, as we noted above, to long delays for farmers in irrigating their crops. Government post-colonial policy denied legitimacy to 'traditional' farming methods and farming livelihoods. Small farmers were labelled traditional and backward. Policy tilted towards promoting a more 'rational' mobilization and management of the available water resources to promote food security. Behind this strategy was a strong, and false, idea that exports guarantee imports, and therefore the logic of the global market had to be followed. An example of this strategy was the growth of the date palm variety 'Deglet Nour', highly praised in Tunisia but which depleted groundwater resources, eroding local date varieties and local knowledge and marginalizing peasantry and subsistence farmers. The financial benefits of the switch to this new variety of date accrued to officials and large investors. Consequently, the oasis economy has never been so dependent on the global market; never have subsistence agriculture and farming in the oases been so marginalized and local biodiversity so impoverished and reduced.

Agribusiness marginalizes small farmers and reduces local biodiversity

Alongside competition over land and water in the oasis irrigated area there has been the emergence of new types of agricultural investment in the steppe zone, which surrounds the irrigated oases and is in direct competition with them. This new agriculture, which has spread very rapidly since the mid-1990s, was encouraged by a new agricultural and water policy designed to attract investors into the agricultural sector and to increase agricultural exports. This new policy entails drawing upon very large quantities of water by, among other things, authorizing private investors to use groundwater more than fifty metres deep. Historically, accessing water at this depth was subject to very strict conditions. However, in order to attract the necessary investment, the state allowed private sector investors for the first time to exploit deeper

new investment → exports → imports.

90

water tables. For small oasis farmers, this 'privatization' of groundwater resources, in favour of investors, reflects increased dispossession and the desocialization of water.

Although there are rules concerning access to deep aquifers, such as applicants seeking to access water below fifty metres being required to submit an agricultural investment project with water-saving technologies, the financial and economic criteria are the most decisive. Every irrigation project requires a budget that covers all investment and expenses. Getting authorization normally requires strong political and administrative relations and sometimes the paying of a bribe. Small farmers are unable to afford such financial conditions, and the majority of such farmers cannot mobilize the necessary capital to cover the costs of such investment projects.

It was therefore mostly urban investors with substantial assets and political connections who had the financial resources to meet the demands of the public authorities. The great majority of these new investors were not farmers. They were businessmen, professionals or civil servants. Sometimes they were public servants (engineers, lawyers, judges), active or retired army officers or senior officers in the police or the National Guard. Sometimes they were returning emigrants or close relatives of people who worked abroad and enjoyed high incomes compared to local salaries. These were the only people able to bear the costs of launching and sustaining an investment project. These investors very quickly created several large irrigated and highly mechanized modern farms with high-added-value products destined for the national market or for export. There was thus very unequal competition for natural agricultural resources (water and land) which exacerbated inequalities relating to access to subsidies, loans and markets. Inequalities led to spatial marginalization of traditional agricultural areas and of small farmer viability.

Moreover, the creation of new irrigated areas on arid lands disturbed the oasis system and impoverished agricultural complementarities: the oasis system was separated from the steppe, which had been an essential and vital component of sustainable irrigation, thus shrinking the productive space of small farmers and limiting them to the irrigated zones inside the oases, which were also decreasing. This process resulted in fewer dairy products, less meat, less olive oil and less cereal production. Many farmers were no longer able to carry out their agricultural activities and were obliged to look for other sources of income beyond their land, and sometimes even outside the agricultural sector altogether. It is estimated that after 1960 'traditional' oases lost half of their cultivated surfaces. Those in the Gabes region, including Chenini, Menzel, Jara and Chott Essalam, shrank from 1,000 to 600 hectares during the same period. At the same time, the total irrigated agricultural surface area in the region of Gabes was doubled from 7,000 to more than 15,000 hectares (Abdedaym 2009a: 179, 247, 249). The enlargement of the agricultural area cannot be celebrated as a success for technical modernization and progress. Rather it confirms smallholder marginalization and impoverishment. It might theoretically be possible to argue that small farmers in the traditional irrigated lands of Gabes will profit from the new agribusiness sector. They might benefit, for example, by becoming qualified workers and technicians on the new modern farms. In terms of the neoliberal philosophy former small farmers will have new opportunities to increase their incomes by 'selling' their labour power to new investors. However, a qualitative survey conducted between 2007 and 2010 among small farmers in the oasis of Gabes showed that only a few of them, namely some Ghannouchis (people from the sub-oasis of Ghannouche), were able to take advantage of the transformations (ibid.: 188).

In fact, since investors have no agricultural knowledge, they seek help from experienced oasis farmers. Those from the oasis of Ghannouche have a very good reputation in terms of competence and honesty. They are particularly sought after. Many investors admit that without the know-how of 'their' Ghannouchis, their projects would never succeed. Thus, certain oasis peasants migrate towards the steppe at the request of investors. Greatly sought after by the investors, the Ghannouchis become the real managers and practitioners of the modern operations. The 'luckiest' or the most ambitious among them become associates, by right, contributing first of all with their know-how and sometimes with a minor investment of their own. But the land and the drilling generally remain the exclusive property of the principal investor. 'Big capital' is able to recruit the better-trained and more competent farmers (according to their criteria), but the process of investment actively marginalizes small farmers and excludes them economically, socially and politically, dispossessing them of their resources in and around the oasis of Gabes.

The competition over resources between two different agricultural sectors disrupts and handicaps the traditional oasis system and has put immense economic pressure on the peasantry. The new irrigated lands in the steppe are incompatible with the ancient oasis system, and the competition over rare common resources, mainly water and land, has marginalized smallholder farmers.

Conclusion

export-led growth.

This chapter has sketched the processes of marginalization and class differentiation of smallholder farmers in Egypt and Tunisia. It has indicated how the processes of marginalization experienced by Tunisian and Egyptian smallholder farmers have been explained positively by the erstwhile political regimes in both countries. The modernization of the agricultural sector has been contrasted with the 'tradition' of smallholder farming. Government rhetoric has tried to meet neoliberal international demands and local financial interests by accelerating rural underdevelopment. It has tried to do so while declaring that export-led growth is delivered alongside improved rural development. Yet we have seen that food sovereignty seems to have been displaced for the sake of neoliberal ideas of food security, even though productivity targets are unmet and rural poverty has increased.

Logically agricultural investment, whose first objective is to maximize profit and to reduce deficits, cannot operate in the way that smallholder agriculture might. The latter aims first of all to ensure local and family food security. The former has to produce for the national or the international market, while the latter produces first of all for the family and the local market. Agro-investors mobilize local resources for consumers who are hundreds or even thousands of kilometres away. Small farmers mobilize local resources to feed themselves or to supply the local market and consumers. Agro-investors exploit resources extensively without worrying about medium or long-term risks. Smallholders preserve the resources, aiming to protect the means of production, reducing the costs of production and consolidating their own food security. The end of the small peasantry certainly means victory for engineers, experts, modernists and agro-investors. But it will first of all serve to aggravate food insecurity and dependency, local poverty and social and economic marginalization.

Tunisia and Egypt experienced a food crisis during the first half of 2008. It resulted in a sharp increase in the prices of basic food items. Underlying this crisis was food dependency, which intensified with a staggering increase in the prices of cereals and other agricultural products in the international market. The recent political 'explosions' in Tunisia and Egypt highlighted the fact that the two revolutions were initiated by marginalized people and started in the marginalized regions before reaching the middle-class and more wealthy urbanites. In both cases, marginality constituted a great opportunity for change. The new leaders in the two countries must keep that in mind and work for improved access to resources for all and the redistribution of economic benefits. Post-revolution agriculture and food policy will need to challenge existing global and local policy status quo. The marginalized people who have initiated the revolutions will remain attentive to any risk of counter-revolution.

Notes

1 This chapter is based on provisional or final results of several years of research and field surveys conducted in Tunisia and Egypt. It is part of two research projects carried out under the auspices of the Social Research Center (SRC), American University in Cairo (AUC), in collaboration with Egyptian anthropologist Reem Saad. The two research projects are 'Poor women and access to agricultural resources: implications for agro-biodiversity in MENA' (2005/06), funded by IDRC (International Development Research Center), and 'Poverty dynamics, access to resources and social change in rural MENA; gendered approach; the case of Egypt and Tunisia' (2007–11), funded by the Ford Foundation.

2 These censuses are conducted every ten years by the Ministry of Agriculture and Land Reclamation. The last census was published in 2002 and related to the situation in 2000.

3 1 feddan (Egyptian unit) = 0.42 hectare = 1 acre.

4 These data are calculated using the official agriculture censuses of 2000, 1990 and 1980 (Ayeb 2010).

5 This point has been developed in many different references, among them Abdel Fadhil (1990: 18), Bethemont et al. (1980: 75) and Saad (2002: 105).

6 The legislative elections in Egypt reserve seats for professional categories such as peasants. The candidate who represents them is supposed to be a farmer himself. In reality, they are generally people occupying different professions and 'owners' of inherited plots or investors in the new reclaimed lands in the desert.

7 A claim made in the opposition newspaper *Al-Ahaly*, 19 July 1997 (quoted by Saad 1999).

8 All numbers, data, statistics and figures concerning the evolution of the agrarian system, including numbers of farms/farmers, the surfaces, the status, are from the three official Egyptian agricultural censuses (1980, 1990 and 2000). Using these sources, I have made a comparative quantitative and qualitative study, published for the first time in Ayeb (2010). These numbers consider only farmers located in the Nile valley and delta, plus the urban governorates of Cairo, Giza, Alexandria, Ismailya and Suez. The total number of farmers in Egypt in 2000 was around 3.6 million.

9 Similar patterns for women's work were evident in fieldwork in Fayoum, Egypt (Ayeb and Saad 2006).

References

Abdedaym, S. (1997) *Gestion de l'eau et son impact sur la dynamique des systèmes de production dans les oasis littorales. Cas de l'oasis de Gabès; mémoire d'ingénieur*, France: CNEARC.

— (2009a) *Mutations socio-agro-spatiales et mode de gouvernance de l'eau dans les oasis 'périur-baines' du gouvernorat de Gabès*

(Sud-est tunisien): de la raréfaction d'une ressource à la crise d'un patrimoine, Doctoral thesis, Université Paris 10 Nanterre-La Défense.

— (2009b) 'Raréfaction de l'eau dans les oasis: crise de la ressource ou crise de gouvernance? Cas des oasis du Sud-est tunisien', in H. Ayeb and T. Ruf (eds), *Eaux, pauvreté et crises sociales* [Water poverty and social crises], IRD.

Abdel Fadhil, M. (1990) 'Nouvelle perspective sur l'avenir de l'agriculture et sur la question agraire en Égypte', *Tiers-Monde*, 121, IEDES.

Attia, H. (1957) 'L'organisation de l'oasis (Tunisie)', *Cahiers de Tunisie*, 5(17/18): 39–43.

Ayeb, H. (2010) *La Crise de la société rurale en Egypte: la fin du fellah?*, Paris: Karthala.

— (2011) 'La disparition de la Sekia en Égypte; entre patrimonialisation et exclusion sociale', in F. Ireton and V. Battesti, *L'Egypte au présent*, Collection 'Hommes et sociétés', Actes Sud.

Ayeb, H. and O. Archambeau (2003) *Sur les bords du Nil l'eau en partage*, Documentary film, Paris/Cairo.

Ayeb, H. and R. Saad (2006) 'Poor women and access to agricultural resources: implications for agrobiodiversity in MENA', Report for IDRC.

Bahri, A., A. Hamdane and F. Lebdi (1995) 'Lignes directrices d'une stratégie en matière d'économie d'eau', *Lecture stratégique*, ITES, pp. 115–25.

Bechraoui, A. (1980) *La vie rurale dans les oasis de Gabès*, Université de Tunis.

Ben Cheikh, A. and M. Marie (directors) (1993) *Grands appareillages hydrauliques et sociétés locales en Méditerranée*, Seminar, Marrakesh, October.

Ben Marzouk, M. (1996) *Gestion et suivi des nappes profondes de Gabès, CI du Chott Fedjej et Djeffara*, Report, CRDA de Gabès.

Bethemont, J. et al. (1980) *L'Égypte et le haut barrage d'Assouan; de l'impact à la valorisation*, Presses de l'Université de Saint-Étienne.

Bush, R. (1998) 'Facing structural adjustment', in N. Hopkins and K. Westergaard (eds), *Directions of Change in Rural Egypt*, American University in Cairo Press.

— (2002) 'Land reform and counter-revolution', in R. Bush (ed.), *Counter-Revolution in Egypt's Countryside*, London and New York: Zed Books.

— (2004) *Civil Society and the Uncivil State; Land Tenure Reform in Egypt and the Crisis of Rural Livelihoods*, Civil Society and Social Movements Programme Paper no. 9, United Nations Research Institute for Social Development, May.

Cherif, A. (1994) 'Politique de l'eau et aménagement des campagnes', *Cahiers de la Méditerranée*, 49: 83–103.

CNEA (1977) *Etude de sauvegarde des oasis du sud tunisien*, Note no. 11, Oasis de Gabès, October.

CRDA de Gabès (1985) *Economie de l'eau dans les oasis de la région de Gabès*, Definitive report on the first phase, Comète Engineering.

— (1999) *L'Eau dans le gouvernorat de Gabès*, Report.

Hajji, A. (1994) 'Mise en valeur et réhabilitation des oasis. Essai d'évaluation de l'expérience tunisienne', in *Diagnostic rapide et stratégie de développement en milieu oasien* (specialized course, Tozeur, 7–26 November).

Hassaainya, J. (1991) 'Irrigation et développement agricole. L'expérience tunisienne', *Options Méditerranéennes*, Series B: Etudes et recherches, no. 3, CIHEAM, INAT, pp. 13–17.

Hayder, A. (1991) 'Le problème de l'eau à Gabès: gestion conflictuelle et étatisation', *Fascicule de recherche URBAMA*, 22.

Kassah, A. (1996) 'Les oasis tunisiennes. Aménagement hydroagricole et développement en zone aride', *Série géographique*, 13.

— (1997) 'Population et ressources en eau dans le Sud tunisien', in *Population, environnement et pauvreté* (International symposium, Rabat, 28/29 October).

MALR (Ministry of Agriculture and Land Reclamation) (1982, 1992, 2002) *National Agriculture Censuses*, Cairo.

Romagny, B. and C. Cudennec (2008) 'Gestion de l'eau en milieu aride: considérations physiques et sociales pour l'identification des territoires pertinents dans le Sud-Est tunisien', *Développement durable et territoire*, Dossier 6: Les territoires de l'eau, developpementdurable.revues.org/document1805.html, accessed 25 December 2008.

Saad, R. (1999) 'State, landlord, parliament and peasant: the story of the 1992 tenancy law in Egypt', in A. Bowman and E. Rogan (eds), *Agriculture in Egypt from Pharaonic to Modern Times*, Proceedings of the British Academy, vol. 96, Oxford: Oxford University Press, pp. 387–404.

— (2002) 'Egyptian politics and the tenancy law', in R. Bush (ed.), *Counter-Revolution in Egypt's Countryside*, London and New York: Zed Books.

— (2004) 'Social and political costs of coping with poverty in rural Egypt', Fifth Mediterranean Social and Political Research Meeting, Florence and Montecatini, organized by the Mediterranean Programme of the Robert Schuman Centre for Advanced Studies at the European University Institute, 24–28 March.

Saad, Z. and A. Nagi (2001) *Poverty in Egypt: Concepts, Realities, and Research Agenda*, Social Research Center, American University in Cairo, www1.aucegypt.edu/src/pdr/Pub_Thematic.asp.

Sghaier, M. (1994) *Les agro-systèmes de production en Tunisie: fonctionnement, rôle et adaptation aux changements écologiques et socio-économiques. Actes du séminaires 'agriculture oasiennes'*, Degache: GRIDAO, INRA de Tunisie.

Sondron, F. (1997) 'L'eau n'est plus le lien social en milieu oasien', in *Agriculture et développement durable en Méditerranée*, International seminar, Agropolis, Montpellier, March.

Toutain, G., V. Dolle and M. Ferry (1989) 'The situation of the oasis system in hot regions', *Development Research Journals*, 22, DSA, June.

Veyrac, B. (2005) *Gestion et usages de l'eau agricole; le cas de l'oasis de Chenini Gabès (Tunisie)*, Master's M1, Université de Toulouse le Mirail.

6 | Margins and frontiers

REEM SAAD

Academic literature from a range of disciplines has no shortage of accurate and all-encompassing definitions of the concept of marginality. An example of such definitions is the following:

> Marginality is a complex condition of disadvantage which individuals and communities experience as a result of vulnerabilities that may arise from unfavourable environmental, cultural, social, political and economic factors. Although most discussions of marginality deal with distressed economic and ecological conditions of life, the concept of marginality can also be applied to cultural, social and political conditions of disadvantage. (Mehretu et al. 2000: 90)

Gurung and Kollmair also stress the multifaceted nature of the concept and its connection to a state of disadvantage. They identify two principal conceptual frameworks within which marginality is defined and described: the societal, which focuses on 'human dimensions such as demography, religion, culture, social structure (e.g., caste/hierarchy/class/ethnicity/gender), economics and politics in connection with access to resources by individuals and groups', and the spatial, which focuses on 'physical location' and distance from centres of development' (Gurung and Kollmair 2005: 10). Importantly, they point to the fact that marginality, or rather marginalization, is a dynamic process that develops over time (ibid.: 11).

The richness of the concept and the many sophisticated and meticulous attempts at capturing this richness are not reflected to the same extent in the usage of the concept in development discourse and practice. Within this framework, marginality (together with notions of vulnerability, exclusion and disadvantage) signals a deficiency to be remedied through intervention, and it is often no more than a shorthand covering a range of poverty-related situations as well as social groups.

This chapter departs from this particular understanding and usage of marginality. It does so in order to explore a wider range of meaning related to the concept and condition of marginality. I am particularly interested in exploring the possibility that a state of marginality may provide a greater impetus for change, and may, in some cases, have positive consequences.

I explore two very different and contrasting examples of marginality in Egypt. The first case examines the (mostly subjective) marginality of a group of intellectuals and artists, and the second deals with the ascribed marginality of a low-status tribal group in Upper Egypt. In presenting these two cases, I try to show that the margin may be a space where social-change dynamics are particularly active, and that in some instances we could in fact be looking at a frontier rather than a periphery.[1]

A relevant distinction to this discussion is between cultural and social marginality. Noel Gist employs this distinction in his attempt to characterize the different aspects of marginality of the Anglo-Indian community in India (Gist 1967). According to Gist:

> Cultural marginality refers to the marginal or peripheral position of a group with respect to the beliefs, traditions, social organization, patterned behavior, and systems of values that distinguish it from other groups or communities. Social marginality refers to the position of a group as indicated by the interpersonal or intergroup relationships with one or more different groups, and to the attitudes and 'images' that tend to shape these relationships. (Ibid.: 365)

These two types of marginality capture one aspect of the distinction between the cases discussed below. The case of the group of intellectuals and artists mostly subscribes to the actual or perceived cultural marginality, where the group generally operates within a framework characterized by lifestyle choices. These choices may deviate from the norms and cultural practices of social groups of similar social standing. This, however, does not result in social exclusion or rejection. The low-status tribe in Upper Egypt, on the other hand, shares in the same cultural framework of beliefs, practices and traditions as the dominant majority of rural dwellers in Upper Egypt. Despite that, the group experiences social rejection and exclusion.

Intellectuals and lifestyle choices

My first case study draws on work I have done on intellectuals and artists' lifestyle choices. The special emphasis has been on issues of taste and fashion, and on subsequent research on the transformation of the meaning and value of traditional crafts. My research on lifestyle choices of what I will roughly term the 'intellectual elite' grew out of my long-term engagement with studying questions of change in rural Egypt. One striking observation led me to investigate one aspect of the interaction between village and city. At about the same moment in the late seventies when peasants were using migration earnings to replace their traditional mud-brick houses with concrete red-brick urban middle-class-style houses, Egyptian and expatriate upper-middle-class intellectuals (writers, painters, anthropologists) started building 'traditional' mud-brick peasant-style second homes in various picturesque rural areas around the country.[2]

The elite mud-brick movement has been closely associated with the names of Wissa Wassef and Hassan Fathi (Al-Omari 2003; Ammoun 1987). They were both architects who from the late forties raised the banner of traditional art. Wissa Wassef is best known for establishing a pottery and carpet school in Harraniyya on the outskirts of Cairo, while Hassan Fathi was a renowned architect whose international acclaim was based on advocating the use of appropriate and available building materials, and also on propagating interesting architectural forms, especially domes and vaults. Hassan Fathi's main agenda was to produce affordable housing for the poor of Egypt, which they could build themselves using local materials. That agenda was summarized in the title of his best-known book: *Architecture for the Poor* (1973).

Fathi's best-known project was Gourna in Luxor. It was commissioned by the Antiquities Authority because they wanted to resettle the people of old Gourna who lived above the tombs of the pharaohs and allegedly made their living out of antique dealing. Fathi designed and built a beautiful village which was nevertheless best known as a failure. This was because, apart from much bureaucratic harassment, the people of Gourna did not welcome the project. They did not want to move or live in it. Some villagers did move there eventually, but they very quickly altered the original design to the point where the location became practically unrecognizable from its original design. The most cited reason for the failure of the project was that villagers did not want to be cut off from their means of livelihood, which was antique dealing. But there must also have been other reasons why villagers did not appreciate Hassan Fathi's architecture.

One major reason for the project's failure was the villagers' attitude towards the dome feature of the houses. The dome did have an aesthetic value outside of any particular social meaning. As Hassan Fathi noted, the dome was 'pleasing to the eye' and had a 'satisfying curving rhythm'. In the context of village life, however, the dome has a specific meaning that is mostly associated with death or with religious structures (mosques and churches). It most closely resembles local saints' tombs (usually close to the cemetery). The dome was not considered fit to enclose a dwelling space for the living. But if villagers for whom this architecture was intended did not appreciate it, others did. Hassan Fathi's architectural style inspired members of an intellectual elite to build in his style, particularly mud-brick domes and other distinctive decorative motifs.

While the trend of acquiring second homes in a particular 'authentic' style exists in many places in Egypt, it is most concentrated and crystallized in the village of Tunis, located at the far end of Lake Qarun in the governorate of Fayoum. This colony of Egyptian and expatriate artists, writers, academics and professionals started with the settlement in the late seventies of Evelyn Perrot, a Swiss potter who was a student and disciple of Wissa Wassef, Hassan Fathi's colleague and contemporary. Over time, others were attracted to the area for its beautiful landscape and always with the idea of escaping Cairo and experiencing an alternative lifestyle. My research focused mainly on this group, of which I am a member, but their voice and choices echo those of a wider category. When I conducted my research in the early 1990s, there were clear expressions of a sense of marginality among members of this group. Their work was either not appreciated by the public, or the artists could not lead the kind of life they wished to lead. The group could be described as subjectively marginal, or, to use the phrase employed by Habib Ayeb, exemplified a case of 'chosen marginality' (Ayeb 2009) that partly manifested itself in this flight to a physical and symbolic periphery. The other side of the periphery coin is 'distinction'. As Bourdieu noted,

> Taste classifies, and it classifies the classifier. Social subjects, classi-
> fied by their classifications, distinguish themselves by the distinctions
> they make, between the beautiful and the ugly, the distinguished and
> the vulgar, in which their position in the objective classifications is
> expressed or betrayed. (1984: 6)

Here I am not restricting the analysis to Tunis residents, but to a wider circle. This is a loose social group that includes upper-middle-class artists, writers and academics. They could roughly be described as belonging to the upper middle class, and of leftist political leanings. Their lifestyle and taste practices are very often articulated as deliberate choices, and expressed in statements about 'our culture' and 'what we are about'. Their adoption of ethnic and tradition-inspired tastes in dress, jewellery and architectural styles is a mark of their distinction vis-à-vis their middle-class counterparts of predominantly Western tastes. But in contrast to elements of the 1970s French bourgeoisie who set themselves in opposition to the general aesthetic, the distinction in this case was people-inspired, and it carried a statement that celebrated the traditional.

Rather than denoting exclusion, such choices in fact demarcated the exclusive. Traditional crafts, ethnic-looking architectural styles, furniture, costumes and jewellery that characterized the taste and fashion preferences of intellectual and cosmopolitan elites operated as markers of distinction. The group who adopted this style were the discerning few who uncovered and displayed hidden aesthetic qualities and characterized the 'peasant' and the 'popular' by distinguishing themselves from the upper-middle-class majority of Westernized taste.

It was precisely this aspect of exclusiveness which contributed to feeding the appeal of the fashion trend, and has been instrumental in propagating the taste for the traditional beyond the small circle in which it was initiated. An important implication concerned traditional crafts. The growing demand of urban and cosmopolitan elites was vital in the persistence, as well as the regeneration, of several traditional crafts, and the valuation of traditional and hand-made crafts as art objects was accompanied by a transformation in their meaning and value.

There are various paths through which Upper Egyptian hand-made crafts, for example, have found their way to venues such as tourist shops in Luxor and Aswan, Christmas bazaars in Cairo hotels and galleries, annual exhibits of development projects, fashion shows in the French embassy in Cairo, not to mention exhibitions in various European capitals. In all these places, the crafts have been brought to their urban sophisticated clientele through outside development as well as entrepreneurial interventions of various sorts.

Mona Abaza details the forms and developments of the ethnic-inspired fashion trends among members of the Egyptian upper middle class and the ways in which such trends relate to issues of identity and consumption (2006: 189–217). She asserts that it is hard to tell whether such trends will have a significant impact on culture (ibid.: 211). Although the exact impact of these trends may be hard to measure in a precise manner, an impact undoubtedly exists. I will now present in some detail the case of Nagada, the Upper Egyptian village whose name became the brand of one of the most exclusive fashion establishments in the country. A crucial factor in the Nagada story was how the tastes and demands of the intellectual elite and a drive towards distinction were instrumental in valorizing 'the traditional' and propagating the demand for it across wider circles.

The Nagada story[3]

The town of Nagada in Qena governorate has been known as a weaving village for thousands of years. The village was known for producing textiles made of silk, and was particularly famous for the *'aba'*, a sleeveless outer garment worn by Arab men (Vogelsang-Eastwood and Einarsdottir 2003: 98). In the twentieth century, Nagada specialized in one specific product: the *firka*. This product measures 3 metres by 90 centimetres, and is woven from artificial silk in geometrical patterns of red, yellow and black (Ammoun 1987: 47).[4]

The *firka* was produced for export to Sudan, where it has been in great demand by Sudanese women for use in ritual occasions such as childbirth and male circumcision. The production was controlled by merchants who supplied the yarn, paid the workers for their labour and exported the product to Sudan. One estimate put the number of families that depended on this type of work at 2,000 (www.nagada.net).

By the end of the 1980s, strained relations between Egypt and Sudan had led to stagnation in the export (and therefore production) of this material. Nagada witnessed a major transformation when in the early 1990s a development intervention by the Canada Fund focused on reviving the local crafts. The intervention was pioneered by the then Canada Fund coordinator Naela Refaat, at the instigation of Mohamed Omar, professor at the College of Applied Arts at Cairo University. Naela Refaat described the objectives of the project as reviving the craft of weaving, as well as helping out a distressed population of weavers who lost their livelihoods with the closure of Egypt's border with Sudan. A main objective of the project was to empower the weavers through creating a weavers' cooperative to enable them to market their product independently of the big traders, and to develop marketing links and outlets. It was also hoped that, apart from a cooperative shop, there would be a small museum to display Nagada weaving products (Naela Refaat, personal communication, 9 March 2004).

The Swiss artist Michel Pastore was approached by the project, and he introduced new designs, new material and new techniques. Pastore based the new designs on the traditional pyramidal motif of the *firka*, a change he describes as 'using the traditional as a seed for the modern'. The result was a marked diversification of the Nagada products. At the end of the project the new products were displayed at a large exhibition at the Goethe Institute and met with huge success. From specializing only in *firka* production, the Nagada weavers moved to producing different shawls, tableclothes, bedcovers and various items of clothing. Naela Refaat said that the extent of the success surprised everyone but funding ran out and a difficult phase ensued. Further funding could not be secured for the crucial step of establishing the weavers' cooperative and instituting a viable marketing mechanism, and the project did not materialize as envisioned.

After an uncertain phase, Michel Pastore, in partnership with Lebanese fashion designer Sylva Nasrallah, started the Nagada fashion house, now located in Dokki, an upmarket Cairo neighbourhood. In the beginning they relied mainly on material woven in Nagada. But with time, this started to change to the extent that only a small fraction originated from there. According to Pastore and Nasrallah, one reason for this was the difficulty of supervising production carried out in people's homes. Another more important reason is the increasing diversity of their designs and products, leading to a decreased reliance on Nagada products. They still, however, use what they describe as Egyptian traditional material, which they procure from factories in different parts of Egypt. Significantly, around the end of the 1990s, they turned to other countries such as India, Turkey and Syria for materials. They import only small quantities, which Sylva Nassrallah describes as 'the spice' that adds a special character to their products (personal communication, 16 March 2004). Even the imported material is linked to the traditions of the respective countries. Tradition remains a central concept for Nagada fashion, but we here see a mode of distinction that distances it from the obviously ethnic creations of other enterprises. This distancing could be heard in Pastore saying: 'Nagada likes the traditional, but does not like folklore' (personal communication, 16 March 2004).

Now this is a situation where the objectives of the development project were not achieved as initially envisaged, in addition to the fact that the Nagada fashion house increasingly lost contact with the village. Yet I would still like to argue that this is a hopeful story. This may not be very clear if we speak only with those who undertook this important intervention, but if we speak with the weavers of Nagada themselves, we may get a different picture. In the village, interviews with the weavers revealed a clearly positive evaluation of the transformation that has occurred in their trade. They point to the fact that looms long deserted in people's homes began working again. Despite the decline in demand on the part of the Nagada fashion house, Nagada products have acquired a name not as traditional products but as quality hand-woven fashion wear. Not least, Nagada supplies tourist bazaars in Luxor, Aswan and Cairo with the distinctive colourful scarves, themselves in a continuous process of transformation in terms of design and material. Significantly weavers keep copies of the new designs that Michel Pastore introduced and they use them to make new patterns. The hyperbole often heard that no one in Nagada is now unemployed may not be an accurate reflection of reality, but it is a telling indication of the mood. It may not be easy to quantify the impact of the interventions and the ensuing transformation. I offer, however, two snapshots that will give a taste of this positive change.

The first is of Yunis, the son of a weaver, who works on his loom in the same room where his father works. Younis is a diploma holder who decided to learn weaving and make it his profession. He is one of many of a new generation of weavers. Passing down the skills of the craft to subsequent generations is key to the survival of traditional crafts. Not only is it reasonably lucrative, but the contexts of elite consumption, and the valuation of these products as artistic and unique, have increased the prestige associated with this trade, which could contribute to this craft's appeal to members of the new generation.

The second case is of a new type of scarf intended for sale in tourist bazaars. Contrary to the more conventional tourist scarves that are modelled on the *firka*, this is a new product that benefits from Pastore's designs. It is of a much better quality, and is sold for a substantially higher price than the conventional scarves. This is significant because it illustrates an innovation developed locally, long after the creators of this renaissance had left.

Another recent development that could at least in part be related to the valorization of traditional crafts by intellectual elites is that traditional crafts are becoming the object of official and semi-official attention in an unprecedented way. They are being treated as a valuable part of Egyptian national heritage (*turath misr al-qawmi*) and are celebrated in a manner and language hitherto reserved for ancient monuments. These objects have moved from becoming a sign of good taste to being deployed by the state as markers of national identity. It may be true that dealing with traditional crafts always contained an element of Egyptian identity assertion.[5] But with obvious official and institutional backing, they are moving towards a *central* place in the discourse defining contemporary Egyptian nationalism, and are becoming instrumental in defining and expressing 'what we are about'.

The intellectual elite influence society through their lifestyle choices by setting the standards for taste and fashion. But the spread of the ethnic traditional styles is now regarded as a vulgarization, either through excessive commercialization or through heavy nationalist overtones. Now that their choices have become too fashionable, the subjectively marginal discerning few are abandoning them in favour of other means of distinction.[6]

Ascribed marginality: the Upper Egyptian low-status tribe

The second case study that helps explain the complexity and also the contradictory character of 'marginality' as a term or label to describe a social group focuses on a low-status tribal group in Upper Egypt. I was acquainted with this group during my long-term research activity in the village that I call Manara in the Edfu region of Aswan governorate. Upper Egyptian rural society, especially the three southernmost governorates of Sohag, Qena and Aswan, displays strong features of a hierarchical tribal social organization that dictates, among other things, residential patterns, marriage rules and political and economic alliances. Tribal hierarchy is a powerful determinant of status. The fact that the latter is primarily determined through ascription (as opposed to achievement) has significant implications for constraints and opportunities of social mobility.[7]

At the bottom of the tribal hierarchy, there are a number of low-status tribal groups with hereditary specialization in crafts production or certain professions that are considered lowly. These landless, endogamous groups with hereditary professional specialization are in fact strongly suggestive of the Indian caste system. They include the potters, sieve-makers and blacksmiths. They are partly integrated into village life, but they also tend to identify with larger structures that exist outside their villages of residence. Some of these groups are in fact stigmatized and considered without honour.

The group I am focusing on here is the Hiwan tribal group, who were traditionally snake-charmers specialized in detecting the presence of snakes in houses and also treating snake and scorpion bites. In contrast to the case described earlier of a subjective marginality, the marginality of this group is totally ascribed. Like other similar groups, such as the potters and blacksmiths, the Hiwan live in a district at the edge of the village. They do not practise snake-charming any more; their main economic activity is fishing and the vegetable and fruit trade.

Members of this group have managed to improve their standard of living considerably, and it was aspects of their marginal status which enabled their economic mobility. The fact of their traditional landlessness, and that they are considered outsiders, allows for a freedom of movement and action. Thus there is a strong correlation between a restricted social mobility and a high degree of physical mobility. They specialized in trade and peddling. Their clearest mark of physical mobility, however, and one which enhanced their fortunes considerably, is that they pioneered desert reclamation in the seventies and they now farm a considerable amount of desert land. It is not entirely clear how they came to acquire this land. Their story matches what other villagers say about this matter: that it was their extreme deprivation which led them to be the first to venture into the desert. They worked very hard under harsh conditions, having to transport loads of valley silt on donkey-back for hours under the burning sun. It has to be mentioned that their claim to the land is not secure. They claim squatting rights on state-owned land and, like others in their situation, they face a threat of eviction if they do not 'regularize' their position through buying the land from the government.

Another hidden asset of their marginal and low-honour status is that they are not subject to the same severe restrictions regarding women's work outside the house. In contrast to the other higher-status village women, the Hiwan women work in the fields. This is made even more feasible as they work on reclaimed land away from the sanctions and scrutiny of the core residential community of the village. It is true that little could be done to erase the stigma of belonging to a tribe of dubious origins. Yet it is also true that the Hiwan were able to advance rapidly where economic mobility is concerned.

The Hiwan are internally socially differentiated. And I now present a case from among the most disadvantaged of this group. This case concerns a young woman whom I call Karima. Karima's mother married a day labourer from a distant village who died early, leaving Karima and her younger sister. They live next to their maternal kin and, having no steady source of income, depended mainly on charity. Despite that Karima managed to get her commercial diploma. They are now in a much better position than when I first knew them in the late 1990s. This is mainly thanks to Karima's industriousness and creative work, especially in trade. It has to be said that the very great variety of profitable activities that come under the category 'trade', and the flexibility of the conditions of their practice, has always made it an obvious outlet for underprivileged and marginal groups, providing them with a real option for improving living standards and even for considerable social mobility. The clearest sign of this ascendance is that she managed to rebuild their dilapidated mud-brick house and to furnish it in a style and to a standard that were unthinkable for someone in her condition. Karima started with a tiny 'home shop' selling sweets and tea and sugar to neighbours and relatives. Through connecting with retailers in Edfu city she got into the business of clothes trading on credit in the village.

When I asked her about her shop, her mother said that she buys half-cartons of merchandise. But Karima interrupted proudly: 'No, that was in the past. Now I buy whole cartons and I make orders that are especially delivered to me.' Karima recounts the story of her struggle after she was left in charge of her small family following the father's death.

My beginning was when my cousin was a small child and I was carrying her on my shoulder. She pulled at my gold earring and broke it. I kept the broken ring until one day I told my mother I am going to sell my earrings and buy stuff to sell. At that time I had no idea about anything. I did not know what merchandise [*bida'a*] was or where they buy it from. I went to Edfu city and sold the earrings for eighty-five pounds. If it hadn't been broken I could have sold it for much more. Before that I went to my neighbour and told her I am selling my earrings to buy *bida'a* and I asked her for money to supplement the sum so she gave me twenty pounds. I had savings of twenty more pounds and that was my starting capital. At that time the pension of my [deceased] father was fifty pounds – now it is eighty. I told Sabra [her sister] how are we to manage with fifty pounds only and she told me no we can still make ends meet with what we sell of butter from our buffalo. My mother was completely against the idea. She brought people to dissuade me including my uncle and my cousins. But I was determined. I said these are my earrings. If I lose, this is my business. But you know, it is trade which raised me [*el-tegara heyya elli rafa'etní*].

I went to Edfu with the money. As I was walking the streets I was wondering: what am I going to tell the [wholesale merchant]? Do I just tell him how much is this carton? As I was roaming the streets I ran into a young woman working in a clothes shop. She was called Abir. She found me worried and sad so she asked me what was wrong. I told her: Sister, I came here as a stranger. I don't know any street in Edfu. Sister, do you know how much a carton of oil or sugar costs? She told me I am going to help you. She worked in a shop selling dresses, scarves, skirts and underwear and these things. She told me: How about if I give you some of this stuff for you to sell in your village. She just trusted me and I only gave her thirty pounds and took lots of stuff from her with the agreement of settling the account when I have sold the stuff. After that I went and bought soap and oil and sugar and these things for one hundred pounds. That was all the money I had. Luck had it that I sold all the stuff and made a big profit. I went to Edfu and paid her her money. At that time our buffalo had a calf. I went and sold the calf and gave our partner his share. I took our share and bought bedsheets, school uniforms, dresses and underwear and I was selling a lot – cash and by credit. I made lots of money – about seven hundred pounds. By God, before that we were almost starving. We could barely find enough to eat and our cousins used to give us anything [charity].

But I had to stop dealing in clothes. People started taking for credit things they could not really afford. There were those who owed me 100 and those who owed me 150 pounds and they were not able to repay me the whole sum. So I stopped these things and continued with the rice, macaroni, Maggi [stock cubes], pickles, lentils, beans and so on. I started really concentrating on this and expanding this trade. All this started with 130 pounds. Now I buy the roll of cleaning wire for 33 pounds and a sack of beans for 146 pounds. Now I can generate all our household necessities from my trade. If I want to visit a sick relative or neighbour I take her some juice or a couple of macaroni packs.

Apart from her success in trading activities, Karima was actively engaged in other activities in and outside the village. Though such activities are not considered 'improper', some of them remain atypical for an Upper Egyptian unmarried woman. She was one among a number of the village educated women who took part in the government-sponsored programme to provide employment to diploma graduates through setting up literacy classes. She started a class for some of the village women, which helped her earn some money, in addition to earning the modestly respectable title 'Abla' (teacher or bigger sister).

A less conventional track, however, was her involvement in development and NGO activity at the village level. She managed to get employed for a while in a healthcare project, for which she was required to travel to Aswan City and spend time training, an experience she recounts with pride, being the only woman in the village to have this opportunity. More significantly perhaps, Karima managed to join the board of the village's Community Development Association, a semi-official NGO which is mainly responsible for managing local development projects. She was not only the first woman to be a board member, but also the first person of a low-status tribe to attain such a position. It has to be mentioned, though, that her selection/election to this position met with considerable resistance from the existing traditional leadership. It was also short lived as she could not withstand the hostile attitude of the other members to her presence. A main reason why she could be there in the first place was policy and donor pressures urging greater representation of women on local-level boards.

It was mainly thanks to her compounded marginal status that she could achieve things that were not possible for other young unmarried women of higher status in the village. Belonging to a low-status group and having no paternal kin are the main causes of her marginal status, but at the same time the principal reason why she enjoyed a freedom of movement and action without carrying with her the burden of honour. Karima not only managed exceptional individual achievements, but to a certain extent she was a pioneer and a model for other young women in the village.

Marginality is a complex state and its impact on groups experiencing it is not straightforward. The compounded and multidimensional nature of marginality has implications on wider social processes. Marginality is not, in itself, a force of social change, yet it could serve as a catalyst and a determinant of the direction of change. In the Upper Egyptian case just described, there is a visible trend of change in terms of an easing of restriction of women's public participation and access to public space. This transformation is linked to an increase in the levels of girls' education, an increase in public sector employment for women, and to pressures from government circles and donors alike for women's inclusion in management levels of development projects. Karima's marginal status has no causal connection to these developments. Her actions, though, have shown the way for other women in her community.

In some cases and in some ways, marginality could be an enabling condition and could have positive consequences. Speaking of subjective marginality in particular, Rhoda Unger argued that 'it permits the individual to deviate from normative practices, since she or he is already free from some aspects of societal control' (2000: 167). I have tried to show that the margin could be an arena where entrenched social rules are suspended and where social sanctions are not in full force. It is not a space of chaos but one in which social order itself is in flux. It could be a space for experimentation and possibility that is highly responsive to factors of change, including emerging opportunity; a frontier rather than a periphery.

Notes

1 A propos the dynamic nature of the concept, Gurung and Kollmair make the observation that 'the negative consequences of marginality can even serve as the starting point of innovations and potentials' (2005: 11).

2 For more on this issue, see Saad (2003).

3 This section draws on Saad (2006).

4 Other sources mention it was made of a blend of cotton and rayon (www.nagada.net; Vogelsang-Eastwood and Einarsdottir 2003).

5 For example, Asaad Nadim describes them as expressing the distinctive 'national character' of the Egyptians (Nadim n.d: 4).

6 'Because the distinctive power of cultural possessions or practices – an artefact, a qualification, a film culture – tends to decline with the growth in the absolute number of people able to appropriate them, the profits of distinction would wither away if the field of production of cultural goods, itself governed by the dialectic of pretension and distinction, did not endlessly supply new goods or new ways of using the same goods' (Bourdieu 1984: 230).

7 On the tribal social organization of Upper Egyptian society, see Nielsen (2006: 128–31) and Bach (2004). On tribal hierarchy and low-status tribes, see Gamblin (2004).

References

Abaza, M. (2006) *Changing Consumer Cultures of Modern Egypt: Cairo's Urban Reshaping*, Leiden/Boston, MA: Brill.

Al-Omari, M. A. S. (2003) *Emarat Al-Fuqaraa am Emarat Al-Aghneyaa?* [Architecture for the poor or architecture for the rich?], Cairo: General Egyptian Book Organisation.

Ammoun, D. (1987) *Egypte des Mains Magiques*, Institut Français d'Archéologie Orientale du Caire. 1987.

Ayeb, H. (2009) 'Introduction: marginality: concepts, practices and directions for action', Presented at the workshp 'Marginality: concepts, practices and directions for action', CEDEJ, Cairo, 20 September.

Bach, K. (2004) 'Changing family and marriage patterns in an Aswan village', in N. Hopkins and R. Saad (eds), *Upper Egypt: Identity and Change*, American University in Cairo Press.

Bourdieu, P. (1984) *Distinction: A Social Critique of the Judgement of Taste*, trans. Richard Nice, Cambridge, MA: Harvard University Press.

Fathi, H. (1973) *Architecture for the Poor: An experiment in rural Egypt*, Chicago, IL: University of Chicago Press.

Gamblin, S. (2004) 'Luxor: a tale of two cities', in N. Hopkins and R. Saad (eds), *Upper Egypt: Identity and Change*, American University in Cairo Press.

Gist, N. (1967) 'Cultural versus social marginality: the Anglo-Indian case', *Phylon*, 28(4): 361–75.

Gurung, G. and M. Kollmair (2005) 'Marginality: concepts and their limitations', IP6 Working Paper no. 4, Development Study Group, Department of Geography, University of Zurich.

Mehretu, A., B. W. Pigozzi and L. M. Sommers (2000) 'Concepts in social and spatial marginality', *Geografiska Annaler*, Series

B: *Human Geography*, 82(2): 'Development of settlements', pp. 89–101.

Nadim, A. (n.d.) *Traditional Arts and Crafts from Cairo*, Prism Series 3, Foreign Culture Information Department, Ministry of Culture.

Nielsen, H. C. (2006) 'State and customary law in Upper Egypt', *Islamic Law and Society*, 13: 123–52.

Saad, R. (2003) 'Mud-brick or no mud-brick? Architectural preference in two Upper Egyptian communities', *Jordens Folk*, 38(1) (in Danish).

— (2006) 'Transforming the meaning and value of traditional crafts in Egypt', *Cairo Papers in Social Science*, special issue: *Cultural Dynamics in Contemporary Egypt*, 27(1/2).

Unger, R. K. (2000) 'Outsiders inside: positive marginality and social change', *Journal of Social Issues*, 56: 163–79.

Vogelsang-Eastwood, G. and S. Einarsdottir (2003) 'Some Upper Egyptian textiles', in N. Hopkins (ed.), *Upper Egypt: Life Along the Nile*, Aarhus: Moesgaard Museum.

www.nagada.net

7 | Transport thugs: spatial marginalization in a Cairo suburb

DALIA WAHDAN

Introduction

Road transport was a strategic sector for the deposed ruling regime in Egypt in its quest to make Greater Cairo a 'world-class' city-region. It swallowed government expenditures and global funds and went through structural transformations and World Bank-advocated public–private partnerships to the point of becoming a matter of national security. By extension, transport operators emerged as a potential threat and challenge to stability.

This chapter explores how people living in a Cairo suburb commute daily between various destinations. In doing so it explores how spatial location creates and then reproduces people's marginality and it reveals complex relationships between providers and regulators of passenger transport in and around Cairo. It highlights the spatial dynamics of marginality in Egypt and the consequences of that marginality for residents dependent upon an ailing and overstretched transport network.

Before the government of Egypt (GoE) reconfigured the country's administrative units in 2008 the suburb of Sitta October (6 October) was officially designated a 'satellite city' west of Greater Cairo Metropolitan Region. It is now part of the second-largest governorate in the area after el-Wadi el-Jadid. Since its inception in 1979, Sitta October has been linked to patterns of capital and labour flows associated with consecutive economic reforms, beginning with the Open Door policies of President Anwar Sadat (1970–81) in the 1970s and the liberalization and structural adjustments that took place under President Hosni Mubarak (1981–2011). Its demographic composition has been influenced by jobs made possible through capital investments and the absence or availability of basic services and infrastructure. Similarly, capital and labour flows have had a direct bearing on demand and supply of passenger transport in and around the city.

The structure of local administration has also played a substantial role in shaping transport services. Before becoming a governorate, Sitta October was administered by a city development agency (CDA), the local arm of New Urban Communities Authority (NUCA), a subsidiary of the Ministry of Housing – the apex authority overseeing the affairs of the city and the one which has been mired in accusations of corruption since the 25 January revolution. Decisions over land acquisitions and infrastructure investments were taken by successive CDA directors in consultation with a board of trustees appointed by the minister of housing or more senior officials. However, in 2008 the city became part of a larger administrative unit with a governor, who, according to Egyptian administrative practices, is entrusted with 'presidential-like authority' over his formal jurisdiction.[1] In 2009 the former president decreed a High Council for Development and Planning (HCDP) to oversee land use and acquisition in the city as part of the larger governorate. The deposed president hand-picked the council members, whose decisions over land were usually delivered in utmost secrecy.

The multiplicity of governing bodies with overlapping responsibilities complicated infrastructure provision and service delivery. Transport operators and commuters alike had to negotiate a medley of government offices and changing regulations to provide and receive minimal levels of services respectively. While commuters suffered unsteady, inefficient, inhumane and unaffordable services, for operators, transport was often the only means of livelihood. Making a living as a transporter in pre-revolution Cairo meant operating within a vulnerable economy dependent upon sudden structural jerks with immediate repercussions on households' and individuals' financial worth. It meant interacting with a hostile environment created by a protracted state of emergency. The latter is particularly relevant to processes of marginalization in and around Cairo.

Although non-government transporters shouldered more than half the supply of passenger transport in Greater Cairo (*Al-Ahram Al-Iqtisadi*, 19 December 2005), they continuously struggled against an unrelenting discourse of criminalization. The discourse started roughly in the 1970s when a few entrepreneurs, encouraged by Open Door policies, imported Peugeot seven-seat vans to operate between cities. The government was slow to formally regulate these vans and eventually Peugeot sevenseaters came to be stigmatized as spontaneous transport, *'ashwa'iyat*, and held responsible for traffic congestion, accidents and pollution. Criminalization intensified under the emergency after 1982.

The law upholds a pervasive definition of 'national security'. It subjects citizens to myriad forms of police surveillance under the pretext of maintaining stability for economic prosperity (Singerman 2002). As mentioned, transport was strategic to national security; its operations, particularly in urban areas and main cities, had to be controlled and operators subjected to strict police surveillance. Nevertheless, the close interaction between transport operators, security forces and government agents created an environment for rent-seeking. That enriched a small group within the ruling regime at the expense of operators regardless of livelihood or commuter rights or their needs for effective transport service.

This chapter argues that 'livelihood' is as central as capital–labour relations in understanding marginalization and depicts the livelihoods of transport operators in and around Sitta October before the 25 January uprising to explain the economic, administrative and political dynamics that circumscribe their activities. The chapter demonstrates how the design and regulation of transport gave rise to inequities through spatial practices that privileged sections of the population while marginalizing others. Such practices strangled livelihoods and locked people in perpetual resistance to formal state institutions and agents.[2]

Sitta October

True to his 'Open Door', President Sadat suggested establishing eighteen new urban communities (October Working Paper, 1974) and the New Urban Communities Authority (NUCA) to control them (Law 95, 1979). Since its inception, NUCA has been trapped in debates about the New Urban Communities Programme's (NUCP) economic feasibility, demographic performance and administrative efficiency. Owing to lack of transparency and absence of consistent data, until 2011 the exact number of NUCs was known only to a few (Florin 2005) and their total populations were way below planned thresholds (*al Ahrar*, 10 March 2006).

Public debates tackled three issues: 'organized looting' of lands through a nexus of businessmen and corrupt officials, NUCA's mounting debts, and the failure of the new communities to attract residents owing to lack of public amenities. Since 1991, government-owned newspapers have repeatedly exposed the proceedings of otherwise secret forums discussing the programme's future and NUCA's transformation into an 'economic agency'. Unlike existing cities, NUCs have city development agencies with appointed heads and executive bureaucracies. The development decisions of each community are vested in boards of trustees. These are representatives of various ministries and select investors nominated by their respective city investor associations and appointed by the minister of housing.

Sitta October is one of the actually existing new urban communities. It was planned to be situated 65 kilometres from Cairo's centre to diffuse the dense Greater Cairo Region (GCR) and redirect development away from the fertile delta (Wahdan 2010). However, a presidential decree (504/1979) ordered its relocation only 34 kilometres south-west of Cairo and mired it in dependence on GCR.[3] Simultaneously, Law 59 (1979) encouraged private capital in real estate, offered lands with basic infrastructures at reduced prices, tax holidays for start-up periods and custom exemption for capital goods. Yet the city's proximity to GCR facilitated encroachments on agricultural lands surrounding it, discouraged permanent migration to the city, delayed population diffusion and justified government's laxity in extending infrastructure until the reforms of the 1990s (Fahmi 1986; Hassan 1982).

While the law encouraged land reclamation and urban agriculture in the green belt around the city (the buffer zone against desert winds), from the seventies GoE encouraged foreign direct investments in textiles, electrical equipment, pharmaceuticals and fast-moving consumer goods (Soliman 1998; Fouad 1984; El-Demerdash 1983). Although some industry was attracted, the city did not rise to public attention until after the neoliberal economic reforms of 1991. Since then the city has experienced investment surges when private real-estate developers, encouraged by legal stipulations and money remitted from Egyptians in Gulf countries, engaged in land speculation and development of expensive residential complexes (Mitchell 2002).

In 2001, Sitta October CDA suffered large financial deficits. Despite collecting around LE80 million in revenues it could finance only 66 per cent of the city's expenses (LE120 million) annually (*Wafd*, 19 October 2001). CDA had to ask NUCA for LE45 million to finance pending infrastructure projects. When NUCA supplied LE22 million only, the agency hiked land prices and borrowed from businessmen. The same year, the city topped NUCs in incomplete projects (537 projects) (*Jomhouria*, 28 December 2001). The global financial crisis after 2008 exacerbated the city's prospects and Sitta October Development and Investment Company (SODIC) registered net losses of LE8.3 million (1 January–31 March 2009) compared to LE17.5 million net profit over the same period in 2008 (*al-Alam al-Youm*, 31 May 2009).

Demographically, the city's population grew from 35,477 in 1996 (Egypt Census, 1996) to 154,093 in 2008 (CAPMAS, Sitta October Governorate Census, May 2008). Most residents (those aged between fifteen and thirty and married) were either non-literate or pre-university educated (85.2 per cent). Only 14.8 per cent had completed a bachelor's degree. The surge in the service sector, however, brought in 'professionals' and students from rich Egyptian and Arab families, increasing demand for housing and urban amenities. It also altered the city's morphology as many house-owners rented flats to students and moved out to low-income housing within or out of the city. Around two million commuted daily to the city, including transport and factory workers from the surrounding, more southern governorates of Beni Suef, Minya and Fayoum.

There are few data on basic services but residents in interviews indicated recurrent shortages of water, electricity, bread and public transport. They were also anxious about street lighting, safe public spaces and affordable means of entertainment. Many shopped in GCR, adding to their already high transport budgets. Potable water was a frequent problem, with repeated leakages from drain pipelines (*October News*, 26, May 2001). While power failures frustrated businesses and residents alike, except for a few investors most factories did not provide housing for their workers, adding to a demand for commuting. Although trustees collected approximately LE18 million annually from residents for services, passenger transport remained a private initiative. Similarly, CDA had earlier aborted one USAID initiative for e-government (1999) and slashed the city's website and the industrial and services database that linked industries to state information and decision-making (www.ids.gov.eg), pushing people to physically commute to government premises for daily business.

The city also suffered institutional congestion. Six different authorities preside over its affairs: NUCA, CDA, the board of trustees, Sitta October Investors Association (SOIA), a governor and, recently, the High Council for Development and Planning (HCDP). NUCA takes decisions on land use, pricing, acquisition and allotment on lands that the Ministry of Housing slates for new urban communities. It sets the parameters for appointed CDA directors. The board, constituted of civic and government members, shoulders decisions over utilities and services that usually tilt towards the interests of powerful investors representing and nominated by SOIA. The latter is a private voluntary organization representing local business interests. It is the interface between business and politics, with most members affiliated to the erstwhile ruling National Democratic Party (NDP). In 2008, Sitta October was incorporated into a governorate of the same name and appointed a governor, who constitutionally represented the highest decision-making authority after the president. In 2009, HCDP was established to oversee land transactions in the city. With the exception of the governor, all institutions are the result of GoE neoliberal reforms.

Nonetheless, CDA is entitled to a percentage share of land sales, revenue from licensing commercial establishments and fees from non-governmental service providers, in addition to government grants. The board is also entitled to 2 per cent of projects' licensing and registration. While these arrangements could imply decentralization and relative financial independence, in the context of a chronic lack of transparency the system has generated the politics of graft. In 2006, for example, the head of the agency was arrested in a land scam (*Al-Ahram*, 26 January 2006).

Debt and the city

Three contextual parameters are important to the dynamics of transportation and marginalization in Sitta October. The first concerns the central government and NUCA's revenues, expenditures and debts. After 1984 government revenue deteriorated dramatically. Revenues (from taxes, petroleum, the Suez Canal, remittances and external aid) as a percentage of gross domestic product (GDP) decreased from almost 45 per cent in 1984 to barely 35 per cent in 1989 (Soliman 2005). GoE responded by slashing subsidies from 12 per cent of GDP in 1982/83 to 6 per cent in 1989/90. However, external debt rose to US$50 billion in 1990. GoE signed an economic reform agreement with the World Bank in 1991 which stipulated a fall in public expenditure, but expenditure as a percentage of GDP rose from 45 per cent in 1986/87 to 57.2 per cent in 1987/88.

Yet GoE received a financial reward for supporting the removal of Iraqi forces from Kuwait in 1990. Egypt's foreign debt was cut in half. The situation improved temporarily after the signing of the second Economic Reform and Structural Adjustment Programme (ERSAP) in 1991 but deteriorated after 2000 with rising expenditures and declining revenues. Even after tax reforms, net deficit exceeded 7 per cent and total debts reached 152 per cent of GDP in 2000.

Domestic debt was caused by misallocation of funds, underutilization of resources and increased refunds of payment for housing and real estate owing to lack of infrastructure. In 2001, illegal encroachments totalled 308 million square metres while more than 223 million square metres awaited evacuation from public land (*al-Ahali*, 4 July 2001). Surprisingly, in the same year NUCA could not utilize $34.6 million (at 3.25 per cent annual rate of return) ring-fenced by CDA for tourist villages at the Construction and Housing Bank (*al-Ahrar*, 4 July 2001).

Secondly, the erstwhile Mubarak government consistently made contradictory decisions on NUCP. In 1998, it removed tax exemptions to private service providers, depriving NUCs of enthusiastic initiatives, only to re-enact them in 2001. Similarly, it reduced down payments for medium and low-income residential units (from 50 to 20 per cent of total price) and extended payment periods above fifteen years at reduced interest rates (6 per cent instead of 10 per cent), making cooperative loans available. Even high-income units exceeding 100 metres were allowed front payments of 15 per cent only with half-yearly instalments over fifteen years at a 5 instead of 8 per cent interest rate (*Mayo*, 5 March 2001). The government has even reduced NUCs' school admission age to lure families. However, it did not enact the High Commission for Policies and Economic Affairs' instructions on 13 March 1985 to directly supervise infrastructure provision in NUCs. Instead, the ministry accused heavily indebted NUCA of inefficiency (*Al-Akhbar*, 6 March 2002).

Since 1982 the situation has deteriorated further as NUCA and CDAs were transformed into 'holding companies' contradicting Article 13 of Law 59 (1979), which stated that on completion of infrastructure networks NUCA must hand the new communities over to local government bodies (*mahalliyat*) of 'old' governorates. Instead, CDAs were transformed into independent revenue-generating mechanisms that actually led to retrenchment, which could have stirred public opinion against the deposed regime.

The third parameter concerned the pattern of government expenditures. Since 1997, public money on subsidies has declined compared to expenditures on police and security. In 1997, 4.7 per cent of GDP went to security and in 2002 the number of policemen exceeded one million (21 per cent of all state employees). In comparison, in 2000/01, 4 per cent only of public money went to subsidies. Police expenditure was important. It helped normalize emergency and criminalize selected livelihoods. For example, although 74 per cent of total investments in the new urban communities was foreign and private (Mubarak wal Umran 1999), the regime was not consistently business friendly. For instance, while the gamut of investment and income tax laws was favourable, bank and insurance regulations stifled business with selective legal sanctions. It was customary to raise criminal charges against investors who found difficulties in servicing their debts, especially if they subscribed to opposition parties. Hani Soroor, CEO of Heidelina Pharmaceuticals and head of SOIA in 2001, noted, 'It is a war of attrition and a concerted effort by the National Democratic Party, banks and media to criminalize certain investors, who go against the interests of the bride.'

The newly formed HCDP in Sitta October is another illustration of selective privileging. Established by ministerial decree number 62 (5 February 2009), this cabal of select investors and NUCA officials suddenly enjoyed full discretion over policies and projects deemed in 'the city's best interest'. It is difficult to determine the logic behind Decree 62, especially given that the assigned functions are a carbon copy of the trustees' (Ministerial Decree 101, 1986). While it could be an instance of bureaucratic congestion, the question remains: how is HCDP better equipped than investors-cum-trustees to decide on 'public interest'?

In a personal interview, Khamis Shaaban, general secretary of SOIA, defended the council as a proactive step against land abuses at the critical junction of establishing a governorate and designing a 2025 city plan. He claimed no conflict of interest since the 'trustee board is executive [*tanfizi*] while the council is planning [*takhtiti*]' and added that SOIA vehemently resisted making Sitta October the governorate capital as this 'would play havoc on land markets and business interests'. It would also mean that old bureaucratic bodies would take over with chronic red tape and fiscal deficits. Shaaban gave assurances that 'selected HCDP investors maintained good relations with everybody in the city and were better equipped to eschew bad elements from land markets'.

It seemed that under emergency law governing was a delicate exercise as regime members juggled livelihoods with the absolute power of violence. With 'continuity for the sake of stability' as the driving motor (Singerman 2002: 29), the erstwhile Mubarak regime's modus operandi was to criminalize whoever it thought threatened its survival. It is also within these contextual parameters that matrices of power and urban governance are woven, giving rise to a city constitutionally within a governor's jurisdiction, yet legally and financially under NUCA's control. It is administered by CDA yet managed by selected trustees and developed on the behest of HCDP.

Struggles over transport

The majority of urban Egyptians depend on buses for transport. In 2008, 3,500 buses operated on 400 routes in greater Cairo, carrying around 3.2 million passengers daily. However, 55 per cent of the fleet was obsolete and few lines served NUCs. The General Authority for Public Transport (GAPT) and NUCA exchanged accusations about poor provision, while the Ministry of Transport withdrew from urban transport as part of broader privatization schemes.

The situation in Sitta October is particularly dismal. While GAPT claimed five daily lines between Tahrir Square in Cairo and Sitta October via Giza, residents rarely saw those 'ghost lines' (*Al-Akhbar*, Letters to the editor, 9 October 2002, p. 4). In 2003, GAPT slashed operations to two lines to cut losses. Tariffs were standardized (from LE0.50 to LE2.50), although service remained precarious. Drivers fragmented trips by relaying passengers to private microbuses that were driven quickly to increase daily round trips. The design of the city helped further fragment trips. It is built around an axial road (east–west) with residential neighbourhoods on both sides. The axis connects industrial zones (west) with the ring road and three national highways (east, north and south). Three roundabouts intersect the axis as central junctions for all transport operations in the city. As such they acted as spaces of domination and resistance, where operators pursue their livelihoods in the face of brutal security and venal traffic police.

Government buses (*naql hokoumi*) did not operate inside the city; private transport (*naql ahali*) provided most services. Microbuses and cooperative buses plied on the axial road connecting the city to GCR (east), while *box el-Fayoum* (quarter-trucks; see below) and *makhsous* (private rental vehicles) carried passengers westwards and *tok-toks* (auto-rickshaws) plied between neighbourhoods inside the city. *Rehalat* buses were contract carriages for factory employees, but operators moonlighted. No official loading spots were permitted but operators carved out their 'right to the city' conventionally among themselves. Passengers complained about lack of fixed routes, reckless driving, unfriendly staff, exploitative practices and precarious operations. For instance, *box el-Fayoum* was originally licensed as cattle transport, yet it carried women, children and people with special needs. A typical one-way trip for a single passenger from Essadess neighbourhood (west) to Tahrir Square, Cairo (east), involved *tok-tok* and/or *box el-Fayoum* microbus to the ring road, public bus to Giza and microbus or *naql hokoumi* to Tahrir! Households spent almost 30 per cent of their incomes on commuting (see Laquian et al. 2007).

Two local entrepreneurs attempted integrated city operations but failed. In 2002, Abdul Hamid Al Wahab started operating with LE50 million start-up capital (*Jomhuria*, 24 February 2002). The General Transport Authority (GTA) permitted him to carry out intra-city operations, contravening Law 55 (1975), which did not provide for private initiatives. Nevertheless, before long GTA withdrew permission and in 2004 the ministry swore to abolish 'spontaneous transport' to help restore Cairo's 'civilization façade' (*Al-Ahram Al-Iqtisadi*, 19 December

2005). GTA invited open tenders for ten private companies to operate minibuses in Greater Cairo, and before long minibuses carrying Cairo Transport Company markings appeared in two upper-middle districts. Although this was the first instance of competitive tendering, the process was obscure.

Official statements on urban transport are as contradictory as those on new communities. Nabil El-Mazny, chief GTA engineer, blamed NUCA for failure to integrate transport into city plans and held it responsible for low rates of population growth in the new communities. He added that nineteen companies were selected after open tender. However, interviews with Muhammed El-Banna, CEO of a transport cooperative in Giza, revealed that tenders set prohibitive bus specifications, making it compulsory to introduce Korean buses, which were imported by General Motors, the sole agent and franchise of Mohammed Mansour, then minister of transport (*Al-Akhbar*, 13 September 2005). Sitta October was not covered by the scheme as the city fell between Cairo and Giza traffic jurisdictions, although earlier, Ibrahim El-Demeeri, former transport minister, had declared that the Egyptian Railway Authority had studied the possibility of extending the Cairo metro to the city (*Al-Ahrar*, 6 August 2000).

Rent from the source Transport authorities have long realized the rent potential of private operators. Besides illicit extortion by traffic and security police, in 1987 Cairo and Giza governorates set up a service project to regulate microbus operations by collecting '*carta* from source' (daily tickets from each microbus for every round trip on each route from central points or the source). In 2002, every vehicle paid *carta*. In Giza, 5,727 microbuses and 232 association buses making eleven average round trips per day paid LE5 per round trip per route daily, while in Cairo around 5,700 microbuses and 4,000 other vehicles did the same. In one year the project raised governorate revenues by 40 per cent.[4] Noteworthy is the fact that the project is a 'special fund' not subject to government audit.[5]

Besides using violence, traffic police ensured payment through impounding vehicles and withholding licences without *carta* clearance. This offset operators' profits. In 2009, monthly vehicle instalment charges were around LE3,200 ($530), excluding maintenance, wages and route permits. Routes were purchased for different time periods. A three-month route cost LE650. One microbus could make LE300 a day if it operated outside the city. One round trip took approximately two hours and could yield between LE80 and LE100. However, running a microbus was not lucrative considering that owners paid around LE3,000 per month, in addition to LE650 every three months for each route and a similar amount every four months for maintenance. Motivated by potential revenue increases, Sitta October CDA established a similar project, income from which allegedly improved parking and maintenance in the city.

Flying coffins Auto-rickshaws (*tok-toks*) were introduced to Egypt in 2000. An entrepreneur from Sharqia, north of Cairo, sub-franchised the marketing of the vehicles from Ghabbour, CITI, and affiliates of Bajaj (India) in Egypt. He started operations in Gharbia, yet Simbelawein in Sharqia was the first town to establish small and micro-scale spare-part assembly workshops. The simple technology encouraged local manufacturing of entire vehicles, cutting costs and increasing the geographical spread of *tok-toks*. The Committee for National Security at the People's Assembly estimated that there were 50,000 *tok-toks* in Egypt, leading to the employment of around 100,000 people as drivers, owner-operators, mechanics, organizers, decorators and moneylenders (*Al-Masri Al-Youm*, 25 May 2005). The new industry also involved licensed importers, local dealers, assembly shops and repair and maintenance depots. Local dealers sold *tok-toks* for cash or payment by instalment and buyers chain-sold for profit. In 2006, purchasing a three-seater in Cairo cost around LE9,800. If payment was by instalment there might be a LE4,800 down payment and LE399 instalments over eighteen months (*Al-Akhbar el-Sayarat*, 10 December 2005).

Across the delta *tok-toks* were creatively used to transport voters to and from polling stations (*Al-Akhbar*, 27 November 2005) or reassembled for goods and garbage transport or as mobile fridges (*Al-Ahram*, 25 November 2005). However, the governor of Cairo believed that *tok-toks* would damage the otherwise 'civilized' image of the capital and banned them (*Al-Masaa*, 4 December 2005). Similarly, the Ministry of Industry was reluctant to license them, claiming the vehicles failed to meet the ministry's specifications for cars or motorbikes and hence were not liable for taxation. Meanwhile, *tok-tok* operators faced arbitrary traffic regulations, vehicle confiscation and extortion of large sums of money by way of fines and stand fees. Many *tok-tok*s were set on fire during the violence that broke out during the 2005/06 parliamentary elections in delta provinces; compensation was paid to owners (*Al-Masaa*, 9 December 2005). The illegal status associated *tok-toks* with social 'evils': operating without meters, reckless and below-age driving, running over pedestrians and the raping of innocent girls (*Al-Jomhuria*, 26 November 2005). To add insult to injury *tok-toks* were nicknamed 'stray carts', 'moving coffins', the 'cursed shuttle', the 'daily headache' and 'night rodents', yet no one questioned whether the social evils had anything to do with the government's reluctance to solve the licensing mess.

The vehicle was repeatedly discussed in the People's Assembly. In 2005, a committee assigned to investigate the vehicle's effects on the economy defended the right of operators to their income and claimed that 80 per cent of them held intermediate to higher education degrees. The committee suggested registering *tok-toks* with local government units as 'slow-moving' vehicles, until the Ministry of Interior amended the traffic laws (*Nahdet Masr*, 24 October 2005). The illegal status did not deter operators from asserting their right to their livelihoods, and *El-Ghad* newspaper reported that unlicensed *tok-toks* usually parked and loaded passengers and goods from central *maidans* (squares) in front of police stations, traffic units or governors' offices (*El-Ghad*, 9 November 2005).

In October 2005, the former governor of Sharqia authorized local units to register *tok-toks* for a fee (LE50) (*Alam Al-Mowasafat wal Jawoda*, 1 October 2005). He issued district colour-coded plates to 1,500 *tok-toks* that registered and started paying *carta*. It was not long before operators got wise to the scam. Traffic units declared the scheme void yet continued to receive *carta* and taxes and track down and impound defaulters. Similarly, the governor of Giza authorized registration at local units only to use it to trace and confiscate all vehicles in order to maintain the 'modern' look of the city. Operators paid round LE2,000 to have their vehicles released (*Al-Ahrar*, 29 September 2005).

Operators demonstrated outside the governors' offices in Sharqia and Giza, accusing them of fraud. Both governors alleged that they had been misinformed about *tok-toks*, which they understood to be locally assembled imported units and thus subject to taxation. Demonstrators presented copies of customs and excise release documents to the press, which attested that the vehicles entered the country as intact units. They demanded that GoE explain why *tok-toks* were allowed into the country if there was no intention to license them in the first place. Demonstrations came to an end when operators offered to surrender their vehicles if the governors promised to provide each operator with substitute employment with a monthly income of at least LE150. Nonetheless, demonstrations recurred at ministry level, compelling Mohammed Rasheed, former minister of foreign trade and industry, to authorize new specifications for *tok-tok* design and safety and to start inter-ministerial coordination and initiate amendments to the vehicles' legal status (*Al-Shorouq*, *Sawot Al-Azhar*, 14 November 2005). These incidents revealed the discord within and the failure of government to secure self-generated jobs or to guarantee the right to livelihood.

In Sitta October, around two hundred unlicensed *tok-toks* were operated, mostly by unemployed young men with college degrees or professionals who moonlighted. Most operators came from Sharqia and Fayoum (east and west of the city). When operators first came to the city in 2003, *tok-toks* were both their source of income and their residence. They slept in their vehicles and organized trips along routes closer to their home towns; very few could afford a rented flat. However, when more people started operating, security police imposed stricter measures on their mobility. In 2004 the police recruited two local leaders to monitor operators. To bestow legitimacy, leaders were brought from operators' town of origin; they submitted daily reports on their behaviour and arbitrated conflicts, the intention being to instil self-discipline in operators and thus maintain stability.

Box el-Fayoum The *box el-Fayoum* or 'quarter-truck' originated in Fayoum, one of Upper Egypt's least developed governorates, for the carriage of goods and cattle. Although most trucks were technically out of service with expired licences, to adapt them for carrying passengers, owners mounted a wooden box-like structure on the boot, which opened at the rear. There were around one thousand such boxes in Sitta October, transporting groups or operating on-demand *makhsous*. Though illegal, they fulfilled 90 per cent of the city's demand, carrying passengers across neighbourhoods without fixed routes. Nevertheless, services were seen as inhumane and sometimes immoral. Operators alleged that they were helpless in the face of police practices. Several officers brought 'girls and ordered the truck for a few hours to the outskirts of the city'. If a driver refused, officers impounded the vehicle and abused the driver.

Their precarious legal status rendered *box el-Fayoum* vulnerable. Police officers confiscated vehicles for days without compensation, and used them in raids and during social unrest. Operators faced hardship given an absence of steady income, denial of the right to space for parking and rest, and monetary extortion through *carta* and tickets, as well as physical abuse by security police. Security forces occasionally bandied the slogan 'sons of the city', meaning that only those born in Sitta October would be allowed to operate. The campaigns terrorized operators, who bribed officers in return. Under the deposed Mubarak regime, police not only protected private property and maintained law and order, they also shielded the government from its imagined enemies by consistently threatening their livelihoods.

The majority of *box el-Fayoum* operators did not own their vehicles and worked for a percentage of daily revenue. They were mostly poor and included college drop-outs, but a few were entrepreneurs with micro-enterprises. Typically a driver lived in the city; as narrated by one operator:

> I owned a small factory for plastic Tupperware at Sadat city, but now I work as a driver on a *makhsous* owned by a man who also resides in October. *Makhsous* do not have fixed routes; we operate at random and on request. I evade *carta* and it is difficult to calculate how much I make per day. The car brings from LE80 to LE100 per round. I work seven days a week. And the round starts from seven a.m. [and lasts] till five p.m. There is another round from five p.m. till one after midnight. The arrangement between the owner and me is that I get twenty-five per cent of the income. The car is registered *naql* Cairo [i.e. a goods carriage]. I have a private driving licence [i.e. not as a classified driver] and I carry with me the official *tawkeel* permit from the car owner.[6]

Box el-Fayoum also operated between Sitta October and other destinations to the west and south-west of the city, sometimes going as far as Libya using the Fayoum–Oasis highway, paying bribes at every checkpoint along the way.

The well-to-do neighbourhoods were mostly served by private taxis, illustrating spatial polarization. Taxis and to lesser extent cooperative buses were the only vehicles licensed to operate in these neighbourhoods and along the axial roads and highways to and from the city. However, well-to-do residents preferred private taxis to association buses. Taxis functioned as private vehicles, transporting students daily to and from universities, and making frequent trips to Cairo International Airport. Operators also made several weekly trips to different tourist destinations in Giza and Cairo and operated as tour guides or provided escort services to students and their visiting friends and families. Given the absence of official stands, operators established informal taxi stands and car-pooled, especially at prayer times. Because they carried permits to operate across governorates, as well as in intra-city neighbourhoods, they made a total of LE100–150 per day on average, and worked from 7 a.m. to 12 a.m., and sometimes till dawn. Although they were licensed and abided by traffic rules and regulations, they were not exempt from police harassment. They complained about arbitrary fines (about LE20,000 annually).

On the whole, the transformation of Sitta October into a governorate has expanded and intensified transport demand; private suppliers jumped at the opportunity. More vehicles and new types appeared on the roads and many operators pioneered new unlicensed routes, hoping to make quick profits before the authorities took retaliatory action. However, the increase in supply did not automatically mean better service or equitable outreach; nor did it create a situation of 'perfect competition', where abundance of supply reduced costs and improved quality. Failure was due mainly to high incidences of unlicensed and unregistered vehicles, arbitrary extortion and policing, contradictory traffic regulations, and extensive surveillance by security police working under prevailing emergency conditions. Operators sharpened their versatile 'business acumen' by negotiating all the above. The enactment of a new traffic law in 2005 in and around Cairo complicated matters by increasing and tightening security measures, as well as leading to the installation of more radar stations and checkpoints.

Incorporating ten population-dense divisions into one jurisdiction, without 'integrating' roadways and transport networks, failed to live up to the rhetoric of efficiency and equitable redistribution (see Hooghe and Marks 2003). It did not even fit 'public choice' frameworks, which advocated decentralization as a means to better market conditions and viewed citizens as clients who bought services from local authorities, with the latter vying to adjust supply according to demand. The limited transport options in the city gave rise to a market-like situation in the first place, with all these factors continuing to determine vehicle technologies and service supply, as well as the structure of tariffs and routing patterns – i.e. all aspects of passenger transport.

Administratively, the governorate remains without formal traffic routes. Its thirteen subdivisions are disjointed, with no direct transport routes between any two subdivisions and no central station. The city is traversed by means of fragmented trips, which over-burden resources (fuel, time, energy and money). There is no city-level department of transport, and traffic police function as surveillance and harassment mechanisms, with complaints having to be directed to authorities beyond city limits. And operators lack formal representation in city politics. Except in the case of the auto-rickshaws operators, who have two self-declared leaders, there is no formal union or syndicate representing operators or redressing their grievances. Under emergency law and the strict licensing conditions required for membership of the drivers' syndicate, an independent syndicate seems the only possibility for Sitta October's informal operators if they are to defend their right to a livelihood.

Spatial marginality and livelihoods

This chapter confirms the recognition that urban spaces should be expressions of infrastructure networks working harmoniously to provide inhabitants with shelter, contact, energy, water and means of transportation. This conception of urban space helps us to understand roads, bridges and vehicles as socially constructed technical systems, closely associated with land use and planning and construction technologies, as well as government and para-government regulatory institutions (Graham 2000; Graham and Marvin 2001). They are not just the outcome of experts' rational choices but entities that are perpetually reconstructed through matrices of formal and informal rules, subject to discord, controversy and conflict. They are dynamic reflections of spatial fixity and movement, and thus organically constitutive of urbanization and urban forms.

Nevertheless, this conceptualization does not mean that infrastructures have agency. Rather, it emphasizes the heightened sense of agency expressed through spatial practices of resistance to the militarization of government functions and the tight security measures of the deposed regime (Ghannam 1997; Davis 2006). This dialectic is crucial for understanding the nature of spatial marginality. In the Greater Cairo region and in Sitta October several tiers of decision-making intersected to regulate transport infrastructure. The *tok-tok* case highlights contestations between the technical expertise of research centres and ministries and operators over what is appropriate technology. The vehicle was also indicative of the range of political decisions that confronted popular will over the use of technology as a means of livelihood and dignity.

The route licensing and traffic management of microbuses was another instance of how control of movement in space and time was often enmeshed in conflicting logics. While governors sought to represent the city as a 'civilized' place, ready to accommodate the speed and versatile requirements of global investments, microbus operators sought to speed up turnover of passengers and revenues to cover the direct and indirect costs of running their business. Frequently, logics conflicted. The Cairo governor's ban on microbuses with Giza and Qalubia plates plying their trade within the capital's jurisdiction was a vivid example. Besides exacerbating traffic congestion, it was indicative of how Greater Cairo remained a contested assembly with multiple space–time mobilities. It also underscored how the 'region' was unevenly consolidated in the minds of top decision-makers; governors of Cairo, Giza and Qalubia, and for that matter Sitta October, did not conceive of their jurisdictions as a territorial unit with economic and infrastructural potentials.

Traffic and security police were two intermediate systems subject to the contradictory logics of governors and operators. While executing their orders, they fulfilled their own motivations through extortion, arbitrary raids and checkpoints. The practices of impounding, enlisting and taking vehicles into custody at distant locations ensured that transport was constantly monitored. This surveillance mentality brought into conflict the complex logics of government bodies and operators and caused further fragmentation of space–time urban mobility. Personal gains aside, conjoining traffic, police and state security for the control of transport operators, under the emergency order, was premised upon the complete conflation of the concepts of state and regime security (see Soliman 2005).

These dynamics played out within the contexts of privatization and unbundling of transport infrastructure. Privatization in Egypt has often been plagued with two ambiguities: the first concerns the imposition of privatization as a paradigm from outside the declared will of the government, and the second relates to the implications this imposition has for government institutional structures and functions. Since its inception in the 1970s, GoE has pronounced its determination to take the 'Open Door' policies seriously and in accordance with World Bank stipulations. However, this has often meant tightening and expanding security and policing, which eventually culminated in the declaration of the state of emergency in the 1980s. This entrenched repressive mechanisms of governance at national, governorate and local levels.

This chapter has focused on governorate-level governance and presented examples from Sitta October showing how institutional and structural changes failed to formulate an integrated policy framework to incorporate the city into the larger urban political economy. It has touched upon how privatization opened up a range of contradictions that generated a political economy of space and marginalization in which the erstwhile government was central. While the deposed regime benefited most of the time, it was vehemently resisted. One instance was the resistance of Sitta October investors to unbundling the management of the city, indicating a lack of trust in the wisdom and integrity of the erstwhile government. At their inception, the central government envisaged NUCA and its subsidiary agencies and boards of trustees as versatile agencies, readily responsive to the needs of the 1970s 'Open Door' and 1990s reforms. These agencies succeeded in rolling out basic infrastructures to the fledgling manufacturing industries located in the industrial zones of the city in the 1980s, but failed to sustain this function. National policy frameworks failed to face up to economic transformations on the global scale, and several manufacturing industries struggled with restrictive laws and regulations and failed to compete with the emerging service sectors. Similarly, the infrastructure networks rolled out during the 1980s and 1990s have barely 'stabilized' – i.e. they reached 'closure' even before their full utilization.[7]

Meanwhile, NUCA remained stifled with legislative restrictions concerning self-generation of capital or the issuing of bonds. Similarly, capital required for rolling out infrastructure compatible with the needs of the service sectors was beyond the capacities of both the agency and the board. It was the prerogative of the central government and its large-scale private sector partners to roll out ring roads, highways and communication networks. The choice was usually to construct roadways that link privileged spaces across the city and bypass less privileged ones. Nevertheless, the gradual infiltration of global and regional capital into the city compelled structural and functional changes within local government, such as the transformation of the planning department at NUCA into a special-purpose agency, the emergence of the Parking Management Project as a revenue generation unit, and the creation of HCDP.

While transport planning was still lacking, the Parking Management Project was an example of an ad hoc institution that aimed to regulate the technologies of mobility and the relations around them. The effect of this project on space–time mobility in the city was minimal as it was parasitic on an already contested terrain. Unlike a few new urban communities, Sitta October did not have gates. This made the regulation of vehicle technologies and movements in and out of the city difficult. Except for those governed by the permits sold to microbuses and associations at governorate traffic departments, there were no pre-designed routes within the city. Operators design routes that meet local demand and to avoid the agency's project inspectors. Cairo and Giza apart, routes to other governorates are randomized and operators evade traffic police units and checkpoints or pay personal bribes to avoid impounding.

The expanding economy of the city within Greater Cairo and the large-scale private investments in services encouraged labour inflows from economically weaker governorates. Owing to the relative ease of admission into the sector, the bulk of migrating labour took up transport jobs. The agency and traffic and security police sanctioned those operators irrespective of their legal status, vehicle specifications or the quality and outreach of their services. They were sanctioned at the cost of daily fees and under conditions of constant security surveillance, at times instilling a sense of self-discipline. Security forces appointed leaders from the place of origin of each group of operators in order to regulate their respective constituencies and facilitate revenue generation and in-kind extortions. Leaders were provided with accommodation facilities in the city for operators who wished to remain overnight. This practice facilitated the monitoring of any unwelcome political activities on the part of operators. In response, operators devised counter-strategies to evade these extortions. They used low-tech vehicles to avoid tolling at highways; alternated routes to avoid police checkpoints and radar on highways; struck implicit agreements to share passengers; divided routes among themselves; shifted loading spots to avoid inspection patrols; solved disputes internally without resorting to police; and to a lesser degree resorted to violence. They also altered fares, manipulated seasonal supply and rented their vehicles for illicit purposes.

This chapter has highlighted how the driving motive of governing transport infrastructure and services in Sitta October sustained the economic power of the erstwhile Egyptian elite and its political stability. Those in positions of authority and power achieved their goals through intersecting processes of marginalization of spaces and criminalization of livelihoods, neglecting the importance of an integrated and comprehensive transport network for the new city. It is indeed ironic that the opaqueness, criminalization, rumours and multiple authorities that characterized the mode of governance in the city came to obstruct the vision of the erstwhile regime and made it increasingly difficult for its members to conceive that those who barely survived on the margins were ready to forcefully occupy 'centre stage' in a resilient uprising that brought the frail regime down.

Notes

1 There has not been a woman governor to date!

2 Data were gathered through interviews and focus group discussions with passengers, transporters, cooperative associations and government officials in and around Sitta October over a period of twelve months.

3 Greater Cairo Region comprises

Cairo, Giza and parts of Qalyubia governorates. In 2006, CAPMAS estimated that 18 million individuals lived in the region.

4 Documents from the project office in Giza.

5 Special funds are not accounted for in central government budgets and are exempt from taxes.

6 Interviews were conducted in parking lots across the governorate during operators' resting hours.

7 In government operations a utility reaches closure when it breaks even financially *and* starts to depreciate in technical terms.

References

Bayat, A. (2000) 'From "dangerous classes" to "quiet rebels": politics of the urban subaltern in the global South', *International Sociology*, 15: 533–57.

Brenner, N. (1999) 'Beyond state-centrism? Space, territoriality, and geographical scale in globalization studies', *Theory and Society*, 28: 39–78.

CAPMAS (n.d.) *Population Census*, www.msrintranet.capmas.gov.eg/pls/fdl/tst12e?action=&lname=, accessed 14 August 2010.

Collinge, C. (1999) 'Self-organization of society by scale: a spatial reworking of regulation theory', *Environment & Planning D: Society & Space*, 17: 557–74.

Davis, M. (2006) *Planet of Slums*, New York: Verso.

Devas, N. (2004) *Urban Governance, Voice, and Poverty in the Developing World*, Earthscan.

El-Demerdash, T. (1983) *The Economic Dimensions of Planning New Settlements*, Unpublished master's thesis, Faculty of Commerce, Zagazig University.

Fahmi, N. (1986) 'Almodon aljadida fi misr nashatiha wa tanmiyatiha', *Proceedings of the Workshop on the Social and Economic Development of the New Settlements*, Cairo: National Centre for Social and Criminal Research.

Florin, B. (2005) 'Urban policies in Cairo: from speeches on new cities to the adjustment practices of ordinary city dwellers', in A. Simone and A. Abouhani (eds), *Urban Africa: Changing contours of survival in the city*, London: Zed Books.

Fouad, M. (1984) Comments on 'Planning and institutional mechanisms', in *The Expanding Metropolis: Coping with Urban Growth of Cairo*, Aga Khan Award for Architecture.

Ghannam, F. (1997) 'Re-imagining the global: relocation and local identities in Cairo', in A. Oncu and P. Weyland (eds), *Space, Culture and Power: New Identities in Globalising Cities*, London: Zed Books.

— (1998) 'I'aadat al-taskeen wa istikhdam al-manattiq al-fadaa', *Cairo in Transition*.

— (2002) *Remaking the Modern Space, Relocation, and the Politics of Identity in a Global Cairo*, London: Zed Books.

Graham, S. (2000) 'Constructing premium network spaces: reflections on infrastructure networks and contemporary urban development', *International Journal of Urban and Regional Research*, 24(1): 183–200.

Graham, S. and S. Marvin (2001) *Splintering Urbanism: Networked infrastructures, technological mobilities and the urban condition*, London and New York: Routledge.

Graham, S. and N. Thrift (2007) 'Understanding repair and

maintenance', *Theory, Culture & Society*, 24(3): 1–25.

Hassan, W. N. (1982) *Almoshkila alfardiya alati towajih ossar alameleen fi almodon aljadida wa kayfiyat mowagahat mihnat alkhidma alijtimaiya laha*, Unpublished master's thesis, Helwan University.

Hooghe, L. and G. Marks (2003) 'Unraveling the central state, but how? Types of multi-level governance', *American Political Science Review*, 97(2): 233–43.

Laquian, A. A. et al. (eds) (2007) *The Inclusive City: Infrastructure and Public Services for the Urban Poor in Asia*, Washington, DC/ Baltimore, MD: Woodrow Wilson Center Press/Johns Hopkins University Press.

Lefebvre, H. (1991) *The Production of Space*, trans. D. Nicholson-Smith, Oxford: Blackwell.

Majdalani, R. (2001) 'The governance paradigm and urban development: breaking new ground', in S. Shami (ed.), *Capital Cities: Ethnographies of Urban Governance in the Middle East*, Toronto: University of Toronto, pp. 13–31.

Mitchell, T. (2002) *Rule of Experts: Egypt, Techno-Politics, Modernity*, Berkeley: University of California Press.

Mubarak wal Umran (1999) *Government of Egypt. Ministry of Housing*, Cairo: Amiriya Press.

Pile, S. (1997) 'Introduction: opposition, political identities and spaces of resistance', in S. Pile and M. Keith (eds), *Geogrpahies of Resistance*, London: Routledge, pp. 1–32.

Shami, S. (2001) 'Researching urban governance in the Middle East – introduction', in S. Shami (ed.), *Capital Cities: Ethnographies of Urban Governance in the Middle East*, Toronto: University of Toronto, pp. 1–12.

Singerman, D. (2002) 'The politics of emergency rule in Egypt', *Current History*, January, pp. 29–35.

Soliman, S. (1998) *State and Industrial Capitalism in Egypt*, Cairo Papers in Social Sciences 21, Monograph 2.

— (2005) *Al Nizam Al Qawi wa Al Dawla Al Dha'ifa*, Cairo: Dar Merit.

Sundaram, R. (2009) 'Re-visiting "everyday life": the experience of Delhi's media urbanism', in M. Reiker and K. A. Ali (eds), *Comparing Cities: The Middle East and South Asia*, Karachi: Oxford University Press, pp. 130–58.

Wahdan, D. (2010) *Governing Livelihoods in Liberalizing States*, Saarbrucken: Lap Lambert Academic Publishing.

Wolff, R. and S. Resnick (1996) 'Power, property and class', in V. Lippit (ed.), *Radical Political Economy. Explorations in Alternative Economic Analysis*, New York: M. E. Sharpe.

8 | Against marginalization: workers, youth and class in the 25 January revolution

RABAB EL MAHDI

For thirty years, particularly since the advent of neoliberalism, the concepts of 'marginalization' and 'poverty' have come to replace those of 'class' and 'exploitation' as analytical categories. The reasons for this are many, but the ideological hegemony and political power of a very small class of big businesses served by technocratic states have been paramount. Under this model, the conflictual power relations revealed by the categories of 'class', 'exploitation' and the subsequent 'class struggle' have been seen not to be useful. Rather, the neoliberal model is legitimized by preaching a harmonious power structure in which 'trickle-down', 'efficient use of resources', 'meritocracy' and 'technical fixes' are used to justify and deal with pressing problems of poverty and maldistribution of power and wealth.

In similar vein, the recent uprising in Egypt since 25 January 2011 has been constructed as a non-violent, youth revolution in which social media (especially Facebook and Twitter) are champions. The reduction of the class composition of the dissent is cloaked by a new imaginary homogeneous construct called 'youth': lumping together the contradictory and often conflicting interests of 'yuppies' (young, urban, well-connected professionals from rich backgrounds) with those of the unemployed, often with little or no education, who live in rural and slum areas. The manufacturing of this image has ensured that the values, tools and tactics of the uprising are equally appropriated and reduced for the use of social networks and the Internet in order to fit the narrative (Smith 2011).

The telecommunications revolution from cell phones to social media networks, such as Facebook and Twitter, has compressed time, space and the cost of mobilization, but these tools have existed and been used for political purposes in Egypt since long before 25 January 2011. Moreover, in a country like Egypt, where more than 40 per cent of the population live beneath the poverty line and over 30 per cent of adults are illiterate, it is difficult to conclude that the majority of protesters used Facebook. Any student or close observer of Egypt can readily understand what has happened since 25 January as the culmination of a number of different forms of mobilization in recent years – notably the cumulative effect of protest movements against the war on Iraq in 2003 and Gaza in 2008, the rise of the pro-democracy movement with *Kefaya* in 2004–05, the labour protests that started in Mahalla in 2006 and have spread throughout the country to include more than 1.7 million people since then, and finally the anti-sectarian protests that peaked after the church bombing in Alexandria in early 2011.

Each of these movements created the conditions for 25 January. They brought people together, breaking the barrier of fear; they politicized people over specific issues that they cared deeply about; and they reinstated the dynamics of collective resistance and active expression against different forms of abuse (social, political or economic). The different movements and processes exposed the exploitative nature of the regime's policies on all of these fronts. The revolution was not only about middle- and upper-class youth in Tahrir Square who wanted another president. The revolution was also about young and older people in Cairo, Suez, Arish and Beni Soueif who did not want to die in queues for bread, water or medical care, or to be abused in police stations, or to have to take their children out of school to earn a living.

While much recent analysis seems increasingly to be centred on conceptualizing the 25 January 'revolution' as a result of middle-class 'youth' activism that used Internet social networks, this chapter deconstructs such a portrayal. The Egyptian revolution was the outcome of a historical process, and not simply a momentary explosion. This chapter depicts the 'revolution' as a rhizome, formed through a multiplicity of inputs and roots. To reinforce this argument, the chapter focuses on the labour protests movement that started in Egypt in 2006, understanding it as one of the major streams that fed into the uprising. It argues that labour protest not only played a role in preparing the ground for the uprising which unfolded on 25 January, but also played a decisive role in leading to the ousting of Mubarak. The chapter concludes that the revolutionary process witnessed in Egypt had its seeds in the economic and coercive entrenchment under the state's project of domination that might be labelled 'policed neoliberalism'.

Policed neoliberalism

Despite shifts towards the market economy as early as 1974, with President Anwar Sadat's (1970–81) initiation of what he called the 'Open Door' policy, it was not until 1991 that the Egyptian regime under President Hosni Mubarak signed a letter of intent with the International Monetary Fund (IMF). That agreement committed the government of Egypt to a structural adjustment programme (SAP). For more than ten years after the signing of the agreement, it was the slow pace characterizing the Mubarak regime's move towards neoliberalism which saved his regime from the fate of many others (such as Argentina and Poland) who undertook shock therapy of this type (Paczynski 2009). In normative terms, neoliberalism was a shift in state prerogatives and structure to what has been called by some the 'national competition state', characterized by Soederberg as a 'state in which all policy formulation (economic, political and social) is subordinated to the goal of attracting and retaining the most capital investment possible' (Soederberg 2001: 107). In this model, the state's internal role is viewed either as 'constraining' or 'enabling' for individuals who compete in an open market. And internationally, its role is to compete within the global economy and provide the most attractive conditions for business investors, regardless of how these conditions affect labour or the environment.

This neoliberal discourse on the state emphasizes two points: the importance of the state as an agent of growth and not equity or distribution; and, following from this, the significance of the state's relations with business, as opposed to other classes or social groups (Williamson 1993; Friedman 2002). This can be vividly seen in the statements of the government, predominantly composed of businessmen, as well as the preceding cabinet of Atef Ebeid (1999–2004), wherein the regime proclaimed its achievements, focusing on levels of foreign investment and facilitating the investment environment regardless of the fact that the claimed achievements did not translate into better living conditions for the majority of Egyptians and that government policy increased poverty. The same logic drove tax and labour law and social service provision, such as health and education. Legislation reduced public spending and obligations on business to provide a tax base for the economy while increasing the economic and social costs for the majority of Egyptians, especially the working class. Businessmen were also important advisers to the government in relation to the direction of policy and in the recruitment of their peers into government.

Ideologically, the neoliberal model in Egypt posited a reductionist paradigm of *Homo economicus* (economic man/woman) – the idea that human beings are economic beings driven by the desire to maximize their utility gains. This presented a very specific understanding of political liberalism. Based on Rawls and Dworkin, two widely read political philosophers of modern liberalism, two essentialist concepts related to liberalism emerge: that of 'equal concern and respect' for all citizens, and that of the state's role in guaranteeing the 'autonomy' of citizens to choose and pursue their life projects (Dworkin 1977; Rawls 1993). Under the neoliberal discourse, the two principles were taken to mean neutrality of the state, with the idea of socio-economic equity as an outcome – not as a goal – of macroeconomic policies or the political organization of the state. The principle of equal concern and respect, however, does not say anything about the appropriate level of the state's active engagement with regard to economic distribution. Thus, emphasizing individual autonomy and equal respect has come to mean under this model that every person should be responsible for their own well-being: individuals bear the responsibility for whatever outcome emerges from their competition in an open marketplace. This view ignores the fact that in order for citizens to be able to formulate and pursue a life project, and for them to gain equal concern and respect, the state needs to intervene to alter many structural conditions, in order to level the playing field. Thus, political liberalism understood as state *neutrality* becomes a way to further perpetuate and mask anti-liberal imperatives. In contrast with earlier phases of capitalist development, political liberalism with neoliberalism excludes and denies citizenship rights that include socio-economic, political and civil rights.

The cutting of subsidies and the erosion of public provision of education and healthcare in Egypt were not exceptional – they were part of a universal policy that has accompanied neoliberalism throughout the world. They have been key aspects of transforming 'used-to-be-free' education and focusing the high-quality healthcare services within the private sector, with no equivalent in public services as states shift from public provision for their citizens to the introduction of private providers for the nation's 'customers'. Those who can afford services or a commodity (including education, medical care, shelter and so on) are 'free and equal' to choose from what the market provides, and those who cannot afford to buy their rights through the market are also 'free' not to do so, and even to exit life altogether.

Similarly, the principle of 'individual autonomy' emphasized under the neoliberal model means that people are responsible for their own well-being, and no account is taken of the fact that they have different starting points in terms of their economic opportunities, and hence may be highly unlikely to overcome significant handicaps and disadvantages under market competition. Equally important, the principle has been extended to exclude collective organization. In other words, individuals are autonomous and free to make choices as consumers and competitors, but they are dissuaded and coerced away from organizing for political struggle to demand their rights. Rather they are encouraged to find ways or 'coping mechanisms' to work in accordance with market dynamics that are unfair to them. Citizens' energies are channelled away from 'demanding' rights – either through political struggle or engagement with civil society – to seek subsistence on an individual basis. For example, instead of being active in a union, workers are supposed to seek out an additional job to help them to afford services that were formerly provided by or subsidized by the state, but that they can now 'choose and buy' within the market. In this regard, any observer of the Egyptian government can see the clear contradiction between the government's discourse and action on the necessity of Egyptians 'growing up', as former prime minister Ahmed Nazif said in 2009, and how this same government clamped down harshly on organized labour movements of people demanding their rights. Or how, under the rhetoric of freedom of investment, the regime officials and propaganda machines attack any attempt at market regulation while completely dismissing the other side of the equation, namely freedom of organization. In other words, investors are free to hire and fire and buy and sell as they please, but the masses are neither autonomous nor free to organize collectively for their interests through independent unions or community associations.

A final political feature of neoliberalism was the change in the ruling elite, not only through its unprecedented bias towards big capitalists but through a shift to what is called technocratism and technical fetishism. The modus operandi of the neoliberal technocratic approach is the insulation of decision-making, whereby policy-making becomes the realm of technocrats and experts, distancing it even further from different sectors of society, as representatives of 'particularistic' interests (Oxhorn and Ducatenzeiler 1998; Veltmeyer and Petras 1997). It is an approach that by definition excludes the less powerful from any possibility of directing public policy to their advantage. As David Harvey notes, 'neoliberals are [...] profoundly suspicious of democracy. Governance by majority rule is seen as a potential threat to individual rights' (Harvey 2005: 66). In Egypt, this meant two things: first, a change from populist corporatism, with all the material (though minimal) gains to large sectors of society; and secondly, a move away from state bureaucrats to technocrats as the main front of policy-making.

Thus, under neoliberalism there was a shift away from co-opting important sectors of society through material handouts to state-controlled collective bodies, e.g. state unions, farmers' cooperatives and student bodies. Even though these organizations were anti-democratic and not very inclusive, they did give out material benefits, such as small redistributed landholdings to farmers, subsidies, permanent employment to workers, and free social services. Moreover, they guaranteed at least a minimal response by the state to these important sectors of society. With the neoliberal advent, such corporatist, albeit imperfect, mechanisms became unsustainable economically because of shrinking state revenue, and were politically divisive. The new neoliberal model catered to the interests of the few, and attacked unions and other associations while at the same time supporting remnants of authoritarian control over different sectors of society that the organizations promoted. For example, the state labour unions stopped advancing material gains for the working class, but continued to coerce them into accepting lay-offs and decreased benefits, and into giving up the right to strike (Beinin 2009, 2010). More importantly, issues such as poverty, education, social policy and economic strategy were presented as technical issues that required administrative or limited technical changes/reforms, rather than being politically profound issues that required structural change. In short, the logic of neoliberalism was to depoliticize questions of power and to reduce them to technical questions. Hence, the question of subsidies and free education became an issue of 'reprogramming', and not a question of resource distribution in society.

Concomitantly, such a shift had to have its new executors, well endowed for the mission. Technocrats, mostly foreign educated, apolitical and claiming expertise in a very narrow technical niche, became the new class of political officials, replacing the traditional upwardly mobile, middle-class bureaucrats and politicians. In the Egyptian case, the hub for such individuals became the Policies' Committee of the ruling party. The old picture of *Wakeel el Wezara* (a deputy minister), who is still an employee but a slightly better-paid one, with a Nasr or Fiat 128 car and a ministry driver (and who still has to make ends meet or resorts to petty corruption to pay for family bills), has been replaced by *el maktab el fanny lil wazeer* (the Technical Office) and different extra-public committees composed of upper-class young graduates from private universities with unbelievable salaries and bonuses travelling around the world first-class. Each of these young technocrats (if they had work) was paid the equivalent salary of at least twenty national university graduates. The new technocratic young managers were detached from the realities of daily living that confronted the majority of Egyptians in their daily life: they were divided from Egyptian society by virtue of class background, education and their social standing and lifestyles. This group of technocrats is part of a worldwide trend, recruited from right-wing universities (such as the University of Chicago and Johns Hopkins to name a couple). They mainly received limited technical ideological training with a neoclassical bias, which they argued was the ultimate, universal scientific knowledge.

The Nazif government of 2004 – the last government of Mubarak's reign, composed of openly neoliberal technocrats and businessmen – 'promoted a second wave of privatization and enacted other measures to encourage foreign direct investment', raising unprecedented, justified fears about lay-offs and speeding the move away from the 1952 labour–state alliance (Beinin 2009: 77). Unlike earlier governments, Nazif's accelerated the move towards neoliberalization. The composition of the cabinet shifted from state bureaucrats and academics to technocrats and businessmen. Yet privatization between 2004 and 2006 was more extensive than it was after the beginning of the economic reform programme in 1991. The new cabinet stressed that their mission was to speed up privatization and attract foreign investment in order to accelerate growth, changing laws and regulations to this supreme purpose. Prices, especially for food and transportation, underwent sharp and unprecedented increases, leading to heightened inflation, despite the proclaimed increase in GNP (Egypt News 2008). Moreover, the successive statements made by Nazif about the need to reassess food and fuel subsidies, and for Egyptians to stop depending on the state, confirmed suspicions about the regime's move away from the earlier model of that state which guaranteed socio-economic rights. Policed neoliberalism increased daily coercion and repression of Egyptians and had a clear class dimension. That is, it was not directed exclusively at political opposition and dissent as in the earlier regimes of Nasser and Sadat, but rather was systematically extended to embrace the popular classes, who were seen as a threat to the evolving socio-economic model. Hence, the mushrooming of shanty towns went hand in hand with the expansion of gated communities and the privatization of public space (Marfleet 2009). Because under neoliberalism the regime could not afford to economically appease its population as it used to do in earlier phases, and because the growth model depended on concentration of wealth, the regime had to shift more towards the use of coercion to keep the 'losers' in check. While earlier regimes used a balanced combination of coercion and co-optation (through political and economic means), after 2004 the Mubarak regime, with the fast shift to neoliberalism, was not able to maintain that balance. With the concentration of both wealth and decision-making in the hands of a few businessmen and technocrats, the regime had to resort more to coercion in order to guarantee its stability. However, it is from within this search for stability and increased monopoly over wealth and power that a rising tide of resistance emerged which led to the demise of Mubarak in 2011.

Trade unions, workers and the struggles for justice

Since the mid-2000s, Egypt has witnessed a labour movement that is 'the largest social movement in over half a century' (Beinin 2009: 77). For decades, the idea of Egyptian labour as an active agent within the public sphere and civil society seemed little more than a myth or, at the very least, a legacy not supported by any visible action. And while there has been important labour action since the 1950s, it was both limited and sporadic. Industrial action before 2000, moreover, did not include workers beyond the locale of contention (i.e. the specific plant or workplace). Subsequently, it did not result in new organizational forms of labour and certainly did not include white-collar state employees. In contrast, the wave of labour contention which was ignited in December 2006 in the biggest weaving and spinning factory in Egypt, in the town of El-Mahalla – where nearly a quarter of all public sector textile and clothing workers are employed and where there is the greatest concentration of industrial workers anywhere in the Middle East – marked the start of something quantitatively and qualitatively different.

The workers at Misr Spinning and Weaving Company in Mahalla al-Kubra went on strike when they did not receive a bonus payment that had been decreed by ex-prime minister Ahmed Nazif. Their action marked 'the largest and most politically significant industrial strike since a dispute in the same workplace in 1947' (ibid.: 79). Drawing inspiration from the action of the Mahalla workers, other industrial workers in both the state and private sectors, as well as white-collar employees (postal workers, educational administrators, tax collectors, transportation workers, government information centre employees, and even physicians and pharmacists), staged a series of protests, consolidating a movement that has not subsided since.

The current movement, while quantitatively significant (more than 1.7 million workers are estimated to have participated in actions during 2006–09), also marks a qualitative leap from earlier labour action in Egypt. The overwhelming majority of these strikes and actions were organized by worker-leaders who were not members of official union committees, which in a number of cases were rendered redundant as, in many of the places where struggles emerged, workers and employees elected their own strike committees with responsibility for managing ongoing action, representing workers in negotiations with the authorities and organizing future action. They developed a whole new repertoire of tools to fight employers and the state, ranging from street protests and strikes to extended sit-ins at official buildings (parliament and the cabinet headquarters) and factory occupations that were initiated by the protesters after the revolution of 25 January.

Such independent organization reached its apogee with the real-estate tax collectors forming an independent union in April 2009 – the first autonomous non-state union since the 1940s – following their successful but extended struggle, which started in December 2007. In this respect, the rise and continuity of the movement become clear if events are seen as a continuum and as part of a totality of struggles against state repression and neoliberalism. In other words, the new independent tax collectors' union cannot be seen in isolation from the El-Mahalla strike any more than a postal workers' strike in June 2010 can be seen as unrelated to the achievement of the striking tax collectors. The unfolding organizational patterns within this wave of protests reveal changes within the state–corporatist pact that indicate a dismantling of the basis of authoritarian dynamics from below, led by the working class.

In contrast to the hierarchy and bureaucratic structures of the state-controlled trade unions, labour protest after 2005 created new mechanisms from below that have slowly challenged the institutional basis of state corporatism.[1] Similarly, the emergence of more politicized demands as part of labour protests – including attempts at independent organization during protests by real-estate tax collectors (which actually succeeded), postal workers and administrators of the Ministry of Education, as well as demands for the renationalization of privatized entities during protests at the Ketan Tanta plant and Kafr El-Dawar textile plant – breached long-held state–labour corporatist 'norms'. The movement was adopting systemic and more overtly political demands. And, despite not being a linear or irreversible process, the rise of more politicized demands endorsed by hundreds of thousands of state employees and industrial workers, including a national minimum wage and independent unions (even when not anti-regime per se), marks a break from earlier patterns of partnership with the state and the ruling regime.

Soon after El-Mahalla's first strike, the de facto worker-leaders who emerged from the strike launched a campaign to impeach local union officials who had opposed the strike and who, according to workers, enjoyed close ties with the state-security apparatus and were puppets of the General Federation of Egyptian Trade Unions (GFETU). More than 13,000 workers signed a petition addressed to the General Union of Textile Workers demanding impeachment of the local union committee and the conduct of new elections (interview, Haitham, worker in the Misr Spinning Company, 10 June 2009). After first refusing to meet the workers, regime representatives, including GFETU chief Husayn Megawir, were forced to go to Mahalla to negotiate with the elected strike committee, bypassing the official trade union committee. Thus, 'while the Misr workers did not formally win their demand to impeach the trade union committee, they rendered it irrelevant' (Beinin 2009: 84). Sidelining the official union workers' committee, the chosen strike committee had to operate democratically. 'Workers' representatives reported back to mass meetings of thousands of strikers on the progress of negotiations' (Alexander 2008: 56). Decisions, statements and tactics were based on collective discussions, making it more difficult for the authorities to break the strike from within. Later, in the case of the tax collectors' strike, not only was the strike committee elected and operated according to principles of deliberative democracy, but there have been regular elections since the end of the strike in December 2007. This novel form of organization, contradicting the internal logic of state corporatism, set a precedent and sowed the seeds for independent organization away from state-manipulated elections, which had been so closely associated with organized labour since 1957.

These developments are as useful in demonstrating 'spillover effects' within organizational forms as in highlighting how organizational forms can be adopted and developed further within new sites of contention. However, they did not happen mechanically. Rather, they took place within a dynamic process in which the new organizational forms traversed sites of contention and manifested themselves variously in these different locations. Ultimately, the significance of both these new forms of organization and the increased demands from the labour movement lies in their potential to reshape the social norms and practices binding labour to the state and the latter to society at large. The meaning of these forms of labour protests cannot therefore be overemphasized, given the pivotal role that state–labour corporatism in Egypt has played in stabilizing post-1952 populist authoritarian rule.[2]

Class and revolution

Many assume that 'class' and accordingly class politics were not present within the Egyptian revolution, and that rather it was a youth revolution which filled Tahrir Square equally with the rich and the poor; those working for multinational corporations as well as the unemployed and the urban poor. Similarly, many hold that the 'working class' was not present as an organized agent during those eighteen days, since there was no general strike, or specific sectors of workers present and demonstrating as a group. These are arguments heard at the many conferences in Egypt, and especially in Europe and the United States, after the revolution. It is also the inverse logic of the argument claiming that this is a 'Facebook revolution' made by middle-class youth. At a superficial level, both assumptions might be true, but close analysis of events throughout the eighteen days proves the opposite: that not only was class politics a prelude to the popular uprising on 25 January, but also that the working class was a strong agent that hastened the fall of Mubarak. The working class participated, not in an organized way as unions or workplace representatives, but as individuals in the momentous events at the symbolic site of the revolution, Tahrir Square. But they also participated through clear class action, i.e. labour strikes, especially during the two final days of the protests.

The protests broke out in Egypt on 25 January in the city of Suez, where the military was first deployed and the first martyr fell. According to many protesters, Suez 'kept the fire alive until the 28th' (interview, Sameh Naguib, Cairo, 25 March 2011). It was in Suez that shipyard workers went on strike as early as 26 and 27 January. For these workers, their 'individual' demands for better pay and working conditions were part of the 'national' demands for a better Egypt.

However, it was not until 9 February 2011 that the working class made its presence visible. During what seemed to be a deadlock (with protesters continuing to occupy different squares and Mubarak resiliently refusing to step down), the then prime minister, Ahmed Shafik, and Vice-President Omar Sulieman gave speeches assuring that the situation would soon be normalized, even with protesters occupying the squares. They made it clear that orders had been issued for work to be resumed in the government mega-complex Mogamaa El-Tahrir. During that week, the protesters actually blocked a number of attempts by some employees to get to work. Among many activists there was a fear that they would be marginalized, if not simply besieged in Tahrir

Square, while business went on as usual in the country (interviews with protesters in Tahrir, 6 February 2011).

It was then that a mass wave of strikes and demonstrations by workers in key sectors of the economy spread throughout the country. Strikers demanded improved economic conditions as well as their main revolutionary demand for President Mubarak's removal from office. According to the *Guardian* newspaper:

> Labour unrest has erupted in a wide breadth of sectors, including postal workers, electricity staff and service technicians at the Suez Canal, in factories manufacturing textiles, steel and beverages and hospitals.
>
> A bus strike snarled traffic in Cairo, a city of 18 million where many of its impoverished residents rely on public transport. (Shenker 2011)

In only two days (9 and 10 February), the strike wave had spread from Alexandria in the north to Aswan in the south. It was not a coincidence that Mubarak stepped down on 11 February, only a day after his last speech, in which he declared that he was staying in office until September 2011.

The class politics and hence class interests within the revolution were clear even in the slogans used by protesters. Depending on the neighbourhood in which you were protesting, the slogans were '*Aish, horreya, 'adala igtema'yyia*' ('bread, freedom, social justice') or '*Tagheer, horreya, karama insaniyya*' ('change, freedom, human dignity'). Of course, this was not a strict binary. In some cases a combination of the two slogans was chanted, but the original set of demands reflected the clear dimension of class politics. The demand for 'social justice' had primary presence throughout demonstrations across Egypt. By the time the protesters occupied Tahrir Square, first on 25 January and then again on 28 January, the unified slogan/demand became '*Al-Shaab you-reed Isqat El-Nizaam*' ('the people want the fall of the regime/system'). It is very interesting to note here that the word '*Nizaam*' in Arabic means system, but it is also used to mean the regime. Once again, it is as if this brilliant slogan reflected a momentary unification between groups that wanted a regime change but not necessarily systemic changes that would jeopardize their interests. This is because many protesters were part of the ruling elite, as broadly defined, but many were also people wanting more systemic change that met their class interests in resisting exploitation. There was thus a momentary collusion between the privileged middle and upper classes and the working class. However, it did not last long, as soon after the ousting of Mubarak the media and parts of the middle class started condemning continual working-class strikes, accusing strikers of having 'selfish, parochial demands' (see Gamal 2011).

Conclusion

This chapter has confirmed the presence of class politics in the Egyptian revolution. Based on participant observation in events in Egypt since 25 January, it is clear that this is not a bourgeois revolution, or another of the colour-coded revolutions seen in the Balkans or eastern Europe. The slogans, demands and class composition of participants, as well as the continuing debates on inequality and the distribution of wealth that followed Mubarak's removal, reinforce the class dimension of the revolution. Class politics and class action were present in the revolution in a number of ways. First, through the engagement of more than 1.7 million working-class individuals in contentious workplace action during the period 2007–10, which not only broke the 'barrier of fear' but also, it can be comfortably argued, led to the politicization of millions of workers and their families, who became agents of change. Secondly, they increased the economic and moral pressure on the regime and exposed its incapacity and vulnerability to broader circles in society. Thirdly, class politics and class action enriched the repertoire of contentious tools of society, from reintroducing the idea of occupation of public space to forming organizations beyond the state-sponsored civil society organizations (e.g. independent unions versus the state's general union). Fourthly, during the eighteen-day confrontation, it was working-class people who used their skills in combating state violence (to which they were subjected every day) in order to secure the occupation and preserve the physical space of resistance (primarily Tahrir Square). Working-class people destroyed the physical symbols of the regime, such as the headquarters of the then ruling National Democratic Party. Finally, a wave of workers' mass strikes during the two final days of the confrontation played a stimulating role in hastening the fall of the regime.

The ongoing Egyptian revolution clearly attests to the centrality of 'class' to understanding politics. This contrasts with the newly used analytical categories of 'youth' and 'marginality'. The prominence of class politics within this revolutionary episode lends itself to an understanding of much-publicized and in-vogue conceptions such as 'democratic transition' and 'poverty and empowerment' within the framework of conflictual class relations.

Notes

1 For more details on state corporatism in Egypt, see Bianchi (1986, 1989).

2 For more details on how labour sustained the populist-authoritarian rule of post-1952 in Egypt, see Goldberg (1992) and Posusney (1997).

References

Alexander, A. (2008) 'Inside Egypt's mass strikes', *International Socialism*, 31, March.

Beinin, J. (2009) 'Workers' struggles under "socialism" and neoliberalism', in R. El-Mahdi and P. Marfleet (eds), *Egypt: The Moment of Change*, London: Zed Books, pp. 68–86.

— (2010) *The Struggle for Worker Rights in Egypt: A Report*, Washington, DC: Solidarity Center.

Bianchi, R. (1986) 'The corporatization of the Egyptian labour movement', *Middle East Journal*, 40(3): 429–44.

— (1989) *Unruly Corporatism: Associational Life in Twentieth-Century Egypt*, New York: Oxford University Press.

Dworkin, R. (1977) *Taking Rights Seriously*, London: Duckworth.

Egypt News (2008) 'Food prices spur Egypt inflation to 16-year high', Egyptnews.com, 11 August. news.egypt.com/en/200808113474/news/-egypt-news/food-prices-spur-egypt-inflation-to-16-year-high.html.

Friedman, S. (2002) 'Democracy, inequality and the reconstitution of politics', in J. Tulchin (ed.), *Democratic Governance and Social Inequality*, Boulder, CO: Lynne Rienner.

Gamal, W. (2011) 'Say social rights not partisan demands' (in Arabic), *El-Shorouk*, 23 February.

Goldberg, E. (1992) 'The foundations of state–labour relations in contemporary Egypt', *Comparative Politics*, 24(2): 147–61.

Harvey, D. (2005) *A Brief History of Neoliberalism*, Oxford: Oxford University Press.

Marfleet, P. (2009) 'State and society', in R. El-Mahdi and P. Marfleet (eds), *Egypt: The Moment of Change*, London: Zed Books.

Oxhorn, P. and G. Ducatenzeiler (eds) (1998) *What Kind of Democracy? What Kind of Market? Latin America in the Age of Neoliberalism*, University Park: Pennsylvania State University Press.

Paczynski, A. (2009) *State, Labour and the Transition to Market Economy: Egypt, Poland, Mexico, and the Czech Republic*, University Park: Pennsylvania State University Press.

Posusney, M. (1997) *Labour and the State in Egypt*, New York: Columbia University Press.

Rawls, J. (1993) *Political Liberalism*, New York: Columbia University Press.

Shenker, J. (2011) 'Egypt's economy suffers as strikes intensify', *Guardian*, 11 February, www.guardian.co.uk/world/2011/feb/11/egypt-economy-suffers-strikes-intensify.

Smith, C. (2011) *Huffington Post*, first posted 2 November, www.huffingtonpost.com/2011/02/11/egypt-facebook-revolution-wael-ghonim_n_822078.html.

Soederberg, S. (2001) 'From neoliberalism to social liberalism: situating the National Solidarity Programme within Mexico's passive revolutions', *Latin*

American Perspectives, 28(3), 'Mexico in the 1990s: economic crisis, social polarization, and class struggle, part 1', May, pp. 104–23.

Veltmeyer, H. and J. Petras (1997) *Neoliberalism and the Class Conflict in Latin America: A Comparative Perspective on the Political Economy of Structural Adjustment*, New York: St Martin's Press.

Williamson, J. (1993) 'Democracy and the "Washington Consensus"', *World Development*, 21(8): 1329–36.

9 | National geographical targeting of poverty in Upper Egypt

SAKER EL NOUR

Introduction

This chapter examines recent government policies to redress rural poverty in Egypt under the ousted regime of former president Hosni Mubarak. The rural poor include large numbers of Egyptians who have been historically neglected in public policy planning and objectives. This chapter reviews one policy approach implemented by the Egyptian government: the geographical targeting of poverty in rural Egypt. Geographical targeting was identified as a political priority by the former government of the National Democratic Party (NDP) (Al-Ahram 2010: 1). The policy was applied to the 1,000 poorest villages, and the first phase was completed in October 2010. The adoption of this policy represented a major shift from general payment of subsidies to poor people to a policy targeting those actually identified as being poor. Epstein (2008) has argued that state policies aimed at poverty elimination often fail to achieve their goals. Moreover, state policies do not reflect the actual conditions of the poor, representing rather the views of policy-makers. This study questions the theoretical basis, empirical delivery and implications of geographical targeting programmes in Egypt.

In order to explore the capacity, implementation and outcomes of these programmes in Upper Egypt, I undertook a case study. The geographical scope of my case study was the village of Markaz, in el-Qusiya district in the governorate of Asyut, Upper Egypt. As a result of the case study, I argue that better understanding is needed of the mechanisms of poverty in Egypt, and also that local municipal authorities have a high level of influence, as they are able to select villages for inclusion in – or indeed exclusion from – the programme. In contrast, villagers' own perspectives of poverty were shaped by the need for food security and for access to institutional and natural resources. However, this dimension has been ignored in the Egyptian government project. Analysis of the first phase of the project shows that the role of agriculture in poor people's lives has been ignored.

The geographical targeting approach to poverty reduction

Policies that target poverty are dependent on being able to define who the poor are, and then are able to direct services and subsidies towards these people only. Defining who the poor are is a very complex task, and associated with high operating costs (Assaad and Rouchdy 2006). Several methods to improve these techniques are applied by developed countries and international organizations. These methods include targeting based on family assessment, individual assessment, self-assessment by municipal communities, and assessment based on geographical location (Baker and Grosh 1994; Coady et al. 2004). Evaluating geographical areas that have low incomes is easier than assessing individuals with low incomes (Coady et al. 2002). In general, geographical targeting requires accurate definition of centres of poverty with the highest rates and their poverty trends, and of the benefits and subsidies that people have been able to access in selected areas (Bigman and Fofack 2000). According to the World Bank, the geographical targeting in Egypt is important for many reasons:

> First, [the geographical targeting] provides a clear criterion for identifying the target population and avoids the informational constraints that impede most other targeted programs. Second, it is relatively easy to monitor and administer and its implementation can be greatly assisted by local administrative institutions and nongovernmental organizations. Third, geographic targeting has relatively little influence on household behavior since it is difficult and costly to change the place of residence. Fourth, it is possible to combine the location criterion with other criteria based on individual or household characteristics (Characteristics Targeting) to refine the level of determining eligibility and thereby targeting categories. Fifth, the instruments of geographically targeted programs can include not only direct income transfers to the target population, but also a variety of other measures aimed at increasing the income of the population. Sixth, poverty maps can also help inform decentralization. (World Bank 2007: 21)

Despite the advantages identified here by the World Bank report, the geographical targeting approach does not ensure that the poor are accurately identified. This can be due to inadequate indicators and standards used to define poverty, which do not reflect the actual conditions of poor people. Subsidies can also be distributed to people who are not poor (Chatterjee et al. 2006). Two types of leakage of subsidies can be associated with targeted programmes. The first is from incorrect targeting, i.e. failing to distribute benefits to people who are poor. The second leakage occurs when non-targeted individuals obtain benefits. Accordingly, inequality can increase instead of being reduced.

Geographical targeting is more effective in reducing the ratio of people who are *not* poor yet have been included to people who *are* poor but have not been included in the targeting programme. This is seen to be the case, because obtaining accurate and detailed observations about targeted areas has been shown to increase the efficiency of poverty reduction strategies (Assaad and Rouchdy 1999; Elbers et al. 2002). From an economic point of view, targeting aims to analyse local socio-economic structure and to measure local inequality in the smallest geographical units. That may help in decentralizing the decision-making process. Furthermore, applying such types of programme could lead to a lower leakage of benefits (Coady et al. 2004; Coady 2006). This means that in order to reduce poverty, geographical targeting should be accompanied by a range of other targeted policies. Other targeting programmes might include investigating the background of individual families, and integration of self-targeting and municipal targeting.

Poverty mapping trials in Egypt

Several attempts were made in the early 1990s to study the geographical distribution of poverty in Egypt. For example, Egypt's Social Fund for Development took a first step in 1993, using 1983 statistics as poverty and unemployment indicators. The National Institute for Planning, in collaboration with the United Nations Development Programme (UNDP), made a poverty map that was published in 2008 (UNDP/INP 2008). In 2003/04, the UNDP published indicators for different villages, covering about nineteen out of the twenty-seven governorates in Egypt. Another study was made by the Social Fund for Development in cooperation with the World Population Council, using an approach of small-area estimation (Elbers et al. 2002). This study incorporated data from the 1996 census and 1999/2000 survey, which included income and consumer expenditure data. Estimates in the mapping exercise were made using the standard of cost of living of villages, rather than of families. The last-named study, however, used geographical information systems to draw up poverty maps (Assaad and Rouchdy 2006). Indeed, this last perspective has primarily shaped the framework of poverty geographical targeting programmes in Egypt.

The 2007 poverty mapping study was conducted on the basis of cooperation between the Ministry for Economic Development and the World Bank. The extent of poverty in Egypt documented in that year used revised data from the Egyptian government censuses of 1996 and 2006, and surveys from the Ministry of Health and Population (World Bank 2007). Poverty maps for 1996 and 2006 were prepared, the poor and poorest geographical areas were defined, and the poorest 1,000 villages in Egypt were specified. The study provides a background and rationale for the Egyptian government project that was called 'Geographical targeting of poorer villages', also known as 'The poorest 1,000 villages project'.

Determining poor areas

The study by the World Bank/Egyptian Ministry for Economic Development used a method similar to that used for the 'small-area estimation approach' (ibid.). This method depends on a statistical process to combine survey data and data on family incomes and consumer expenditure with census data. Census data include statistics on population, housing and facilities in order to estimate poverty rates for different geographical units. After assembling the data, poverty maps can be used to show the geographic distribution of poverty. The survey data provide estimations for income and consumer expenditure, for use as an indicator for the state of poverty in different regions, especially for assessing and comparing rural and urban areas.

Censuses in Egypt provide comprehensive data that include population characteristics. Yet censuses do not contain detailed data about consumption levels of goods and services. There are three steps in developing poverty maps. The first is to determine the data that are available for families' standards of living from censuses and surveys. A comparison is made between census and survey data, specifying common variables associated with family living conditions. The detailed list of commonly available data includes gender and age of family members, level of education, school attendance by six-to-eighteen-year olds, working status and type of work of family members over fifteen years of age, nature of accommodation in the house, and utilities. These utilities include electricity, potable water, sanitary drainage. In addition, other variables relevant to the geographical dimension include the location of the governorate where the respondents currently live. The second step involves using the list compiled in step one, as well as the household survey data, in order to estimate the household consumption rate for the seven regions in Egypt.[1] The third step uses the estimates obtained in the second step to set out the family consumption rate for different regions.

Policy-makers use estimates of family consumption to calculate the poverty rates and welfare levels for different geographical areas of the country. The poverty rates are based on the cost of basic needs, in order to assess the approximate family poverty rate for the region (ibid.). Variations among different regions are considered, relating to non-food consumption prices, price changes, and variation of the main necessities according to age and gender. In step three, poverty estimates as well as welfare indicators are built up for different geographical areas. The results are then used to assemble the database for poverty and welfare indicators at regional levels, which in turn can be presented through PovMap computer software for poverty mapping, as part of the geographical information systems, in order to draw poverty maps.

Egypt's poverty map in 2007

The Egyptian government and World Bank study (2007) became the fundamental reference for determining the poorest 1,000 villages for the geographical targeting programme in Egypt. The report used three different definitions:

- *extreme poverty*, defined as the inability to obtain even basic food, with expenditure of less than LE995 per year (ibid.);
- *absolute poverty*, defined as spending less than the amount required to obtain minimal food and non-food requirements. This group was termed 'poor', with spending of less than LE1,423 per year;
- *near-poverty*, defined as equivalent to spending barely enough to meet basic food needs and slightly more than meeting essential non-food needs. Spending for this group was on average between LE1,424 and LE1,854 per year.

The three groups combined were defined in the World Bank report as '*All poor*'. The minimum food basket based on actual consumption patterns of the poor was estimated using data from Household Income, Expenditures, and Consumption Surveys data (HIECS) (CAPMAS 2001).

Our analysis of the Egyptian government and World Bank study final report showed that using these assessment criteria:

- The absolute poverty rate had fallen from 24.18 per cent in 1990/91 to about 19.14 per cent in 1995/96. It also declined to 16.74 per cent in year 2000/01.
- Following this period, the poverty rate increased again to 19.56 per cent during the year 2004/05. However, the extreme poverty rate increased from 2.0 per cent in 1996 to 2.90 per cent in 2000, and rose to 3.80 per cent in 2005.

- In 2005, the 'all poor' rate was 40 per cent of the population, representing 28 million people. While 13.6 million – around 19.6 per cent of the population – were in absolute poverty, around 14.5 million, 21.0 per cent, were categorized as 'near poor'. Furthermore, 2.6 million, 3.8 per cent of the population, were estimated to be 'extremely poor' (ibid.).

According to HIECS data, poverty in Egypt during 2006 was not acute. However, there were many people living on or around the poverty line, meaning that a minuscule monthly decline in consumption of only LE4 will increase the numbers of people living in poverty by 2.3 per cent. In contrast, a small improvement in poor people's income can remove around 2 per cent of poor people, taking them above the poverty line.

The report also showed that poverty had a strong regional dimension in Egypt. Upper Egypt was the poorest region in the country; its poverty rate was 18.6 per cent in urban areas, but 39.1 per cent in rural areas. For Lower Egypt, poverty rates for the rural areas were 16.7 per cent, some 7.7 per cent higher than for urban areas. That is, the poverty rates in Upper Egypt's rural areas were twice the levels of rural areas in Lower Egypt. The report indicates that almost 40 per cent of Egyptian villages had a poverty incidence ranging between 50 and 70 per cent, most of them located in Upper Egypt. Furthermore, about 95 per cent of poor villages in 2006 (based on the fifty, hundred or thousand poorest villages classification) were located in Upper Egypt. In addition, about 80 per cent of these villages are in just three governorates:

- 36 per cent in Minya governorate;
- 24 per cent in Asyut governorate;
- 20 per cent in Sohag governorate.

Finally, from the poorest 1,000 villages in 2006, 252 villages (25.2 per cent) were in Minya governorate, while 129 villages (12.9 per cent) were in Asyut governorate.

The census and survey data used to establish the poverty map of Egypt ignored other important information relating to services delivered by local administrations. This information includes health services and education, the ratio of teachers to students, rates of absence of teachers, and environmental and agricultural issues. The current agricultural and environmental data lack important details regarding land use, soil degradation, water networks, irrigation and agricultural drainage systems. Moreover, the World Bank report recommended that economic growth should be considered the primary mechanism for poverty reduction, in addition to two anti-poverty strategies targeting the poor. The first of these was to provide poor people with basic social services such as initial healthcare, nutrition services and primary education. The second principle was to identify the support networks for assisting poor people unable to benefit from economic growth, or those exposed to disasters and other crises (ibid.: vii–ix).

Geographical targeting and social policies in Egypt

From 1950, the Egyptian government adopted universal programmes for poverty reduction, targeting poverty among low-income people (Al-Gibali 2008). Despite the consequences of economic reform after 1991, the Egyptian government argued that poverty reduction through state assistance was important. This situation was changed after 2004 by former prime minister Ahmed Nazif. His aggressive neoliberal government adopted a strategic shift, in order to rationalize social spending. Deposed president Mubarak devoted part of his election programme in 2005 to underlining the necessity to adopt new strategies that targeted poor people. The stated objectives of these new strategies were to reduce the incidence of poverty, within the framework of the 'Project to improve the standard of living of priority social welfare categories' (Information and Decision Support Centre, Egyptian Cabinet 2006: 10).

The Ministry of Social Solidarity began to develop plans that aimed to meet the basic needs of the poorest 40 per cent in Egypt. These goals could be achieved by developing a system of social benefits through a new targeting mechanism. Previous strategies received substantial levels of support from the World Bank and UNDP (El-Khawaja 2010). The Ministry of Social Solidarity identified two approaches in order to achieve the new strategic goal. The first of these was geographical targeting of poverty, which could be continued under the poorest 1,000 villages project. The second approach was to review the subsidized benefits and combine them, converting them into financial support. The first pilot experience of conditional financial subsidies took place on a limited scale in Asyut governorate, and at Ain el-Sira in Cairo governorate. El-Khawaja (ibid.) concluded that the second approach was ignored by the national media. The national media focused on 'Geographical targeting of the poorest 1,000 villages', which represented the turning point in moving from a global untargeted approach to the adoption of targeting methods in Egypt's social policies.

Targeting the poorest 1,000 villages: project design and implementation

A ministerial group for social development was established in 2007. The group comprised representatives from the ministries of Housing, Health, Education, Transportation, Higher Education, Social Solidarity, and Local Development, in addition to the Social Fund for Development. The main objective was to produce a new framework for social policies in Egypt. The minister of housing, utilities and urban development, Dr Ahmed Al-Maghrabi, was assigned to be the group reporter. The task of this group was to prepare and design the policies required for project implementation. As group reporter, Dr Al-Maghrabi noted that 1,141 villages would benefit from the geographic targeting of poverty programme.[2] The programme would cover a total of 12 million people, spread over nine governorates:

- Al-Minya, Asyut, Sohag, Beni Suef and Aswan governorates (1,030 villages);
- Helwan and 6 October governorates (18 villages);
- El Behera and el-Sharqia governorates (93 villages).[3]

The total cost of the geo-targeting of the poorest 1,000 villages was estimated at LE30 billion.

The Ministerial Group for Social Development (MGSD) set seventeen development indicators for villages that had been targeted, with these indicators representing the priority directions that the project was trying to develop. These indicators evaluate levels of civil society participation, basic services, electricity, health services, emergency healthcare, basic education, social security, the environmental situation, solid waste, new job creation, sports services, literacy level, fire services, civil defence, public roads, urban planning and development of human capital. In general, the local government is responsible for both supplying these services and monitoring what has been achieved (Social Contract Centre 2010).

In April 2007, the MGSD formed a supervisory committee under the leadership of the Central Agency for Reconstruction, which comes under the authority of the Ministry of Housing. The MGSD included representatives from all the ministries and agencies involved. Other institutions were also involved in this process, including the Social Fund for Development, the Youth National Council and the Women's National Council (ibid.). The committee could submit decisions to the MGSD for approval, and during May 2007 inaugurated the action plan.

The implementation of the 'Geographical targeting of the 1,000 poorest villages' project was divided into three phases, in addition to the pilot phase. For the pilot phase, the MGSD selected two 'local villager units'. 'Local villager units', or just 'villager units', are administrative units within governorates. Smaller than cities, they are communities that also include within them a number of sub-villages (this is covered in more detail later in this chapter). The two units selected by the MGSD were Nena Villager Unit in el-Sharqia governorate and Alasaid Villager Unit in Beni-Suef governorate. The pilot phase covered fourteen villages, with a total of about 70,000 residents.

Implementation of Phase 1 began in October 2008. It lasted two years and included 151 villages located in twenty-four communities (local villager units) in six governorates:

- Sharqia governorate: 31 villages;
- Behaira governorate: 19 villages;
- Minya governorate: 30 villages;
- Asyut governorate: 22 villages;
- Sohag governorate: 26 villages;
- Qena governorate: 23 villages.

Phase 2 began in July 2011 and includes a further 912 villages. These villages belong to the forty-three local villager units and are spread over the four governorates of Minya, Asyut, Sohag and Qena. The implementation of this phase is scheduled to last for three years.

Phase 3 includes the development of seventy-eight villages in the four governorates of Helwan, 6 October, Beni-Suef and Aswan. The implementation process of this phase is scheduled to start in July 2014 and, like Phase 2, to last for three years. The project is due to end in 2017 at the end of Phase 3, with the implementation of all three phases due to be complete by then (UNDP/INP 2010: 33).

Geographical targeting of poverty: Asyut governorate

This section examines project organization and problems related to the project methodology and implementation at local level. Data for my analysis came from my case study of Mer Villager Unit in Markaz. The data were collected from Mer Villager Unit and one of Mer's sub-villages, Nazlet Salman. Analysis of this case study made it possible to examine the poverty mapping methodology and alternative methods that could be used. It also helped to give a better understanding of the characteristics and mechanisms of poverty in Upper Egypt, as well as facilitating the consideration of policies that would be more effective in reducing poverty levels.

The World Bank study rated Asyut government as the third-poorest governorate overall in Egypt, after Minya and Sohag governorates. According to the framework for the geographical targeting project, Asyut governorate was the location for 236 of the villages that were to be targeted at some stage of the project implementation. These villages are the home of 2.8 million residents, with 1.4 million of these people estimated to be poor (World Bank 2007). Phase 1 of the targeting project included twenty-two villages in three local villager units in Asyut. One of these was Mer Villager Unit, comprising eleven villages with a total population of 90,000 people. Phase 1 of the geographical targeting project was aimed in part at local villager units. At a micro-level of analysis, there were several problems associated with the selection of villages classified as poor. There are technical problems related to data accuracy, concepts of poverty and the local reality, as well as political problems of governance. Moreover, there were issues concerning the role of local leaders, electoral politics and the limitations of the implementation timetable, which finished in October 2010.

Project operational structure in Asyut

It was observed that the project administration team defines the 'local level' of the project not as a village level but as embracing the entire Asyut governorate. From 1973, all issues related to rural development projects were officially assigned to a government agency, the Reconstruction and Development of the Egyptian Village (RDEV). After 1994, the National Programme for Integrated Rural Development, *Shorouk*, became the official umbrella for integrated rural development (El Sawy 2002). The political impetus of *Shorouk* was lost after 2002, owing to problems related to centralization and the diminution in political priority and corresponding reduction in financial support, but particularly to the project's lack of success in actually changing the level of poverty in the country.[4] Nevertheless, the Village Observer Office in Asyut governorate, representing RDEV at governorate level, remains the main source of our data about the rural development.

The criteria that are used in the village selection process, to decide which particular villages will be included in geographical targeting programmes, are an important factor that affects the project outcomes. Phase 1 of the project included 151 villages nationally. The selection process for these villages lacked statistical standards, and villages were selected directly by the MGSD. Six governorates, two of them in Lower Egypt, were selected as the target area for this project. The previous World Bank report indicates that 95 per cent of all the villages that make up the 1,000 poorest villages project are located in Upper Egypt. However, Phase 1 of the project was unaware of this fact, and selected two governorates in Lower Egypt, mainly for political reasons (World Bank 2007).

In our case study at Mer Villager Unit, it was found that three factors significantly affected the selection process and mechanism. The first was the impact of key actors at governorate level, and of local leaders of the NDP. The second was the role of local administration and administrators of villager units, including groups of sub-villages. The third was the data quality at local level, which influenced the village selection.

Administrative and local power

Two local forces influenced the selection of my case study in Mer Villager Unit. In the first phase of the project implementation, two actions were taken which had important implications. The first of them was by the Egyptian government, and the second by locally elected leaders. The director of the Asyut Village Observer Office, representing RDEV at the governorate level, declared that:

> In the last year, 2007, the governor asked me to provide him a list of the poorest five villages and the richest five villages. [...] Later, I was surprised by an administrative request to include five villages in Phase I of the geographical targeting project. Moreover, among the five villages in the list sent by the governor, for inclusion as poor villages under the administration of the poverty reduction programme, were two that had previously been classified as rich villages. In addition, when I questioned this issue, I was told that the governor did not like evidence showing that his governorate was in a bad condition, containing many poor villages. (Interview, director of Village Observer Office, Asyut governorate, 2009)

There are many examples of instances where local authorities tried to manipulate the actual situation in the governorate, which showed the poverty and development conditions in the governorate in a poor light. In addition to this, local leaders, members of parliament and National Party members aimed to steer the project towards benefiting their villages, as their ability to bring benefits to their villages helps them to be rewarded in congressional elections and legitimizes their re-election. One local leader, a member of parliament, said: 'If you were told that by stating that your village is a poor one, you will get up to five million Egyptian pounds, then what do you expect me to say? [...] It is not about the fact that your village is poor or not. It is the ability to seize opportunities, and is about competition among the members of parliament regarding their respective committees before the election time' (interview, member of parliament, 2009).

This example shows the impact of local forces on behalf of certain villages during Phase 1 of the project, and illustrates that local leaders have the ability to include/exclude certain villages from the project selection process when it does not match their political interests. While the World Bank study identified the poorest villages, subsequent political interactions at national and local levels had a major impact on the target process implementation.

The village and targeting

Although the poverty map was constructed based on the geographical unit or 'village', the selection of villages for Phase 1 relied on the local villager units, the *wehda qarawya mahalya*. This means that the design of the poverty map ignored the nature of the administrative structure currently used in Egypt. However, this design was very influential in the application of the project. In Asyut governorate, twenty-two villages were selected for Phase 1, located within three local villager units.

The village is the smallest geographical unit in the Egyptian administrative structure. The local administration law (Act no. 43 of 1979, Local Administration System) defines the village as a villager unit, *wehda qarawya mahalya*, which includes a central village administrative unit called *Qarya Om*, or mother village, and a group of smaller villages called *Qora taba'a*, 'hidden' villages (often known as sub-villages). This leads to technical problems that ignore the local reality and the administrative divisions of different regions in Egypt. According to the poverty map, there are different rankings among different sub-villages within the same villager unit. However, local administration and labour organizations at governorate level are verified through the villager units. This highlights the problem of inconsistency between the poverty map project outcomes and the fact that administrative payments are based on the unit of the village rather than on the sub-village.

Nevertheless, the project implementation methods used to facilitate the work at local administrative level cause a high centralization of services in the mother villages (villager units). That is, the current methods neglect the sub-villages. The situation in our case study, Mer Villager Unit, illustrates this problem, as the sub-villages are excluded from the project services. For example, while the governor made several field trips to Mer Villager Unit, followed by other field visits by the project's Local Executive Committee, Mer's sub-villages, such as Nazlet Salman, were not visited at all during follow-up field visits. Thus, this targeting methodology could lead to targeting the villager units, or mother villages, and to excluding the sub-villages, which are generally poorer than the mother villages.

Returning to the case of Mer, everyone I spoke to said that 'Mer is a very rich village'. Its agricultural land is considered among the best in the whole of Asyut governorate, and I was also told that in Asyut there is a proverb in common use which runs, 'Even the poor man who farms in Mer is not a poor man'. Our general observation confirmed that the project services were centralized in Mer, although the village already has institutions and services such as an agricultural credit bank, an agricultural extension centre, a cooperative association, schools for all levels of education, a youth centre, and two non-governmental organizations (NGOs). In contrast, the sub-villages of the Mer Villager Unit were lacking in most of the above services and institutions.

Data validity and reliability

An additional problem associated with the geographical targeting project in Egypt which emerged from the case study fieldwork was the reliability and validity of the data that were used to assess poverty at the selection stages before implementation. There are many critical analyses on the accuracy of data in Egypt (El-Issawi 2007). The field study in the sub-village of Nazlet Salman within the Mer Villager Unit showed high levels of inconsistency with the results of the 2006 census[5] and estimated data of 2007. One aspect of the data inconsistency found in the study was the observations on education, housing and even village size. For example, while the census data estimated the sub-village size of Nazlet Salman to be 14.54 square kilometres (CAPMAS 2007a, 2007b), an engineer from the agricultural society mentioned that the village, with all its houses and agricultural land, was no bigger than 1 square kilometre. Census data show that 66 per cent of the village buildings are brick. Yet field evidence indicates that there are about four hundred houses in the village, and concrete buildings represent around 86 per cent. The proportion of brick buildings was therefore just 14 per cent, rather than the 66 per cent recorded in the census.

For education data, official records indicate only fifteen residents with a university qualification in the village, yet my enquiries noted fifty-seven residents with such a qualification. There is also a disjuncture between the official alleged truancy rates of 65 per cent and the estimated truancy rate given by teachers during 1995, which was no more than 1 per cent (CAPMAS 2007a). One teacher in the village concluded: 'I have been living here, in the village, since 1995 and each year about fifty students are enrolled. Their data comes from health records and their truancy rate before the end of primary school does not exceed one per cent' (interview, local schoolteacher, 2009).

This means that the data regarding the truancy rate do not match those in the 2006 census data. There are social reasons that increase data inaccuracy. In the census questionnaire, data collectors were hesitant about asking private questions relating to the household and family conditions, which sometimes led them to make estimates about households rather than requesting actual information.

Poverty relief projects

On 12 January 2010, the governor of Asyut said in his interview with *Elyoum Elsabi* newspaper that the development process in Mer Villager Unit, with its ten sub-villages, would cost about LE305 million. The bulk of this amount would be distributed as follows:

- LE220 million for sewerage projects;
- LE20 million to build twenty-four residential buildings;
- LE10.6 million to develop health units, including purchasing four ambulances and constructing a new health centre in Nazlet Salman sub-village;
- LE32 million devoted to building five new primary schools, one secondary school, and expanding the existing five schools;
- about LE7 million to build six multi-purpose sports fields, youth centres, and to develop the existing village administration unit buildings;
- an additional LE7 million allocated to support the environment by planting trees in the streets, cleaning, improving recycling and garbage disposal, and finally developing the social solidarity units.

Specifically, Nazlet Salman sub-village will benefit from the targeting project. According to the implementation plan, the project plans to introduce a health unit, a football field, an elementary school, small loans for the poor, two housing blocks in Bani Hila' village, two fire engines, and a tractor to deal with village solid waste and sanitation systems. As a result of the case study fieldwork, we have several comments on the proposed projects under the targeting programme in general, and those planned for Nazlet Salman in particular.

However, in Nazlet Salman sub-village, the existing schools were replaced before, and have been in use since 2007. In addition, the village does not need health units, as there is a health unit 500 metres north of Ghalah village, one of the sub-villages of 'Dairout Markaz. While Nazlet Salman is a sub-village of el-Qusiya Markaz, it would be better to allow Nazlet Salman villagers to benefit from the nearest health unit instead of establishing a new unit. Finally, there is a problem associated with the project's housing design. The project plans to construct two buildings of four floors, housing eight apartments to serve eight poor families, instead of constructing rural houses that are needed by people whose main source of income is from farming. The construction of these apartments does not take any account of farmers' needs, such as storage and specified areas for their animals.

Although the World Bank's study of the poorest 1,000 villages project in Egypt illustrated that rural regions should be the priority geographical target area for this project, agricultural activities, as the main factor in Egyptian rural areas, have been ignored. The project mainly focused on the educational, development and health capabilities[6] in Mer Villager Unit. Moreover, the project focused on establishing certain facilities: schools, health units, youth centres, etc., which is similar to the traditional concept of integrated rural development. The current project objective therefore overlaps with other projects carried out by different agencies (UNDP/INP 2003: 101).

The World Bank, in its publication *World Development Report 2008: Agriculture for Development* (World Bank 2008) made a number of recommendations for agricultural development, and highlighted the importance of the social role of agriculture and smallholder production to food security in the world. The report clearly showed the need to link anti-poverty policies to agricultural development. It also focused on several prerequisites for agricultural development (ibid.): equal access to agricultural land, health, water and education. In addition to these, it noted that qualitative and quantitative support of public investment, and improving how markets function, all lead to better development outcomes. Other factors include enhancing the performance of agricultural production, improving access to financial services, reducing the levels of risk that farmers are exposed to, promoting innovation in science and technology, and developing more sustainable production and environmental services (ibid.).

In Egypt, as elsewhere, the relationship between rural poverty and agricultural policies is closely correlated. The geographical targeting project in Egypt totally ignored this reciprocal relationship. For example, Law 96 of 1992, which arranged the rental relationship among landowners and tenants, had the effect of increasing rural tenants' vulnerability to high costs of production, and rents for agricultural land increased sharply (Ayeb 2010; Abdel Aal 2002; Saad 2002; Bush 2002). In addition to changes in tenure, high prices for raw materials such as fertilizers, pesticides and seeds accentuated this vulnerability (Socialist Papers 2004). In summary, many problems that confronted small farmers, tenants and landless people, and which increased levels of rural poverty, were totally neglected in the poverty alleviation project.

Local definitions of poverty

In contrast with the views of poverty that emerged from the geographical targeting project, we can distinguish two concepts of poverty in the village:[7]

1 The *poor village*: this is a village that lacks public services and institutions, and has limited agricultural and potential reclaimed land, as well as high levels of emigration.
2 The *poor household*: this refers to a family that does not have land, or which owns less than one feddan; which may have sons working abroad, and has to rent agricultural land to feed the children and animals (interview, local informant, 2009).

Poverty is clearly linked to the agricultural sector. Access to agricultural land is a central index for defining the poor village and poor people. The terms 'poverty' or 'poor' are used to refer to households rather than to define individuals in the village. On the other hand, agricultural landownership is used as the main index for measuring household poverty levels and households' capacity to hold livestock and take decisions on where to try to make a livelihood (i.e. whether or not to emigrate and try elsewhere). Hence poverty, in the sense of lacking food security, is only one dimension of the concept of poverty that is used by villagers. This concept of poverty thus focused mainly on poverty linked to access to resources, employment and food security. Here, we are combining two concepts of poverty. The first concept is 'poverty of institutional capabilities', which refers to the *poor village*, as defined above. The second is the concept of 'poverty of access to livelihoods', which represents the situation of family poverty, the *poor household* defined above. We have combined the local view with the national view.

The national view is derived from the findings of a report jointly published by the UN Food and Agriculture Organization (FAO) and the International Fund for Agricultural Development (IFAD), *The Status of*

Rural Poverty in the Near East and North Africa (FAO/IFAD 2007), which characterized the poorest families in rural Egypt as follows:

1 Family does not have access to agricultural land; the majority of the poor are either landless or tenants, or owners of very small farm holdings.
2 Family has limited access to health and other social services.
3 Family has difficulties in obtaining a job at a steady salary.
4 Family in rural areas with high dependency ratio (i.e. ratio of persons who are economically dependent on those who provide for them).

This illustrates that poor people in rural areas have limited access to natural resources. Small-scale farmers suffer from the lack of water for irrigation and are often forced to use drainage water. Moreover, Egyptian small-scale farmers generally operate with high farming costs, lower yields, and with the areas that they are able to farm scattered, rather than concentrated in one holding. Access to resources and services has an important bearing on whether people are poor or not. In addition, access to resources leads to empowerment of the poor and stimulates economic growth. Policy measures in Egypt which aim to mitigate poverty need to improve the access of poor households to production and non-production assets. These measures could include improved access to irrigated land, irrigation water, livestock, education services, healthcare, clean potable water, social security and employment.

Conclusion

This chapter examines the 'Geographical targeting of poverty in rural Upper Egypt' project. The project's theoretical framework, prepared by the World Bank in collaboration with the Egyptian Ministry of Investment, has also been explored. Phase 1 of the project implementation in Asyut was evaluated. By setting out the fieldwork for my case study, I have endeavoured to explain different local dimensions that have had an impact on the project implementation processes. As a result, the case study has aimed to identify the local concept of poverty at the village level by adopting the views of rural people themselves, matching these to the founding aims and plans underlying the project.

Although the geographical targeting of poverty project was mainly aimed at supporting people living in poverty and reducing the leakage of benefits to non-poor recipients, little was achieved in this regard. There were many reasons why the project was unsuccessful in this, and why the intended policies did not achieve tangible outcomes. The first phase of the project did not focus on the poorest geographic area, according to the project reference study. Instead, local and national political considerations overruled the project design. These political considerations clearly diverted the regional distribution of the project and how it targeted areas and people. While some of the targeted areas were in northern Egypt, other project activities were located in Upper Egypt's rural regions. The latter areas were found to be more politically oriented, as for example in Asyut governorate.

The results of the case study illustrate that the people who were targeted did not benefit from the project. Accordingly, the main objectives of the targeting programmes were not fully achieved. The agricultural dimensions were completely ignored. The absence of the agricultural dimension was observed at the planning and implementation stages of the programme, and particularly in the first phase of the programme. The method of geographical targeting of poverty defines poverty as being based on consumption and welfare indicators. This definition neglects the local perception and people's own perspectives of poverty. The poorest farmers define themselves as people with insufficient assets, with fewer employment opportunities, and low financial capacity. In addition, poverty refers to a lack of access to healthcare, clean water and education services. These definitions were not taken into account during the programme geographically targeting anti-poverty measures on the poorest 1,000 villages in Egypt.

Notes

1 Egypt is made up of twenty-seven governorates. Census data divide the country into seven major regions: urban governorates, urban Lower Egypt, rural Lower Egypt, urban Upper Egypt, rural Upper Egypt, urban border, rural border. The poverty map study calculates seven poverty lines, based on the basic needs of the different regions.

2 I observed some variation in different statements regarding the number of the villages targeted under the project. The project and the minister of housing stated that 1,000 villages were to be targeted. In contrast, some newspapers have mentioned the figure of 1,141 villages, while the executive director of the project refers to 1,153 targeted villages.

3 From a speech by the social solidarity minister on 'New social contract policies: towards integration of economic and social policies': www.ndp.org.eg.

4 El Sawy (2002) indicates that out of total investments of LE18.2 billion earmarked for the programme during the period 1997–2002, by January 2000 only LE1.5 billion had actually been disbursed.

5 One of the data collectors who participated in the 2006 census in Nazlet Salman told me: 'I pointed

to ask families about the number of their children and their age. However, I thought that it was shameful to ask questions about the household assets and furniture. So I used to make an estimation based on the external appearance of the house.'

6 The state has adopted a concept of 'poverty of capability', which indicates that the availability of better basic education and better healthcare would lead directly to improved quality of life and thus increase the ability of a person to improve their income and escape income poverty.

7 Both concepts were extracted through the discussion sessions with different groups of villagers, as well as through the reporter meetings. The dialogue mainly concentrated on defining: the poor people in the villages; the characteristics of socio-economic development; the poverty of the village; and criteria used in poverty classification. Based on local classifications of poverty, for example, families that have no agricultural land either of their own or rented to feed their children and farm animals (buffalo) are the poorest. This group was followed by families that own less than one feddan and whose members work for other farms, or who have a son working in Libya. In contrast, families that have 2 feddans of land are not considered poor.

References

Abdel Aal, M. H. (2002) 'Agrarian reform and tenancy problems in Upper Egypt', in R. Bush (ed.), *Counter-Revolution in Egypt's Countryside: Land and Farmers in the Era of Economic Reform*, London: Zed Books.

Al-Ahram (2010) 'Mubarak: the next five years for the poor and the marginalized', 11 November, p. 1.

Al-Gibali, A. F. (2008) 'Towards an integrated framework of subsidy policy in Egypt', *Strategic Papers*, 18(183), Cairo: Al-Ahram Centre for Political and Strategic Studies.

Assaad, R. and M. Rouchdy (1999) 'Poverty and poverty alleviation strategies in Egypt', *Cairo Papers in Social Science*, 22, Monograph 1 (Spring), American University in Cairo.

— (2006) 'Poverty and geographic targeting in Egypt: evidence from a poverty mapping exercise', 13th Oil Annual Conference: Its Impact on the Global Economy, Kuwait, 16–18 December.

Ayeb, H. (2010) *La Crise de la société rurale en Egypte; la fin du fellah?*, Paris: Karthala.

Baker, J. L. and M. E. Grosh (1994) 'Poverty reduction through geographic targeting: how well does it work?', *World Development*, 22(7): 983–95.

Bigman, D. and H. Fofack (2000) 'Geographical targeting for poverty alleviation: an introduction to the special issue', *World Bank Economic Review*, 14(1): 129–45.

Bush, R. (2002) 'More losers than winners in Egypt's countryside: the impact of changes in land tenure', in R. Bush (ed.), *Counter-Revolution in Egypt's Countryside: Land and Farmers in the Era of Economic Reform*, London: Zed Books.

CAPMAS (Central Agency for Public Mobilization and Statistics) (2001) *Household Income and Expenditure Consumption Survey (HIECS), 1999/2000*, Cairo: CAPMAS.

— (2007a) *The 2006 Population Census*, Cairo: CAPMAS.

— (2007b) *Population Estimations of 2007*, Cairo: CAPMAS.

Chatterjee, S., S. Aburar and G. Estrada (2006) 'Geographical targeting of operations for poverty reduction', *Poverty and Social Development Papers*, Technical note No. 1 (July), Manila: Asian Development Bank.

Coady, D. (2006) 'The welfare returns to finer targeting: the case of the Progresa Program in Mexico', *International Tax and Public Finance Review*, 13: 217–39.

Coady, D., M. Grosh and J. Hoddinott (2002) *The Targeting of Transfers in Developing Countries: Review of Experience and Lessons*, Washington, DC: World Bank.

— (2004) 'Targeting outcomes redux', *World Bank Research Observer*, 19(1): 61–85.

Dubois, J.-L. and F.-R. Mahieu (2002) 'La dimension sociale du développement durable: réduction de la pauvreté ou durabilité sociale?', in J.-Y. Martin (ed.), *Développement durable? Doctrines, pratiques, évaluations*, Paris: Les Éditions de l'IRD (Institut de Recherche pour le Développement), pp. 73–94.

El-Issawi, I. (2007) *The Egyptian Economy in Thirty Years*, Cairo: Academy Library and Third World Forum.

El-Khawaja, D. (2010) 'Le ciblage géographique: les nouvelles priorités des politiques sociales de l'Égypte', Paper presented to the seminar 'Les questions sociales, politiques publiques et des réformes en Afrique du Nord et le Moyen-Orient', 13 April, Paris: École des Hautes Etudes en Sciences Sociales (EHESS), Unpublished document.

El Sawy, A. (2002) '"Intentional ambiguity": the legislator to look at local government in Egypt', *Journal of the Renaissance*, 13, October, Cairo: Cairo University Faculty of Economics and Political Science.

Elbers, C., J. O. Lanjouw and P. Lanjouw (2002) 'Micro-level estimation of welfare', *Policy Research Working Paper*, 2911, Washington, DC: Development Research Group, World Bank.

Epstein, T. S. (2008) 'Poverty, caste, and migration in South India', in D. Narayan and P. Petesch (eds), *Moving out of Poverty*, vol. I: *Cross-Disciplinary Perspectives on Mobility*, Washington, DC: World Bank.

FAO (Food and Agriculture Organization)/IFAD (International Fund for Agricultural Development) (2007) *The Status of Rural Poverty in the Near East and North Africa: Enabling Poor Rural People to Overcome Poverty*, Rome: FAO/IFAD.

Information and Decision Support Centre, Egyptian Cabinet (2006) *Study of Poverty and the Characteristics of the Poor in Egypt*, Cairo: Centre for Information and Decision Support, Council of Ministers.

Saad, R. (2002) 'Egyptian politics and the tenancy law', in R. Bush (ed.), *Counter-Revolution in Egypt's Countryside: Land and Farmers in the Era of Economic Reform*, London: Zed Books.

Social Contract Centre (2010) Web page on Phase 1 of the 'Poorest 1,000 villages' project (in Arabic), www.1000qarya.gov.eg/programs/programs.aspx.

Socialist Papers (2004) Issue VII, October/November, Giza: Centre for Socialist Studies.

UNDP (United Nations Development

Programme)/INP (Institute of National Planning) (2003) *Egypt Human Development Report 2003*, Cairo: UNDP/INP.

— (2008) *Egypt Human Development Report 2008*, Cairo: UNDP/INP.

— (2010) *Egypt Human Development Report 2010*, Cairo: UNDP/INP.

World Bank (2007) *Arab Republic of Egypt: A Poverty Assessment Update*, World Bank, Ministry of Economic Development of the Arab Republic of Egypt, Report no. 39885-EGY, Washington, DC: World Bank.

— (2008) *World Development Report 2008: Agriculture for Development*, Washington, DC: World Bank.

10 | Working with street kids: unsettling accounts from the field

KAMAL FAHMI

Introduction

In Latin America, Africa, Asia and eastern Europe, children and youth living on the streets are commonly referred to using the term street children. In North America and western Europe, the term homeless youth is used interchangeably with that of street children to refer to this population. Since the beginning of the 1980s, this social phenomenon has been increasingly preoccupying policy-makers, researchers and development planners. Despite the widespread concerns and the numerous intervention programmes, the street children phenomenon is escalating persistently worldwide and confusion still remains regarding the definition and conceptualization of these young populations living and surviving under circumstances that most would find unbearable (De Moura 2002; Cree et al. 2002).

This chapter draws on a participatory action research project started in 1993 with street children in Cairo. I was the principal in charge of this project. My responsibilities included overseeing the design and implementation of the different phases of the project and recruiting and training the street workers, in addition to being an active participant myself. A full account of the project can be found elsewhere (Fahmi 2007).

I want to focus specifically on the methodological difficulties and the ethical issues encountered by the practitioners, who were at the same time both researchers and street workers in the project. The proximity to the street kids required difficult emotional work for the researcher-practitioners that is often hidden in research accounts. While the accounts of some of the incidents related here may appear sensationalist, my purpose in relating them is twofold: I want to document some of the situations of extreme marginality and exclusion that we came to witness and, by the same token, demonstrate the depth and complexity of the ethical dilemmas faced by practitioners. The major challenge for the street-work practitioners who work with excluded populations is ethical in nature. This is because of the value-laden, ambiguous, complex and uncertain character of many of the situations in which they become involved, and for which established academic knowledge is of limited use, and which, in addition, often require an immediate response. Hence, street-work practitioners constantly need to construct their own experiential knowledge based on the skill and the spontaneous and intuitive savoir-faire that they bring to their function. Moreover, the strength of this kind of reflective, praxis-based practice resides in its ability to tackle ethical dilemmas with a dialectical sensitivity. That helps to elucidate the issues that emanate from within the grey zones of practice and to avoid the trap of Manichaean moralism (ibid.).

Street children

Street children is the generic term used to refer to groups of children who develop a special relationship with the street whereby it becomes their main habitat. The frequency of the term's use seems to suggest that such a group exists as a homogeneous phenomenon. Indeed, these youngsters do look alike. They wear shabby, dirty clothing and can be seen begging, performing petty jobs, working, or just wandering about with no apparent purpose. They share an appearance of abandonment that may lead observers to single them out as street children. However, although these children look alike, they have different family characteristics, life histories and prognoses. Many researchers believe that the expression street children is in itself problematic, giving a distorted message because it conveys an implicit assumption that these children are alike and that they live on the streets in the same way and for similar reasons. Actually, street children comprise a diverse population in terms of their individual characteristics, their motivation for being on the street and the extent of their participation in street life.

Preliminary field investigation indicated that street children mostly do not exist on the streets as isolated individuals. To be able to survive on the street, one has to establish some form of strong (if informal) paternal/family relationship to improve one's chances of survival. Thus, street children are associating most of the time with other children, youth and adults of both sexes in what seem to constitute groupings that can be viewed as street milieus within a street society. It is within the context of the street society that the socialization of deviance takes place and influences the identity construction of street children and youth. Thus, in order to capture the complexity of an individual's existence on the street, we need to elucidate the organic daily ties that the individual maintains with surrounding street milieus (ibid.).

Participatory action research (PAR)

The choice of PAR to 'do something' regarding the phenomenon of street children was consistent with our view that street children are far from being mere victims and deviants. These kids, in running away from alienating structures and finding relative freedom on the street, often become autonomous and are capable of actively defining their situations in their own terms. They are able to challenge the roles assigned to children, make judgements and develop a network of niches in the heart of the metropolis in order to resist exclusion and chronic repression. Thus, for research and action with street kids to be emancipatory, it is necessary to acknowledge and respect the human agency the kids display in changing their own lives. Fundamental to PAR is its 'bottom up' approach, which seeks to empower affected communities by involving them in defining needs, identifying problems and developing potential solutions.

Paulo Freire is generally considered to be the father of PAR (Finn 1994; Gaventa 1993; Hall 1981; Selener 1997). The ideas expressed in *Pedagogy of the Oppressed* (Freire 1970) and the concepts of *liberating dialogue* and *critical consciousness* developed in *Education for Critical Consciousness* (Freire 1973) continue to be basic tenets of the type of PAR that maintains a focus on power and its relationship to knowledge production. Freire's understanding and commitment to praxis, as well as his attempt to develop a methodology for involving disenfranchised people as researchers seeking answers to questions raised by their daily struggle for survival, were guided by his grassroots field immersion for many years.

The PAR design was evolved with the objectives of penetrating street children's milieus and establishing a meaningful participatory presence using a street-work methodology;[1] understanding the magnitude, underlying factors and conditions, and persistence of the street children phenomenon; developing with the individuals and groups concerned community-based alternatives to institutionalization.

A very important achievement of the project was the recruitment and training of street workers who acquired the skills and knowledge of street-work methodology. These workers were difficult to identify and recruit given the absence of this kind of practice in Egypt. None of the social workers we contacted were willing to go into the streets and link up and 'be with' the kids in their life settings. It seems that for a great majority of social workers this kind of activity is not consistent with a professional view of what social work is. We thus had to rely on informal networks to identify and recruit lay persons with a view to educating, training and equipping them on the job with the necessary skills and knowledge using a reflective methodology. Initially two workers, one male and one female, were recruited and trained. Through snowball recruiting, these two workers subsequently introduced and participated in the training of additional workers.

The training and coaching of street workers took place using a reflective methodology inspired by the work of Donald Schon (1983, 1987, 1995) on experiential learning. Schon strongly argues that research and theory need not necessarily precede practice in a linear and deductive fashion. Instead, he maintains and demonstrates that people's practical experience can be used to produce theories inductively through a process of reflecting on that experience. In this process, the integration of theory and practice is worked on through cyclic and systematic reflection. In discussing and analysing the uncertain and complex situations that are encountered in the field, practitioners become actively engaged in identifying the contradictions and theoretical assumptions implicit in their work. They thus strive to dissect the various perspectives for interpreting situations within the field context and to articulate the basis for their intuitive actions and their meaning and impact, as well as the inevitable ethical dilemmas that their actions raise.

The first task for the street workers was to infiltrate the living milieus of street kids by means of a gentle and unobtrusive process. This demands considerable tact and talent on the part of the street workers in order not to perturb daily routines or the regular course of events. Indeed, street workers must demonstrate numerous qualities, a partial list of which includes: sensitivity; knowing how to observe and listen, the ability to make connections and to take time to understand; belief in the capacities of the youth and in his or her potential, accepting differences in language, values and culture, and respecting youth and those surrounding them; the ability to establish their own limits and recognize their own strengths, weaknesses and fears; availability; and having a spirit of initiative.

During the project the team succeeded in establishing a meaningful and sustained presence in street children's milieus in about ten locations in Cairo. Given the fact that the street children phenomenon exists within a wider context of street society, the street workers related not only to the children, but to the street communities as a whole. In so doing, they were very careful not to disturb the existing modes of organization.

Once a meaningful presence had been established and relationships with children and other members of the street milieu had reached a comfortable level of mutual trust, it became important to create a physical locus within the area/territory in order to start establishing a sense of group belongingness and solidarity. Thus, a drop-in centre was opened in April 1997 to serve as a landmark or point of reference for a concrete community movement to advocate alternatives to institutionalization. Many of the children and other members of their milieus participated in the process of setting up the centre. Medical care, shower facilities and simple meals were offered to the children. The focus in the drop-in centre was on building up the strengths and skills of the children, not on removing them from the streets. The process of programme development was based on experience and participation, and contextualized within a non-formal education framework (Epstein 1996; Leite et al. 1991; UNICEF 1987).

Methodological challenges

Most researchers agree that getting accurate information from street children and youth is not an easy task (Aptekar 1994; Bemak 1996; Young and Barrett 2001). For different psychosocial reasons many of these youngsters have lost all confidence in adults, and, because of constant abuse and exploitation, it is impossible for many children to believe that an adult approaching them has anything but an ulterior motive in mind – offering something but wanting as much or more in return. Therefore, initial contact, the offering of friendship and the building of acceptance, confidence and trust require great skill and sensitivity on the part of the intervening adult.

Furthermore, these youngsters have developed an extraordinary capacity to tell stories. Lying about their ages, family background, the reasons for being on the street and the givens of their street lives is all part of their well-rehearsed scripts. There are many reasons why children manipulate information: they are wary of adult authority in general and fear the police in particular. Manipulating information has a psychological function that allows the children to get back at a society that devalues them. Falsified information also serves to keep society at bay in terms of the details of their lives; autonomy has become the precious compensatory benefit of not having the protection of a family, school or village, and they should not be expected to give it up readily. Indeed, it seems that manipulating information is not, as many would argue, a reflection of the individual's deviance but rather a necessary skill for survival under alienating conditions. Accordingly, the validity of gathered information and projection of adequate intervention depend on the degree of trust that exists in the relationship between the data collector and the child/youth. The development of such trusting relationships requires so much time and investment of the self that it cannot be afforded under the circumstances in which the majority of research is conducted.

The majority of research on Cairene street children is descriptive and/or quantitatively oriented (Bibars 1998). Although it highlights general characteristics and trends of which it is important to be aware, it does not provide a deep elucidation of the complex interplay between the socio-economic, cultural and ethical factors that shape and influence the phenomenon in question. Most of the research on street children has overlooked the existence of street girls and focused on the boys as though they are living on the street in isolation from the street communities in which they mingle and socialize with other boys, girls and a wide variety of adult street people (Aptekar 1994; Lucchini 1996). As a result, the street context in which the children and youth live and survive has been neglected and, unsurprisingly, insistence on adopting 'rescue' approaches has led to the burning out of dedicated practitioners.

To counter these methodological difficulties, a participatory action research approach was chosen in order to implement a programme of front-line street intervention using an ethnographic methodology of street work. This allowed access to and implantation in the street milieus of street children and youth who were difficult to approach through conventional outreach methods. Participatory action research is a field intervention that is simultaneously coupled with a research activity, which primarily serves to orient, adjust and consolidate the intervention/action itself. Thus, the aim is to institute an ongoing process of qualitative research and evaluation whereby the collection and analysis of data are used to elucidate the different aspects and dynamics of the realities of street children and the street milieus that they frequent. In other words, the street intervention encompassed two major activities that simultaneously fed into each other. The ethnographic street work aimed at developing ties of trust and solidarity with street children and their surroundings by joining them on the street and, by the same token, gaining knowledge regarding their realities through the collection and analysis of pertinent data. Specifically, the above-mentioned methodological obstacles were dealt with in the following manner.

First, the implementation of a carefully designed street-work methodology allowed unobtrusive social infiltration (Punch 1986, 1994) into different street milieus and organizations frequented by street children and youth, many of whom were considered to be 'hard-core'. This was achieved gradually and tactfully over a period of more than two years and allowed street workers to gain not only the trust of key members of targeted street milieus, but also access to first-hand information and data right at the front line of the phenomenon in question. This was the first time in Egypt that a street-work methodology was implemented.

A team of street workers of men and women established a meaningful, interactive and intensive participatory presence in street milieus in about twenty locations, located in the areas of Pyramids Road, Faisal Road, Giza railway station, Giza Square, El-Manial, El-Sayyeda Zeinab, El-Mohandesin, Tahrir Square, and downtown. The street workers' intensive and participatory presence, as well as their non-judgemental approach and attitude of solidarity, culminated in the building of a strong rapport with the children. As a result the children started to relate, maybe for the first time, to adults who respected them, cared for them, related to them on their own terms, accepted them for what they were and, most importantly, listened to them and did not betray them. With time and sustained presence, the street workers were integrated into the spaces of the daily street lives of children and youth. They came to be perceived not only as good 'buddies' but also as resource people who were available and accessible. Street workers became companions and accompanied the children in their daily joys and struggles, offering not only help during emergencies but also, and more importantly, the opportunity for genuine social support and resocialization actions whereby children and youth gradually relearned to trust adults, who, because of past experience, were perceived as threatening and oppressive.

Secondly, the scope of data collection was enlarged to include qualitative research tools, such as informal discussions and dialogues, semi-structured interviews, life accounts, social trajectories and others. This allowed the accumulation of qualitative data regarding the factors that push children and youth away from their families of origin, as well as the dynamics of street socialization that guide and sustain them in street life.

Thirdly, the scope of the research sample was enlarged to incorporate not only girls and young women, but also key figures from the children's surroundings in the streets. The street workers maintained good relations with these adults and were able to co-opt some of them, who began to act not only as key informants but also to play an increasingly active role at the drop-in centre and to be influential in the community organizing process being initiated.

The special relationships of trust that street workers build with street kids – whose experiences with adults and mainstream societal institutions have been largely negative – not only demand the investment of a considerable amount of time, but also a sustained, meaningful and participatory presence in the street milieus where these youngsters live. It is through such a presence that 'intimate familiarity' with ongoing community life is achieved, and that street kids, both individually and in small groups, come to realize that there are adults who genuinely care for them. By establishing relationships and a sustained presence in the street milieus frequented by the kids, the street workers are able to develop relationships that were not exclusively, or necessarily, 'help oriented'. Instead, the objective was to develop rapport and relationships that are basically ones of acceptance, trust, complicity and solidarity, created by the repeated sharing of the ordinary, warm and tender gestures of everyday life: laughing together, seeing each other in different situations that might even be ridiculous, allowing the other to experience and express different emotions, playing and having fun, contemplating, creating, going for walks, joking, and allowing the other the right to experience crisis, to express disappointment, fear, suffering and a desire to die. As such, the primary role of street workers is to offer their 'being' through the use of self in a sustained participatory presence in the everyday life of the kids they come to know.

The importance of carefully recruiting, training, educating, supervising and coaching street workers cannot be overstated. Indeed, the selection of street workers itself requires a great deal of caution. Many people volunteer for this kind of work because they feel sorry for street kids and want to help them. Individuals who have such feelings often encounter problems once they start working. Depression is the most common consequence, as workers become overwhelmed when they imagine how sad and desperate they themselves would feel if they had to face the adversities of the streets. Well-meaning individuals who do not understand and control their feelings may actually harm the children they wish to help by strengthening the children's feelings of exclusion and making them feel helpless.

In accompanying the kids through their everyday living in street milieus, street workers capitalized on the use of the self as a powerful tool for mutual trust-building. However, the genuine interest and care they displayed with regard to the kids were accompanied by disturbing emotions that the street workers needed to manage. On a practical level, it is necessary to appreciate the physically and emotionally demanding nature of direct, day-to-day street work. The workers relate not only to the kids, but also to their surroundings and the street community as a whole. This included a wide variety of street adults who, in some capacity or another, influenced the daily existence of street kids: natural leaders, police informants, street food vendors, tea-makers, security agents, street employers, grocery and coffee shop owners, shoeshiners, commercial sex workers and others, who were part of the kids' surroundings in the streets. Although many kids were forming attachments with individual workers, the workers began to realize that such gratifying relationships could also be very taxing if they were not adequately managed.

In the following section some of the main challenges that the street workers encountered while undertaking this participatory action research project over its duration of eight years will be elaborated in more detail.

The kids' manipulations and the workers' acculturation

An ongoing complication in this project was the tendency of the kids to manipulate. Presenting untrue, well-rehearsed stories about experiences, family background, current situation, age and reasons for leaving home is often well integrated into the behaviour patterns of street kids. This misrepresentation seems fundamental to survival and is related to an ability to manipulate the environment. The street worker becomes another facet of the environment through which the kids must successfully manoeuvre in order to survive. Consequently, street workers had to learn to accept a degree of 'healthy manipulation' from the kids, who were seeking to maintain a sense of control. This also facilitated the development of a relationship between the child and the street worker based on the child's terms and not just the worker's.

Moreover, there is a delicate balance to be observed by street workers, who not only have to maintain professional integrity and identity, but also be versatile enough to move comfortably in the street child's domain without trying to become one of the children. There is a danger of 'false acculturation', whereby street workers over-identify by assuming cultural characteristics that are unnatural for them. All of the above required the maintenance of a high level of engaged support and self-investment.

Invisible others: the gatekeepers

Prior to infiltration work, we had hypothesized that street kids did not live on the streets in a bohemian or individual way. Rather, we assumed that in order to survive, most kids would join some kind of group or street organization in which the leaders might not welcome outsiders poking their nose into their affairs. As such, we expected that the kids contacted by the street workers were being observed and had to inform their peers, as well as the leaders, about what was going on. A non-obtrusive form of infiltration was deemed necessary in order to avoid a rapid rejection by the milieu, providing another reason to be covert. This hypothesis required the street workers to be very careful about how they presented themselves, the impressions they gave and the questions they asked. The leaders had to be neutralized. In addition, the state security agents and informants, who were bound to be mingling with the kids and their surroundings, had to be taken into account. They, too, had to feel that we were sufficiently benign for them to let us proceed with our work.

These invisible others were thus the gatekeepers who had to authorize and not hinder our access to street milieus. Their being invisible meant that our messages to them regarding who we were and what we were doing had to be conveyed indirectly through the kids and the street individuals with whom we established contact and relationships.

Managing emotions: fear and prejudice

During early participant observation work, our fear had to be acknowledged – fear of violence, of being ridiculed by the kids, or of looking stupid, and, certainly, the fear of being unable to handle sensitive situations that might suddenly arise on the street. We realized that many of our fears originated in the stereotypical mass fantasy about the wildness and havoc of street life and the belief that street kids would readily, for the sake of survival, commit violent acts. We had to remind ourselves constantly not to let these prejudices exaggerate our fears and unduly immobilize us. Later, as the work progressed, many of these prejudices were challenged. Most of the violence is directed against other members of the group, seldom against outsiders. The crimes committed by street kids are of a petty nature, e.g. stealing drying laundry and goods in marketplaces. Contrary to widespread belief, over the eight-year duration of the programme, no evidence emerged tying these kids to the drug industry or to terrorist groups, as is often assumed.

Street workers also needed to come to grips with the repugnant appearance of many of the kids. Barefoot, wearing shabby and dirty clothes, most had dirt on their faces, arms, feet and on every exposed part of their bodies, which were often also covered with scars. Their fingernails were quite long and full of dirt. It was difficult not to feel unnerved after shaking hands with them, and as the closeness of the rapport with them increased, so did the physical closeness so characteristic of Middle Eastern societies, which further intensified our feeling of discomfort.

However, this initial apprehension dissipated gradually as the development of a closer rapport with the kids made us less disturbed by their physical appearance. Subsequently, we found out that most of them enjoyed and appreciated personal cleanliness. Access to water and washing facilities was indeed one of their main problems. Interestingly, we also learned that the dirt on some kids' bodies was self-administered, using mud. They resorted to this practice while they were begging, hoping to elicit enough disgust among prospective donors that they would contribute some change hurriedly in order to get away from these 'filthy young monsters'. Furthermore, we came to appreciate that long fingernails are maintained for defending oneself against assault. Later, when the drop-in centre was opened, the street workers felt no hesitation about helping some of the younger children to shower. Periodic hairdressing of all the kids and application of medicated lotion became a regular practice in order to minimize hair lice.

Witnessing destitution

During this early participant observation work, one of the most tormenting issues that project workers had to handle was the feeling of being incapable of providing much help regarding some situations of utmost destitution and misery facing young children. One late winter night we met two girls holding hands and going around parked cars trying to identify a convenient sleeping spot. The older girl, who was seven or eight, told us that they had to sleep under a car so that they did not get picked up by the police. Under her arm, she was holding a piece of cardboard to use as a mattress for her and her younger sister, who was crying desperately. 'She is very tired and wants to sleep,' said the older sister, who looked exhausted and pale herself. She nevertheless made the effort to explain to us that they had fled from a police raid on nearby 'Ataba Square earlier in the evening, where their mother had been arrested. We knew that an urban upgrading plan was about to be implemented in the area of the square. This, as is often the case, was accompanied by the eviction of street people, who had managed to eke out a living and make a kind of habitat around this busy square for many years, surviving by selling tea, soft drinks and food to travellers waiting for buses at a main terminal located in the vicinity of the square. The dilemma for the older sister was that she did not really feel secure sleeping under a car. She was worried that she might not notice if the car started moving and that it might run them over. It was getting late and cold when it occurred to us to ask the doorman of an apartment building whether he would let the two girls sleep in the building's entrance hall for a few hours. To our relief, he agreed.

Later, in my warm bed, I was thinking of the strong desire that I had felt to bring these two girls home, to make them safe and comfortable and to accompany them to look for their mother the following day. Such situations occurred repeatedly afterwards, and we had to learn to acknowledge the painful limits of our ability to help.

Sensitive issues: drug consumption and sexuality

The intensification of accompaniment work described above allowed us access to an array of morally sensitive information, especially with re-gard to drug consumption and sexual matters. We had to deal with uncertain, complex, ambiguous and value-laden situations that raised ethical and moral dilemmas. Supplementing our own observations, many kids increasingly confided to us details of behaviour regarded, in the context of traditional societies like Egypt's, as highly immoral. Adults who witness or come to know about such behaviour are expected to severely reprimand the deviant and take necessary action to correct him or her.

We adhered to a strong belief that accompaniment of deviant popu-lations demands an increased tolerance with respect to use of drugs, violence, sexual activities and all those values and lifestyles usually condemned by mainstream norms and considered detrimental to the well-being of children and youth. Yet we remained confused as to whether this tolerance required us to accept any kind of behaviour. Recognition and acceptance of difference were indeed major issues with which we grappled throughout the programme. Below are some examples taken from situations in which we were confronted with issues related to drug consumption and sexuality.

In the meagre literature on street children, drug consumption and sexual matters are usually referred to as sensitive issues, and represented in terms of abuse, addiction, promiscuity, exploitation and high-risk behaviour, such as prostitution, homosexual activity and anal intercourse (De Moura 2002). This representation, permeated by the negative aspects attributed to street life, often ignores the debate regarding the ethical questions raised by these sensitive issues in favour of the moral obligation of 'protecting' the children (see, for example, Young and Barrett 2001). Researchers are advised to assess carefully the possible negative impacts on street children before divulging information regarding abusers and the children's spatial survival strategies to avoid retaliation from the police or other abusers. This 'protectionist' discourse is employed at the expense of dismissing and excluding other aspects of the lived experience, such as exploration, pleasure and adventure, which are not exploitative and can even be empowering at times. In exploring closely the issue of glue sniffing and drug consumption, we came to understand that in the context of street life there are very good reasons to engage in the use of inhalants: peer pressure, the need to belong to a group and the fear of isolation, to name a few. Moreover, the anaesthetic effect of glue helps to block out not only 'bad thoughts', but also hunger pangs and the effects of harsh weather. In this sense, glue sniffing is vital for street survival. However, we were also concerned about the possibility of cognitive deterioration and detrimental repercussions on the nervous system, which are widely believed to result from the use of inhalants. As such, we were at a loss as to how best to react when children informed us about their drug consumption and sniffed glue – sometimes provocatively – in our presence. On the one hand, we felt that criticizing, discouraging or condemning this kind of behaviour was obviously negating the unique context and circumstances associated with it. On the other hand, we felt an urge to 'protect' the children from the detrimental health effects of drug consumption. It was not without pain that we came to realize that for any prospect of behavioural change in drug consumption to emerge, the living circumstances of the young 'addicts' themselves needed to change.

Our initial concern may have concealed some of our own value judgements, prejudices and ignorance. We did not differentiate between varied usage of inhalants (moderate, occasional or chronic), and we assumed that every kid who sniffed glue must be an addict. It was only later that we came to observe and understand that many kids used drugs socially and were not drug dependent. We also learned that the alleged negative effects of inhalants in the form of cognitive and personality disorders were far from being conclusive (Jansen et al. 1992). Therefore, it became important not only to be aware of the unique street circumstances that led to glue sniffing, but also to start identifying and discerning differences in usage.

The gap between our own social location and the street kids was even more apparent when reflecting on sexual matters. The street workers felt ill at ease discussing the kids' sexual promiscuity, even though it did not seem to elicit much shame or guilt on the part of the kids. It must have elicited great discomfort among the workers as our discussions – as in the literature – tended to focus on issues of prostitution, paedophilia, sexual abuse and exploitation. This tendency among the street workers resulted, once more, in an overemphasis on the protective dimension, blocking deeper reflection.

Drug abuse and sexual exploitation are commonplace in street culture; however, representing the kids' sexual relationships and use of drugs solely in terms of exploitation and abuse not only excludes other pleasurable aspects, but also confirms the victim label. To accompany the kids in a meaningful way, we needed to identify, recognize and relate to both the victim and the actor in them. Furthermore, the street culture context in which the realities of abuse and exploitation are lived and experienced needed to be borne in mind.

In Egypt, open and public discussion of sexual matters is generally frowned upon, and deviant behaviour is whispered about and severely condemned. However, in private, a rather surprising tolerance is observed among both the affluent and less privileged classes. The two cardinal rules for indulging in unacceptable sexual behaviour, such as premarital, extramarital, homosexual and anal sex, are silence and secrecy. Thus, the challenge for me was to establish enough trust with the street workers for the whispers to become louder and for them to acknowledge painfully the inevitable hypocrisy/paradoxes that often colour mainstream values. That was the prerequisite for embarking on a process of critical analysis not only of the realities and lived experiences of street children, but also of our own.

As stated above, through the dialogical relationship with the street workers, we came to recognize that by referring to the kids' sexual behaviour only in the negative terms of exploitation, abuse and risky behaviour, we were negating any possible pleasure or exploration/ experimentation that might be there as well. The majority of the kids had reached an age at which their sexual maturity and their bodily changes aroused curiosity and the desire to discover and experiment. We also observed that both boys and girls were often involved in sexual relationships that were not necessarily exploitative but had more to do with exploration, intimacy and even love. From our privileged position in the daily lives of the kids, we witnessed the genuine, sincere and intense emotions associated with many of these relationships. This made us think that the absence of parental restraint may have been of positive benefit to the street kids by enabling them to experiment more freely in comparison with kids growing up with the security of parental love and protection.

We also came to understand that the sexual and physical abuse of street kids was not committed by their peers or adults in their milieu as often and as brutally as we had imagined. Instead, the abusers were too often the very same individuals whom society had appointed as their protectors: the various policing agents and their informants (Human Rights Watch 2003). Exploiting the exclusion and voicelessness of the street kids, these abusers committed their acts of abuse quite freely, confident that the kids' voices would be easily muted and never reach a sympathetic ear. We knew that reporting such abuse would not result in any significant change, except for our removal from the scene. Both governmental and non-governmental organizations know about the abuse and exploitation of street children, yet a law of silence prevails: the threat of the counter-accusation of defaming Egypt is too intimidating.

It was perhaps the paedophilic and homosexual relationships which were the most difficult to accept. Struggling with the issues that these relationships raised helped us realize that acceptance of the other in the work of accompaniment did not require accepting or sanctioning just any kind of behaviour. Instead, it meant not suppressing the other's words and experience and being non-judgemental, realistic and capable of facing facts, rather than ignoring them. It also entailed recognizing the right to trial and error. Accepting the other required us to reject the desire to control the other, and to engage instead in a reflexive dialogue that invites the questioning of certain assumptions without inducing feelings of threat or pressure, but empowered by an evolving critical consciousness.

Silent practices

This attitude of recognition and acceptance of 'the other' enabled the gradual incorporation of certain silent practices, especially in relation to reproductive health issues. The children's sexual promiscuity required us both to convey general information and advice about reproductive health and to dare to distribute condoms and take the risk of being severely reprimanded in the event that we were found out. However, the relationships of mutual trust established with the kids prevented the disclosure of this silent practice, even at times of difficult negotiations with street leaders. In other words, there was a moral obligation on both sides not to divulge information that could hurt the other.

Another 'tricky' silent practice was the accompaniment of teens and young adults during their pregnancies in a cultural context where pregnancy outside marriage is so severely condemned that the very life of the female is threatened. The shame that she incurs justifies killing her to eliminate it. Therefore, we were quite alarmed when young women and teenagers became pregnant, even more so when they decided to keep the baby. In addition to our concern that they were putting their lives at risk, we were worried about the difficulties of giving birth and nurturing an infant on the street. With time we were able to identify and develop several rudimentary emergency resources for such situations, including a shelter and a sympathetic gynaecologist who monitored pregnancies until delivery and performed abortions when necessary. However, the burden of nurturing the infant when the mother's own survival was so precarious inevitably led to entrusting the baby to an acquaintance, often with an informal agreement that the mother could not see her newborn again.

We experienced other dramatic situations when newborns had handicaps or were in precarious health. I still recall the sad incident involving Samar. A few weeks after giving birth, Samar came to us one morning at the drop-in centre, holding her newborn tight in her arms. She was looking very worried and told us that she did not know what the matter was – the baby was dead. As she was a single mother with no birth certificate for the infant, it meant that the legal procedure for burial could not be followed. If the mother had gone to a hospital or a police station, she would have been considered a criminal offender, been humiliated and locked up. A couple of leaders hastily decided to take the baby to the hospital. On their way, as they told us later, they realized that they could not come up with a convincing story with respect to the identity of the baby and how they found him. In order to avoid possible legal repercussions, they decided to bury the baby according to tradition.

This incident, like many others, occurred within what might be called the grey zone of practice. Such incidents often took place suddenly and created some shock as well as panic given the uncertainties they evoked and the immediacy of action they required. Witnessing such incidents made us vulnerable from a legal perspective. The burial incident related here reflects a situation of extreme marginality in which the baby had no civic name, i.e. he did not officially exist, and as such no burial permit could be issued. Further compounding the situation was the non-recognition of Samar's status as a single mother.

Some of the kids' silent practices also raised difficult dilemmas.

One example involved Mervat, whom we came to know shortly after she had run away from her village in the governorate of Minia, about 300 kilometres south of Cairo. She was about twelve years old, with white skin and blonde hair (such features are less common in Egypt and highly valued). She was quite witty, as well as good looking, and was successful in gaining our love, care and attention. Despite her age, origin and physical features, all of which made her particularly vulnerable in the street, Mervat managed to extract herself from precarious situations with the least possible damage by relying on her boldness, her capacity for seduction and her unusual survival instincts. In fact, her family situation, as we came to observe later, was quite stable, and her father had complied several times with her wish, expressed to him in a heartbreaking letter, to return home and had come to Cairo to take her back. However, Mervat always ran away again, and even helped her younger brother to do the same.

Mervat wanted to continue her street lifestyle, and it was clear that she had adapted exceptionally well in terms of taking greatest advantage of the free and adventurous aspects of street life, as well as experimenting with a variety of petty jobs usually reserved for boys, such as shoeshining and fire-eating. Mervat was also a convincing liar, displaying the proper emotions and gestures for whatever dramatic situation she was relating, and naturally, she wanted to become an actress.

At the age of sixteen, four years after running away, Mervat was developing into a mature and charming young woman, and in her street career she had managed to become a leader. Acquiring this status was contingent upon her ability to establish that she was not an easy sexual prey for speculating males, and this was no easy task. Unlike some other females, who become leaders by acting tough and hard, inflicting on themselves additional razor cuts, and dressing and behaving like men, Mervat, although she smoked, sniffed, took pills, played karate and worked like the boys, was feminine and quite proud of it. Acting tough in order to survive and establish status was not her strategy. To avoid sexual harassment from males, Mervat managed to establish a tacit pact with two key figures in the street locality where she spent most of her time. These two men, a police informant and a tea-maker, were her friends and, using the clout of the first, they always tried to be the first exploiters of female newcomers to their street locality. The two males had a pact with Mervat whereby she quickly linked up with female newcomers and led them to the den of these two exploiters. In return, Mervat was not only spared the viciousness of these two monsters, they also provided her with protection from other preying males, as well as from police harassment and abuse. This protection, as well as Mervat's attributes, including her ability to read and write, definitely afforded her a privileged status among the leaders.

Mervat's example was one of many that made us realize that, in street culture, values are often paradoxical. For each value, one inevitably finds its very opposite. Group solidarity and intense individualism appear to go hand in hand. Selfless sharing and selfishness are equally widespread. And although tolerance is valued, there is no compunction about betraying a friend in order to avoid problems. Our bewilderment and feeling of unease over these paradoxes were attenuated when one day one of us said, after some reflection, that she would, in all likelihood, deceive her buddies if her own survival were seriously threatened. This made us realize that these paradoxes do not reflect behaviour and characteristics specific to street children. Indeed, they are aspects of human nature.

Violence

While we consciously attempted to implement a democratic family structure – constantly reminding ourselves that the culture of the street possessed its own logic and articulated its own normative value claims – there were times when value clashes caused what seemed like strong and insurmountable emotions. For example, one morning a group of kids arrived at the centre holding Hassan, a young boy around ten or eleven years old, by the arms. Hassan was obviously in great pain and could hardly walk. They told us that Hassan had been forcibly 'taken' by Tarek, an older kid of about fifteen, who also visited the centre. While trying to comfort Hassan and reach the doctor over the phone to ask him to come earlier than usual, the street worker with whom Hassan had a special rapport looked quite disturbed by the situation. A few minutes later, when Tarek walked recklessly into the centre, this street worker grabbed him and proceeded to beat him up. As we watched, with mixed emotions, this physical punishment of 'the monster', and before any of us could intervene, the street worker stopped as suddenly as he had started and walked away.

Later, the street worker told us that he could tolerate deviant behaviour such as homosexuality and paedophilia, but he could not tolerate sexual assaults. Our grappling with the issue inevitably led us to wonder about the psychological repercussions of sexual violence on the victims. Over the eight-year duration of the programme, we came to face several other situations similar to the one experienced by Hassan. The kids told us many other stories about their experiences of being sexually assaulted. It was definitely surprising to us that these kids did not seem to have been particularly 'damaged' by the event. Although they would tell us about such incidents only when enough confidence had been established, observing the ease with which, among themselves, they humiliated each other jokingly over being forcibly taken helped us to contextualize the incidents of sexual assault. We came to understand that one of the very early pieces of advice that newcomers to the street obtain from their peers is a repeated warning to protect themselves against such assaults. However, newcomers also learn that most peers have experienced being taken by force, which is usually marked by a razor cut on the face inflicted by the offender. Despite the obvious cruelty involved in these assaults, we wondered whether the trauma could result in better survival skills. We also wondered whether the fact that there was no shame attached to these public incidents alleviated the emotional and psychological repercussions of the assault. What seemed certain to us was that if kids brought up in a safe and secure family were exposed to this kind of brutality, the lack of awareness of the coming threat and the subsequent alienation that usually follows would make the situation more complicated for them than for street kids. The apparent absence of psychological damage to many street kids who are exposed to sexual assault may, after all, be explained in the words of Hamada, a seasoned kid who, in reply to our bewilderment regarding the frequency of these assaults, told us: 'It's only natural; when you are young you get taken, and when you grow up you take.'

Conclusion

Successfully engaging in the participatory action research project with street kids required workers and researchers to exercise myriad skills. The 'intimate familiarity' developed with the children often involved being implicated in unpredictable situations in which uncertainties and ambiguities gave rise to a large number of difficult ethical issues. From the outset, reflexivity became the mode of survival for the workers in feeling their way through these dilemmas, acquiring and developing their understanding of phenomena and containing the difficult emotions that were produced.

As reflexivity was instituted as a group activity, participants developed the capacity to attend to the lived experience of the other, to consider the viewpoint of the other with respect to oneself, and thereby develop a critical self-consciousness. This developed the capacity for intentional and meaningful activity in a context rife with complexity and difficulty for all concerned.

In 1993, when the PAR reported here was first initiated, officials in the Egyptian Ministry of Insurance and Social Affairs and the Ministry of the Interior did not recognize it as a phenomenon worthy of study or interest. The concern expressed by certain international organizations such as UNICEF and the ILO (International Labour Organization) was trivialized in an apparent attempt to dismiss it altogether. According to the officials, there were only a limited number of children and youth to be found roaming the streets of Cairo; they were well known to security officials and the situation was under control. Many of these officials advised us not to adopt the concerns of *foreign* organizations, which they viewed as intent upon defaming Egypt.

It is interesting to note that at the time the term street children was not used in Egypt in reference to the population in question. Vagrant kids was the most common term used by both the public and officials. The official adoption of the literal Arabic translation of the term street children took place only in 1998 when Suzanne Mubarak, wife of Egypt's then president, used the term in a public address. Following this, it was adopted by the National Council for Childhood and Motherhood (NCCM), which was closely associated with Mrs Mubarak, who used to chair its Advisory Technical Committee. Since then the issue of street children has figured on the NCCM's agenda as one of the most pressing social problems.

With regard to changes at the policy level, the NCCM announced in March 2003, in a spectacular ceremony that received lots of media coverage, a national strategy to 'eradicate' the phenomenon of street children (NCCM 2003). In this strategy, the core of the discourse and recommendations we had developed over the years of PAR with the street kids was adopted: the diversity of the phenomenon and its organic link with street societies, the importance of viewing the kids as active social actors capable of participating in the search for the means to improve their situation, the necessity of establishing drop-in centres and shelters that the kids can voluntarily join, developing training courses to sensitize public servants concerned with the phenomenon, and so on.

Despite the fact the NGO under whose umbrella the PAR was undertaken had a good working relationship with NCCM (with whom we shared our views and analysis of the phenomenon), the council, notwithstanding its influence, did not do much to prevent the dismantling of the association. It was clear that the act of adopting our discourse and recommendations – almost word for word – was one of co-optation. While it is true that the adopted policy appears sophisticated and constitutes a powerful tool for the Egyptian state to use to respond to accusations of maltreating street children (Human Rights Watch 2003), still no efforts to implement it have resulted in any meaningful change. It remains to be seen whether in the post-25 January 'New Egypt' NCCM will be able to act effectively.

Note

1 Street work as a form of social intervention is characterized by a practice of 'immersion' in the living milieus of targeted marginal and marginalized populations in order 'to be with them'. For a full account of this methodology and its historical background, see Chapter 2 in Fahmi (2007).

References

Aptekar, L. (1994) 'Street children in the developing world: a review of their condition', *Cross Cultural Research*, 28(3): 195–224.

Bemak, F. (1996) 'Street researchers: a new paradigm redefining future research with street children', *Childhood*, 3: 147–56.

Bibars, I. (1998) 'Street children in Egypt: from home to the street to inappropriate corrective institutions', *Environment and Urbanization*, 10(1): 201–16.

Cree, V. E., H. Kay and T. Key (2002) 'Research with children: sharing the dilemmas', *Child and Family Social Work*, 7(1): 47–56.

De Moura, S. L. (2002) 'The social construction of street children: configuration and implications', *British Journal of Social Work*, 32: 353–67.

Epstein, I. (1996) 'Educating street children: some cross-cultural perspectives', *Comparative Education*, 32(3).

Fahmi, K. (2007) *Beyond the Victim: The Politics and Ethics of Empower-ing Cairo's Street Children*, New York: American University in Cairo Press.

Finn, J. L. (1994) 'The promise of participatory research', *Journal of Progressive Human Services*, 5(2): 25–42.

Freire, P. (1970) *Pedagogy of the Oppressed*, New York: Herder & Herder.

— (1973) *Education for Critical Consciousness*, New York: Seabury Press.

Gaventa, J. (1993) 'The powerful, the powerless and the experts: knowledge struggle, in an information age', in P. Park (ed.), *Voices of Change: Participatory research in the United States and Canada*, Connecticut: Bergin & Garvey.

Hall, B. L. (1981) 'Participatory research, popular knowledge and power: a personal reflection', *Convergence*, 14(3): 6–17.

Human Rights Watch (2003) 'Charged with being children: Egyptian police's abuse of children in need of protection', *Human Rights Watch*, 15(1), hrwo.org/reports/2003Egypt 2003/eghpto203.pdf.

Jansen, L., R. Richter and R. Griesel (1992) 'Glue sniffing: a comparison study of sniffers and non-sniffers', *Journal of Adolescence*, 15: 29–37.

Leite, L. C. et al. (1991) 'A school for street children in Rio de Janeiro', *Environment and Urbanization*, 3(1).

Lucchini, R. (1996) *Sociologie de la survie: l'enfant dans la rue*, Paris: PUF.

NCCM (National Council for Childhood and Motherhood) (2003) *Strategy for Protecting and Rehabilitating Homeless Children (Street Children) in the Arab Republic of Egypt*, NCCM Project Document, Cairo.

Punch, M. (1986) *The Politics and Ethics of Fieldwork*, Beverly Hills, CA: Sage.

— (1994) 'Politics and ethics in qualitative research', in N. K. Denzin and Y. S. Lincoln (eds), *Handbook of Qualitative Research*, Beverly Hills, CA: Sage.

Schon, D. (1983) *The Reflective Practitioner: How Professionals Think in Action*, New York: Basic Books.

— (1987) *Educating the Reflective Practitioner*, San Francisco, CA: Josey Bass.

— (1995) 'The new scholarship requires a new epistemology', *Change*, 27(6): 27–34.

Selener, D. (1997) *Participatory Action Research and Social Change*, New York: Cornell University Participatory Action Research Network.

UNICEF (1987) 'Paulo Freire and the street educators: an analytical approach, care alternatives for street children', UNICEF Regional Office for Latin America and the Caribbean, Bogotá.

Young, L. and H. Barrett (2001) 'Ethics and participation: reflections on research with street children', *Ethics, Place and Environment*, 4(2): 130–4.

11 | Marginalization and self-marginalization: commercial education and its graduates

MOUSHIRA ELGEZIRI

Introduction

Vocational education was established under Mohamed Ali in order to serve the needs of the burgeoning modern army, but it did not witness real progress until the 1952 revolution. At that time, the new regime decided to accord it special attention to push forward its plans for economic growth and development. A surge was witnessed in the expansion of technical schools with three streams: industrial, agricultural and commercial. In particular, the latter was feminized and closely associated with women's 'natural' leanings towards non-manual office work. Because of its focus on clerical work, commercial education was associated with white-collar public sector employment and promises of social mobility.

In the years following Nasser, technical education deteriorated. President Anwar Sadat's (1970–81) Open Door policy created the conditions for the rise of new social groups and the changing class landscape in favour of the rich and a dual system of education that favoured private education at the expense of public schools. Economic power demonstrated by private tutoring became parents' only way to remedy the deterioration in the quality of education, further disadvantaging the poor. In addition, the decline in public sector employment following the privatization process of the 1990s during the presidency of Hosni Mubarak (1981–2011) meant that holders of commercial diplomas who were typically employed in the government and public sector had no prospects in the labour market. According to the 2006 Egyptian Labour Market Panel Survey (ELMPS), as government employment declined between 1988 and 2006, female participation rates also declined and women who were employed in the government were withdrawing from the labour force (Assaad 2006: 26).

With those socio-economic shifts, successive government education policies continued to neglect technical education and use it only as a way to limit university enrolment (see Richards 1992; Specialized National Councils 1980: 34). Successive governments, however, have been unable to completely dismantle Nasser's socialist policies and could not do away entirely with what came to be known as the gains of the revolution. The result was ambiguous policies that placed graduates of technical schools in a limbo situation. The government of Egypt (GoE) opened university doors to technical school graduates, while making it practically impossible for them to enrol in higher education. The dilemma was further exacerbated by high unemployment among new entrants into the labour market. At the same time, technical education has developed over the years into a low-status type of education associated with economic poverty and limited prospects in the labour market. No serious attempt has been made to address the problems of technical school education and graduates in a radical manner and all reform measures have been haphazard and cosmetic. The overhaul of the education system was deemed a priority after the revolution of 25 January 2011, particularly as it relates to questions of social justice.

This chapter explores how young women from poor families have internalized the changing macro-socio-economic context of education and work. It examines how they make educational decisions and how those decisions ultimately result in reinforcing their marginalization. I argue that decision-making is socially embedded within families and largely reflects the understanding of their sense of limits. First I trace the evolution of technical education from a promising to a marginalized dimension of education provision and how it has grown to be identified with the poor. I then present the results of interviews with female commercial school graduates who 'chose' to follow the commercial school route even when they had the possibility of following the general academic track leading to university.

The 1952 revolution and education

The decision to make education free and compulsory from the ages of six to twelve and to open secondary schools to anyone who completed primary education was taken in 1950, two years before the revolution (Richards and Waterbury 1996: 119). Within this context, technical education became part of the formal secondary school system (Hyde 1978: 2).

It was not until the 'Consciousness Phase', 1956–60, of Nasser's presidency (Ibrahim 1982: 379) that the regime devoted a more concerted effort to enforce equity and redress the long deprivation of disadvantaged groups of basic social services. During this phase education acquired special weight and significance. The regime expanded all levels of schooling, including technical education. It launched a massive school building programme, using the motto 'a school every day', and between 1951 and 1976 primary school enrolment increased by a factor of four (Waterbury 1983: 218).

Nasser's regime emphasized the importance of introducing technical and vocational training in order to meet the country's rising needs for skills and know-how as it moved towards industrialization and modernization. The plan was to bring technical education within the overall plan for the country's development. At the time of the 1952 revolution secondary school students were overwhelmingly in the general academic secondary stream that prepared students for university; just 16 per cent of the approximately 115,000 students then enrolled were in technical schools (Szyliowicz 1973). The main challenge faced by the 1952 revolution was to improve the image of technical education. It took Nasser and his colleagues' intensive discourse to enhance the value of work and instil pride in manual work by asserting the centrality of factories for the country's industrialization. Nasser wanted to dispel the colonial legacy that Egypt's strength lay with its agricultural sector rather than with the development of its industrial base. The regime reiterated its commitment to social justice and people's control over tools of production as well as the need for planning and a vibrant public sector to lead the development process (Hopwood 1982: 138). By 1960 the shift to technical education had begun: just 60 per cent of students were in general secondary education. By the mid-sixties enrolment in technical secondary schools had increased fourfold, more than general academic secondary enrolment, but it was still lower overall than the latter (Faksh 1976: 240). By the late 1960s, as total secondary school enrolment approached 300,000, technical education dominated: fewer than 20 per cent of all secondary students were then in the general academic branch (Antoninis 2001; Szyliowicz 1973).

For women, until the early sixties, domestic roles influenced their education. The 'female cultural schools' that targeted girls before the 1952 revolution with their emphasis on learning of 'domestic work with the maximum of economy and good taste, and along up-to-date lines' (Boktor 1963: 63) continued to attract women while boys were increasingly encouraged to choose from a variety of educational institutions (Hyde 1978).[1] Gradually, however, within the climate that emphasized the need for public mobilization to respond to the exigencies of nation-building, women were equally required to take part in the new national project of industrialization and economic development, while not neglecting their primary task of looking after their families.

By the early 1960s the revolution was concerned with changing people's attitude towards girls' education. In 1953 only seventy-four girls were in commercial education and none in the other two technical streams (Abou Zeid 1970: 32). Gradually girls began to enrol in industrial schools. This started in 1959/60 with a modest number of 23 girl students rising to 810 in 1964 and to 13,661 in 1979 (Metwalli 1989: 114). Girls enrolled in a limited range of specializations that were regarded as fitting women's nature and aptitude, such as fine mechanics, electronics, beautification and leather manufacturing (ibid.: 91–3). Their enrolment in agricultural schools took place much later in 1976/77, with 616 students, rising to 4,869 in 1978/79 (ibid.: 222; Sanyal et al. 1982: 214).

Girls also entered commercial schools. Their number rose from 819 in 1955/56 to 10,000 in 1961/62 (Boktor 1963: 6), and while in the same year the number of girls attending female cultural secondary schools was five times more than those in commercial secondary schools, by 1961/62 their number in the latter schools was one and a half times more than in the former (ibid.). By 1968/69 the number of girls in commercial education was drawing closer to the number of boys: 49.8 per cent of pupils were boys, 50.2 per cent girls (Metwalli 1989: 166). By 1977/78 girls outnumbered boys in commercial education (at 51 per cent) and they soon established the tradition of forming a majority in commercial schools (Sanyal et al. 1982: 214).

The five-year plan (1960–65) led to an increase in industrial production and the introduction of a number of important new industries, including iron and steel, rubber and pharmaceuticals. These boosted work opportunities. On the agricultural front land reclamation and development projects, and the imminent expansion of cultivable land resulting from completion of the High Dam, provided additional employment for university and technical school graduates (Institute of National Planning 1963: 33–4). Work opportunities were abundant for graduates of industrial and agricultural schools; they were absorbed in the new factories and agricultural centres, and worked within the scope of their specialization, which was often not the case before the revolution. By 1959 only 5.7 per cent and 5.6 per cent of the graduates of the two technical streams, respectively, were reported unemployed (Boktor 1963: 65). As for graduates of commercial schools, only 4.9 per cent were unemployed. Areas of their employment included accountancy (40.1 per cent), clerical work (24.7 per cent) and commerce (5 per cent). The rest were in miscellaneous jobs (ibid.: 66). Female Cultural Schools for Women gradually lost appeal and were phased out. The majority of their graduates became housewives, fulfilling the expectations of this particular type of education: to prepare educated homemakers (ibid.: 65–6).

In the years following the revolution, the regime had considerably expanded the middle class and created demand for the new education institutions. For the deprived and marginal groups before the revolution, particularly the rural poor, education in its entirety became associated with the status of and opportunities for social mobility. The state played an active role in raising people's social expectations when in 1963 it launched an employment scheme that guaranteed a job for all university and technical school graduates in the government bureaucracy.

The earlier cohorts of men and women who joined technical schools after the 1952 revolution and were then employed in the public sector were children of the families that were the early beneficiaries of the socialist decrees. Most of their parents had migrated from the rural areas in search of a livelihood and pursued the hope of securing work opportunities in the wake of the drive for industrialization in 1960–65. As education became free and could lead to employment, these families wanted to give their children an education opening up the opportunity for clerical work. Upward educational mobility indeed took place and reached its apogee from the mid-fifties till the early sixties, the height of the revolutionary phase.

Problems of education: marginality and inequality

Nasser's state-led import substitution industrialization provided Egypt with significant industrial infrastructure, but there were serious problems with the performance of the public sector. It had been used to absorb the increasing numbers of graduates and to provide subsidized commodities. The pressure to deliver on both these state demands slowed the pace of industrialization and the government failed to launch the second five-year plan of 1965/66–1969/70 (Hinnebusch 2003: 220). This failure, among other things, jeopardized the position of the large subordinate segments of the low-level state-salaried employees. They had the largest stake in the regime's plans for economic and industrial growth. They were lifted by the state from the bottom ranks of the market to the bottom rank of the bureaucratic hierarchy, and they were also the main losers in the stalled modernization project.

Nasser's redistributive policies were soon challenged as the population rose from close to twenty million in 1951 to over thirty million in 1970 (CAPMAS 2000). Schools could not keep pace with the increase in the number of pupils; they began to operate a two-shift system and quality of education deteriorated (Williamson 1987: 126). Those of the country's meagre resources earmarked for services like education were swamped by population growth and most of the resources were expended on the salaries of the people who operated educational facilities.

After Nasser's death in 1970 Anwar Sadat turned Egypt towards the West in a policy of liberalization known as the Open Door policy (*Infitah*). The opening up implied a reconfiguration of state policy away from Nasser's concerns with improving the living conditions of the poor towards the interests of the rich. The latter included landed interests, the bureaucratic bourgeoisie of the sixties and the commercial bourgeoisie of *Infitah*, who engaged in financial activities, contracting, import and export and wholesale trading (Imam 1985: 261–71). Within this context, education was gradually transformed into a tool of social distinction and closure which undermined the principles of social justice that had characterized it since the 1952 revolution (see Abdel-Fadil 1980).

A dual system: private and public education The first set of pressures on the education system manifested themselves around the launch of the Open Door policy in 1973. This was also the time when discussions took place about establishing the first private university in Egypt (Ayubi 1980: 407). Private universities were deemed necessary to meet the demand of graduates of private schools with foreign language instruction and better-quality education. Also in the early 1970s, education became a main promoter of socio-economic advancement and government employment. It became more accessible to children of the privileged classes and less to individuals from lower social strata. By the end of the sixties only about a tenth of university students were children of workers and peasants, who represented over 82 per cent of the population. In contrast, over 85 per cent of the students were children of professionals and white-collar Egyptians, who constituted only about 15 per cent of the population (ibid.: 417).

Successive governments encouraged private investment in education to meet the demands of returnees from the Gulf countries, among other middle-class groups, who came back home in the wake of the first Gulf War in 1991. Middle-class families became dismayed by crowded schools and their demand to give their children an educational edge spurred businessmen to produce model schools that combined modernity and criticality of foreign school curricula with the authenticity of Islamic and Arab culture.[2] The result was a gamut of public and private schools.

Many layers of education institutions emerged which catered to differ-ent socio-economic levels.[3] Public schools have seriously deteriorated because of poor resources, overcrowding and obsolete curricula. Down in the hierarchy were technical schools.

Law no. 101 of 1992 allowed the establishment of private fee-paying universities (Ammar 2005). The number of private universities mush-roomed, reaching seventeen by 2007.[4] While there has still been a commitment, *de jure*, to the principle of free education in public universities, the last thirty years has witnessed a surge of fee-paying foreign language departments in public universities. This has created distinctions not only between fee-paying private universities and free public institutions, but also within the latter.

Private tutoring Private tutoring is an area where inequalities are most flagrant. After the compulsory primary stage, continuing in higher levels of education is contingent upon obtaining high scores. Sheer demographic pressures and poor pedagogic resources have played a significant role in the proliferation of private lessons to allow students to obtain the necessary grades to progress in the system. Overcrowded classrooms and multiple shift systems have resulted in an extremely short school day of about three hours and a lesson time of less than half an hour in some schools. Parents have resorted to private lessons to make up for the deficient system at school.

Since the 1990s private tutoring has become pervasive. It represents the largest household education expense (ETF and World Bank 2005: 26) and may account for 25 per cent of family annual income where children are in secondary education (Assaad and Elbadawy 2007: 3). The importance of families being able to mobilize financial resources increases as students approach the general secondary stage. The three-year secondary school stage climaxes in the general secondary national examinations (*Thanaweya Amma*). The score in these exams determines entry into higher education and the specific faculties in which students can study. As expected, students from the highest wealth quintiles are much more likely than poorer students to receive private lessons. In urban areas the average tutoring expenditures among the richest are five times more than among the poorest (ibid.: 11–14).

Private tutoring is *de jure* an illegal phenomenon but is widely prac-tised. It takes place in both private and public schools and is often offered by the schoolteachers themselves. Whereas in the former it is largely determined by the high income of middle-class parents and reflects their keenness to provide their children with a competitive advantage, in the latter it is mostly used as a remedial measure to make up for the poor quality of education and the lack of interaction between teachers and students in the classrooms.

Private lessons are also used to pacify teachers who, in their endeavour to augment their low salaries, pressurize (and sometimes blackmail) students to take private lessons with them, at the risk of otherwise failing. In a survey of public preparatory schools published in 2000, almost 60 per cent of the students felt teachers treated them differentially, with 25 per cent attributing this treatment to whether or not they took private lessons with them (El-Tawila et al. 2001: xvi). Rates for private lessons varied according to, among other things, the type of school, teachers' competence and status and the teacher's judgement of the economic standing of the student's family. Private lessons ensure a smooth transition in the educational system both in terms of passing the exams and moving up in the system, but they impact negatively on learning. As students rely on private lessons, they do not feel the need to attend school regularly. And teachers do not give due attention to classroom instruction since the subject matter will be taught privately. The result is that students' actual educational performance and attainment may not improve and they may ultimately end up repeating school years at later stages (Birdsall and O'Connell 1999).

School drop-out Many children drop out of school, often before completing primary education (Langsten and Hassan 2009), though the drop-out rate has improved. During the period from 1963/64 to 1969/70 the drop-out rate ranged between 19.4 per cent and 23 per cent (Abdel-Fadil 1982: 355). In 2010, despite diligent government efforts to improve school enrolment and retention, 8.5 per cent of young people aged eighteen to twenty-one dropped out of school before completing compulsory education, and 5.1 per cent dropped out at later stages (Population Council 2011). Similar to its role in private tutoring, wealth plays an important role in determining school drop-out rates across all levels of schooling. Students from poor households are at least three times more likely to drop out at the end of the primary and preparatory schools than students from rich households (Suliman and El-Kogali 2001; World Bank 2002).

The enrolment of girls and their drop-out rates are claimed to be gender-related. Some attribute it to the preference for male siblings in case poor families cannot afford to send all their children to school (Sultana 2008). Others claim that as girls reach puberty their mobility, including going to school, may be restricted (Ibrahim and Wassef 2000;

Mensch et al. 2003). Costs associated with travelling to school are particularly important, and these can also jeopardize girls' education chances as opposed to boys'. The demand for them to do domestic chores also jeopardizes girls' schooling (Assaad et al. 2010). Finally, the labour market, and particularly the private sector, discourages female employment owing to its non-conducive work environment and salary scales that are more favourable to men (Assaad and Arntz 2005).

Technical education: the 'choice' of the poor If poor households manage to resist withdrawing their children from schools at the early primary and preparatory stages to send them to the labour market, they reach another decision-making point at the end of the preparatory stage. This is when many parents 'opt' to send their children to technical schools.

Branching to general secondary school (leading to university) or to commercial, agricultural and industrial technical education (which theoretically offers the chance to go to university and higher institutes), takes place at the end of the three-year preparatory (middle) school (see Figure 11.1). Qualification is mainly a function of scores in the last year of preparatory school, with those who obtain high grades going to general academic secondary and others with low grades channelled into technical education.

The determinants of drop-out rates for pupils are complex (Assaad et al. 2009). A range of factors may be responsible for such a decision. These are financial, the student's learning abilities, school environment, access to infrastructure and services, influence of teachers, and relationship with peers (see El-Tawila et al. 1999). Boudon (1974) does not see individuals governed by the 'primary effects' of their families' financial situation and class culture throughout their school years. Rather, he sees educational trajectories as a sequence of events. At their early stages of education, children are influenced by primary effects which may affect their performance, but not their aspirations. At later stages, at branching points, secondary effects come into play when rational choices are made on the basis of parent and student evaluations of benefits and costs and constraints and chances of success; students make different choices appropriate to their class positions. The poor are concerned about calculating the costs of university education versus the expected social and monetary returns (Becker and Hecken 2009). Thus, they may opt for technical or vocational education or an apprenticeship with direct access to the labour market rather than a more theoretical university education and the uncertain prospects of white-collar employment (ibid.).

11.1 The structure of the education system in Egypt (*source*: Ministry of Education 2006)

At decisive branching points, poor Egyptian families make their own calculations giving primary consideration to the availability of financial resources. As indicated above, for Egyptian families children's progress in the educational system is not guaranteed without private lessons, which is a large extra financial burden. Decisions will also depend on the impact families expect education to have on their child's life and the entire household. For many poor families a child in school is a lost opportunity for income generation for the entire family. I argue that the primary effects of the family, in terms of the material and financial resources it makes available to children, are important in decision-making. Equally important, however, is family habitus, which internalizes class culture and mediates between individuals and their social worlds (Bourdieu 1977). Family habitus continues to play an important role beyond the early stages of education and is central to understanding how decisions are made at branching points. Many of the problems of technical education are not strictly unique to this stream. Obsolete curricula, poor-quality education, the stress on memorization and rote learning, authoritarianism and lack of interaction in the classroom, ailing structures and high-density classrooms are typical of the Egyptian public educational system, both general and technical streams. As alluded to above, what mainly distinguishes technical education from other types is its association with the poor.

Earlier work has shown that the wealth differential for the transition into secondary education is small (Langsten and Hassan 2009). This is confirmed by the modest difference between the poor and the wealthy in the number of those who complete preparatory school and who fail to enter secondary education (Table 11.1, column 3). This cannot, however, be interpreted as reflecting socio-economic equality in the transition into secondary school. Inequality is maintained by tracking poorer students into technical secondary, while wealthier students overwhelmingly go to general secondary (Table 11.1, columns 4 and 5).

Regulations of the education system have reinforced inequalities. Once they have followed the technical education route, young people find themselves in a cul-de-sac, with few opportunities to grow and advance socially and professionally. Technical education provides no option for its students to change from the technical to the general stream, although the opposite is possible, i.e. general secondary students can always switch to technical education. When they fail and use up their chances to repeat a general secondary school year, general secondary students have the option to 'change paths' (*tahweel massar*), almost always to the commercial stream. The social bias and inequality

TABLE 11.1 Preparatory completion and type of secondary school attended (among those who have completed preparatory); young people, 15–19 years of age, 2006 (percentage distribution)

Wealth quintile	Completed prep.	Sample size	Secondary school attended			Total	Sample size
			None	Tech.	General		
Poorest	44.9	972	6.9	68.5	24.6	100.0	435
2nd	60.5	894	5.6	58.9	35.6	100.0	540
Middle	65.3	816	3.8	58.0	38.3	100.0	533
4th	78.4	638	3.2	44.0	52.8	100.0	500
Richest	87.4	809	1.3	23.4	75.4	100.0	706
All	65.8	4,129	3.9	48.3	47.9	100.0	2,714

Source: ELMPS, 2006 (author's calculations)

TABLE 11.2 Type of technical secondary school attended by year (percentage distribution)

Programme	1991–92	1995–96	1999–2000
Agriculture	12.2	10.2	10.0
Industrial	45.1	45.2	44.7
Commercial	42.7	44.6	45.3
Total	100.0	100.0	100.0
Sample size	(391,717)	(556,014)	(656,167)

Source: 'Statistics of pre-university education years 1991, 1996, 2000', Ministry of Education (2006: 105)

implications of such regulations are obvious: technical school students can experiment only with their own stream.

Technical secondary education has expanded since 2000. Its growth has been more significant than the expansion in general academic secondary education. Even as the balance in secondary school enrolment began to shift back towards general secondary, in the late 1990s technical students still constituted about 65–70 per cent of all those enrolled in secondary school (Antoninis 2001; NCERD 2001).

In the 2005/06 school year, with almost 3.5 million students in all types of secondary education, technical education students constituted 56 per cent of all secondary school students, while public general secondary school students represented 33 per cent, Al Azhar religious education 8 per cent[5] and private general secondary 3 per cent (Ministry of Education 2006: 273). Paradoxically, at the height of the labour

TABLE 11.3 Type of technical secondary school programme attended, by gender, 2005/06 (percentage distribution)

Programme	Boys	Girls	Total	Sample size
Industrial	62.3	37.7	100.0	992,057
Agricultural	77.1	22.9	100.0	223,386
Commercial	33.8	66.2	100.0	745,719

Source: 'Statistics of pre-university education years 1991, 1996, 2000', Ministry of Education (2006: 105)

market problems and the decline of the public sector, enrolment in commercial education continued (Table 11.1), with girls forming the majority of its students (Table 11.2).

The beginning of the crisis: who pays the price?

The expansion of university education and job guarantees for university graduates dramatically increased demand on higher education. Provincial universities were opened between 1970 and 1979 to meet the increased demand (Cochran 1986: 71), which rose from 191,483 students in 1971 to 660,357 students in 1984 (Richards 1992: 27). Free university education also meant that despite inducements and propaganda to improve the image and emphasize the importance of technical education, families still preferred a general rather than any other type of secondary education for their children that would lead to university (Fahmy 1973, in Hyde 1978: 93).

By the late 1960s, and even though university had benefited some of the disadvantaged groups, the poor were increasingly aware that

TABLE 11.4 Type of higher education attended by type of secondary completed, age 25–29, 2006 (percentage distribution)

Higher education attended	Secondary completed		Total
	General	Technical	
None	3.9	89.3	57.8
Institutes	7.8	7.0	7.3
University	88.3	3.8	35.0
Total	100.0	100.0	100.0
Sample size	805	1,378	2,183

Source: ELMPS, 2006 (author's calculations)

university was not for them (Ayubi 1980). For poor families education was not free as once promised. Private lessons to improve academic performance and ensure good grades in school leaving exams were mainly a function of economic power and financial means. Gradually, technical education, which prepared students for the labour market, was recognized as more suitable for the poor. In fact it became an appealing destination. The employment guarantee scheme, effectively enforced till the mid-1980s, also applied to graduates of technical schools, and a tradition had been established that graduates of technical education could earn the respect and income of employment in the public sector and join the middle-class salariat. Moreover, a diploma from a technical school certified completion of twelve years of education even if it did not lead to university.

Technical secondary education was looked upon by the GoE as a way of easing the stampede to universities, to limit the number of university graduates and control unemployment. In 1984 a fundamental policy decision was taken to reduce university enrolment. For several years enrolment fell by about 3 per cent per annum. By 1989 the total number of universitystudents had been reduced by nearly 100,000, a decline of some 14 per cent (Richards 1992: 19). This coincided with a reduction in economic growth and unemployment among the university educated rose to 9.2 per cent in 1986 from 6.7 per cent in 1976 and 3.1 per cent in 1960 (Fathi 1991: 117). Moreover, Law no. 139 of 1981 for technical education tried to streamline technical education to cope with the demands of the Open Door policy. The main intention, however, was to prepare it to absorb 70 per cent of secondary school pupils in the 1980s. The main brunt was borne by the commercial schools, which alone were responsible for hosting 60 per cent of the graduates of preparatory schools (Specialized National Councils 1980: 34).

It was clear that the plan for commercial schools to absorb excess students was not drawn up in response to any real demands in the labour market. With the drying up of clerical job opportunities in the public sector and the failure of the Open Door policy to generate sufficient work opportunities for young graduates in the 1980s, graduates of commercial schools were the main losers; there was clearly no need for additional graduates from that stream.

The decision to continue to channel students into commercial schools was taken on pragmatic grounds. Unlike for industrial and agricultural schools, the equipment of commercial schools did not entail the high costs of setting up workshops and laboratories and supplying them with expensive machinery and tools. Moreover, among the three streams of technical education, commercial schools accepted students with the lowest scores.[6] Thus, decision-makers, including governors, felt they had more freedom to use technical education to respond to emerging public needs. With increased decentralization, governors had more autonomy to decide areas of priority, and with the availability of commercial education, they had a flexible and inexpensive facility to fulfil the aspirations of poor families to provide their children with the right level of education for government employment. Governors used their discretionary powers to open new classrooms and even set up new specializations, such as 'commercial services', to absorb incoming students and appease public demand (Metwalli 1989: 171; Specialized National Councils 1980: 35). Educators and labour market observers nevertheless questioned whether there was any real need for commercial education in the context of the general slump in the economy. They wondered whether it was not time to close this stream altogether. Universities had already produced large numbers of graduates from the faculty of commerce – the same specialization as the commercial technical schools – who were job hunting and certainly had more opportunities in the market than graduates of technical schools. However, the situation remained unchanged and no steps were taken at that time to modify commercial education for fear of unfavourable public reaction.

Chronic problems of technical education

The persistent paradox of technical education is that although the system generated large numbers of graduates, there were shortages in skilled labour and specific specializations. By the mid-1960s there was debate about the mismatch between the skills of technical school graduates and the needs of the labour market, a problem that has continued to impact educational and employment policy planning (Szyliowicz 1973: 269; see also Galal 2002: 6–7).

In contemporary Egypt technical school students have two possible avenues for higher education. The first is to enrol in some branches of public universities or seek admission to the Open University. The second is to join middle and higher institutes. However, according to Table 11.3, neither of the two options offers genuine possibilities for educational advancement for young people. While the majority of students (88.3 per cent) who finish general secondary schools make their way to university, almost exactly the same percentage of students who went to technical schools stop at this level with only 3.8 per cent going on to university. At the same time, there is virtually no demand on middle and higher institutes from either general or technical school students (only 7.8 per cent and 7.0 per cent respectively).

But what are the options for students in the technical stream and why, despite their availability, has technical education remained a terminal degree with its graduates not going on to university?

Middle and higher institutes To reduce the pressure on university education, in 1957 the GoE started to establish middle and higher institutes to provide training for technical school graduates. These were in various professional fields, including fine arts, music, agriculture, commerce and industry. In 1971 a large number of higher institutes was introduced to complement the technical schools and accommodate increased student enrolment. Middle and higher institutes had about 21,000 students in 1973, increasing fivefold to about 105,000 in 1989 (Richards 1992). The total continued to grow, though at a slower pace, to about 164,000 students in 2006/07 (Hozayin 2007).[7]

These institutes were originally designed to provide specialized, practical training in areas that were not covered by the universities. Missions had been sent to European countries within which students completed a year of fieldwork, and more than four thousand students benefited from that scheme between 1956 and 1964 (Szyliowicz 1973: 285). However, institutes were subsequently criticized on the grounds that their expansion had serious implications for the quality of what they had to offer. As with technical schools, their increased emphasis on specific rather than general skills weakened the chances of their graduates in the labour market. They soon lost their edge of providing practical training as they were skewed towards theoretical education. The distinction between the institutes and the regular universities gradually disappeared. Students complained that institutes did not upgrade their knowledge and did not provide anything more than what they had already acquired in their technical secondary schools. They stated that they received a 'second class' education in those institutes (Richards 1992: 12).

University Technical school graduates have two options for higher education. The first is through regular enrolment in university. In the technical school leaving exam, if students obtain scores ranging between 70 and 75 per cent, they are allowed to enrol in the less prestigious university faculties (such as Arts and Commerce). With the more auspicious faculties – such as engineering for industrial school students – an accreditation examination is required based on

TABLE 11.5 Type of higher education attended by type of secondary school completed and wealth quintiles, young people, age 19–23, 2006 (percentage distribution)

Wealth quintile	Upper intermediate	University	None	Total	All
TECHNICAL					
Poorest	1.5	0.4	98.2	100.1	274
2nd	3.2	0.0	96.8	100.0	378
Middle	4.6	1.4	94.0	100.0	416
4th	6.9	3.4	89.7	100.0	320
Richest	12.2	8.0	79.7	99.9	237
Total	5.3	2.3	92.4	100.0	1,625
GENERAL					
Poorest	10.3	74.1	15.5	99.9	58
2nd	16.2	76.6	7.1	99.9	154
Middle	15.4	76.3	8.3	100.0	169
4th	17.6	78.2	4.2	100.0	307
Richest	8.2	90.1	1.7	100.0	575
Total	12.5	83.0	4.5	100.0	1,263

Source: ELMPS, 2006 (author's calculations)

additional curricula and study. The other option is the Open University, which was introduced in different branches of current Egyptian universities between 1990 and 1991 (Heggy 1991). It mainly targets graduates of technical secondary schools and others who obtain low grades from general secondary schools. The Open University offers a flexible system of study, requiring only one day of attendance during the weekend. The fees amount to an average of LE1,400–1,800 (US$254–327) yearly.[8] The only caveat is that five years must elapse after leaving secondary school for one to enrol in university.

The fact is that very few technical school graduates enrol in any type of higher education, as Table 11.4 underscores. Those figures challenge the two main assumptions underpinning the rationale behind the Open University: the first is that graduates of technical schools find work within five years after leaving school, and the second that the work they find is lucrative enough that they can afford to pay for university tuition.

University enrolment by wealth quintiles further illuminates the association between technical education as a terminal degree and poverty. Table 11.5 shows that the overwhelming majority of technical school students in the poorest quintile stop after obtaining their secondary diploma. Only as we move gradually to higher wealth quintiles do students start going to university and higher institutes, although in modest numbers. On the other hand, the opposite is true in the case of general academic students. Interestingly, we should note that the general academic track invariably leads to university for both poor and rich students.

Recent developments

Based on advice from the World Bank in the 1990s, the Egyptian government opted for a long-term slow process of change to create a balance between general and technical education (50/50 enrolment). This was to be achieved mainly by converting commercial schools into general secondary schools, moving towards the total elimination of commercial schools (Ministry of Education 2006: Annex 2, p. 101). The process was reported to have met with public resentment. Commercial education has always been considered the lowest threshold of education that was relatively inexpensive and did not require private tutoring. As a result of public resistance, the government had to interrupt the process without meeting the target. Out of a total target of 315 schools only 201 schools had been transformed up to 2003/04 (ibid.: Annex 2, p. 102). Until any radical change takes place, some cosmetic modifications, including new teaching technologies and multimedia, are reported to have been introduced in core curricula for both the general and technical tracks (Megahed 2002).

By 2001 nearly half the public sector firms had been sold off with a consequent increase in unemployment (Hinnebusch 2003: 220). Despite the momentum given to the formal private sector and some noticeable growth (7.4 per cent per annum in urban areas and 8.7 per cent in rural areas in 2006; Assaad 2007: 21), it has not been able to meet rising employment demands. The continued decline of public sector employment has coincided with the rise of the informal sector. Public sector employment dropped to 25 per cent in 1998 from 60–70 per cent in the 1970s; the proportion of new entrants in the labour market whose first job was informal rose from less than 20 per cent in the 1970s to 60 per cent in the 1990s (Radwan 2007: 42). At the same time, the share of public sector employment fell from nearly 100 per cent in the mid-1970s to less than 20 per cent in the early years of the millennium (Amer 2009: 210). The informal sector[9] constitutes 55 per cent of the Egyptian labour force (World Bank 2003: 81), and has been unable to generate 'decent work' for the young, the majority of whom are graduates of technical schools who undertake survival activities (Radwan 2007). More worrying is that informality has not been a temporary situation: 95 per cent of those who were employed in informal jobs in 1990 were still in informal jobs in 1998 (Mokhtar and Wahba 2002, cited in World Bank 2003: 83).

Why go to university? In 2007 I conducted qualitative research with eighty-five women who had graduated from commercial schools. Thirty-five of the women were between the ages of forty-one and sixty and had been employed in the public sector. Fifty of the women were between twenty and forty, mainly engaged in the informal sector. The investigation explored the education decision-making process among the younger women. In examining their education decisions, I tried to grasp the pattern of socio-structural dynamics that shaped those decisions (Bertaux and Bertaux-Wiame 1981: 37).

Some students who achieved low scores in the preparatory school leaving exam did not aspire to qualify for general secondary. For them, conditions made the prospect of general secondary undesirable or impossible. In some cases, the scores were so continuously poor that following the technical track was the only choice. Behind this choice, however, lie a number of factors, including poor financial means, personal abilities and a discouraging school environment.

Yet some students had fared well in both primary and preparatory school and had the option to go into general secondary education, the formal route to university, but despite this possibility, they decided not to follow that option. Given their financial means, families had made it clear to children that education was an available option if they wanted but it had to be within their financial means and not constitute an additional burden on them. Children often interpreted this caveat as an invitation to apply their sense of justice and choose equality with their siblings.

Those who had the choice

EQUALITY AND IMPLICIT UNDERSTANDING Children had a moral responsibility towards their families, particularly as they went through periods of difficulty. In situations of economic crisis, for example, the uncertain path of general secondary and university education, or any procrastination that delayed entry into the labour market, was implicitly and explicitly rejected. The thought of pursuing education or other individual projects was seen to have been selfish. In particular young men felt it was their 'natural' responsibility as men to support their families. They realized that any delay in earning money was a threat to the entire family that they could not afford.

Family responsibilities did not discriminate between male and female children. Some women were aware that they had good potential and that opportunities might be lost if they devoted themselves to family responsibilities. Yet there was generally no bitterness, rather a sense of oneness fuelled by a common understanding that they – men and women – collectively faced a disadvantaged situation. Women insisted that it was not male indolence or procrastination in trying to improve their lot which caused their financial problems, but rather ferocious realities beyond their control. To that extent, young women were ready to use all the possibilities their education afforded them to rescue a family business from going bankrupt, for example. That often meant not only postponing education plans but also marriage.

In some families, both male and female children forsook their education and worked together to save the household. When Asma's (thirty-two) father died prematurely at the age of thirty-eight, he left a carpentry workshop and eight children: three boys and five girls. His eldest daughter was only fourteen and the youngest son six months. The family tried to get workers to run the shop but did not succeed, and they were losing money. Eventually they sold the workshop. The eldest daughter, who was in the preparatory stage when her father died, gave up her education and worked in a garment factory. She was soon joined by another sister. Now that his sisters had taken that step, the oldest among the boys felt it was also his responsibility as a man to support his family, so he too dropped out of school. Family responsibilities were daunting. Asma's mother had to send one of her daughters to live with her paternal aunts in Alexandria.

As the five older siblings now brought home income from their various jobs, the four younger children, including Asma, were able to complete their education. Asma was a good student and had plans to study law at university. She qualified to enter the general track, but instead decided to take the commercial diploma route, to the dismay of her teachers, who had high hopes for her. 'Mother was very pleased at our success and diligence. I don't remember that she ever had to tell us to study or do our work. I used to come home after school and do house chores with my younger sister and sometimes my younger brother also helped.' In this and many other cases, the choice of the technical track was derived from moral obligations towards the family and the need for equality among siblings. There were many other cases like this.

DISABLING CHOICE: CLASS AND GENDER INSECURITIES At the end of the preparatory stage parents have to demonstrate their readiness to support their children's educational journey. This pledge is necessary as preparations for the general secondary exams require not only special financial arrangements for private tutoring, but more importantly a statement on the part of the entire family that they are psychologically ready to go through this onerous and tense process. As students prepare for the transition into preparatory school, their fear of general secondary education mounts and, even when they qualify for it, they hesitate and eventually decline the opportunity. Nagah (twenty-seven) describes her family's feelings towards the general secondary stream: 'My family wanted me to go to general secondary. But they said it was very tough and needed hard work and a lot of study. We heard in the papers that students commit suicide. I didn't want to go through a depression or have a mental breakdown. It was much easier to go into technical education.'

None of the family, including the young women, had confidence that they were fit for and could successfully go through the general academic education process. Many women associated studying for general secondary with sickness. Mariam (twenty-eight) described her intense preparations for the exams and then her later disappointment when she still could not obtain the qualifying scores for general secondary. Most respondents described at length their fear of specific academic subjects, particularly foreign languages. Their struggle with particular curricula had a strong impact on their choice to take an easier route. Two points became important here. The first was the fear of the English language that was shared by most siblings in the same family.

Respondents noted that learning foreign languages was technically and pedagogically difficult mainly because it was not in their 'social sphere' and was not used within their circle of acquaintances. There was a sense of collective helplessness and lack of intellectual and other cognitive resources to deal with such problems.

The second important point that emerged was that it was common for students to switch from general to commercial education in a procedure known as *tahweel massar* (changing paths). Some participants claimed that in their schools as many as five out of nine classes shifted from the general to the commercial track. Students would enter the general secondary stream, try it for a while, find it difficult and leave it to transfer to the easier commercial track.

Once they shifted to commercial education, women fared well. Not only was the curriculum much easier but the entire atmosphere was more relaxed and less competitive. For a while, they also enjoyed preferential treatment from teachers as their very acceptance into general secondary education was proof of their privilege. Unlike others who were forced to pursue the technical track, they – at least – had the choice to try general secondary.

Yet even this alleged privilege was used by some school managements to put them down and ridicule them. Young women who changed from general to commercial tracks posed administrative problems for school staff as it meant that they had to find them places in schools that were already full. Instead of celebrating the fact that 'brighter' students were joining the commercial track, the girls were rebuked for not realizing earlier that they were not good enough for academic secondary. A school principal was reported as telling one of these girls: 'Why be arrogant and insist on general secondary when you know that you would not be able to cope with it? Why not choose the easy road from the beginning?'

The labour market and university education

For students who had no choice and those who did alike, there were negative feelings about the kind and quality of education they would get in commercial schools. They were aware it did not give them an edge in the labour market. Many students realized that commercial education was 'just one level above illiteracy eradication', and their degrees would be 'just a piece of paper'. But there was also a general understanding that rampant unemployment has left its mark on everyone, including university graduates. This served to 'reassure' students that they were not the only ones to suffer.

The daunting experience of siblings and others who had university degrees in finding work was often referred to in women's narratives. Nonetheless, once admitted into the commercial school several participants believed the commercial diploma was a solution to a temporarily disadvantaged situation. They were hopeful that eventually things would improve and they would be able to enrol in university. Some of them worked hard to obtain university qualifying scores while others did not even try. The Open University option remained elusive. At the same time, the majority of participants had misgivings about the value of continuing education in higher institutes. In their opinion, they were not much different from the technical schools they attended.

Conclusion

There is no doubt that the 1952 regime had an egalitarian vision in which education played a central role. The expansion of education benefited some of the disadvantaged groups. In the years immediately following the 1952 revolution many more girls and boys from poor backgrounds were enrolled in schools and institutes of higher learning in marked contrast to their families. Technical education provided the state with the possibility of driving industrialization and development and imposing a new image of a modern society in which individuals acquired their status from their work and their contribution to societal progress. The vision held true for a short period of time when the economy performed well and when educated individuals had access to jobs in public sector companies and factories. But once this arrangement became unsustainable, things fell apart.

The state attempted to enhance the image of technical education but with limited success. It failed to eliminate social polarization, status barriers and the manual/non-manual divide. At the same time, the quality of education offered at technical schools and the poor output it produced did not enhance its public image. Successive governments failed to present the technical stream as a viable and important alternative to academic education. In this sense technical education reflected the ebb and flow of Egypt's modernization project.

Very few technical school graduates go to university. Government policies have reinforced this trend by virtually closing this door to them. Those who go to technical secondary schools continue to be disproportionately poor (World Bank 2007). Technical education is now offered, not for educational or professional reasons, but rather on social and political grounds – to ease the burden on higher education and as a safety net to ensure at the same time that those who have been deprived of entry into university are not out on the streets (Gill and Heynemann 2000: 402–3). Within this bleak picture, commercial education, with a majority of female students, has grown to be particularly vulnerable over the years. Despite this realization, some women joined the commercial track, even when they had the choice to follow the general track. This chapter has explored how self-marginalization took place.

Educational decisions are a function of disadvantaged contexts and are not separate from the structure within which they are exercised; rather they are derived from women's definition and understanding of their families' collective disadvantage. Women internalize their structural constraints and possibilities and act upon them. Notwithstanding the role of personal abilities in education, the interviews showed that women act as agents in deciding their educational trajectories, what their limits were and what they could realistically achieve. The decisions young women took are not separate from their families. In fact, sometimes they are a result of parents' own dreams that failed.

The dream to go to university is a dream that stands alone and seems divorced from the steps that lead up to it. Women and families did not identify with the university track and could not locate themselves within it. Both parents and children lacked confidence in their abilities and were more comfortable within the realm of technical education, which did not challenge their social and financial abilities. Technical education has developed to be the poor people's fallback position. They could aspire to go to university, but if they failed to take that route, which was almost always the case, they still had their bastion of technical education. They were aware that their position was disadvantaged relative to other graduates with more education, but again, with pervasive unemployment, they were not that different from university graduates; their prospects in the labour market were until that point uncertain.

Notes

1 Commercial education has always been regarded as the a natural continuation of the 'female cultural schools' that targeted women before the 1952 revolution and afterwards, while males were encouraged to attend technical industrial and agricultural schools (Hyde 1978; see also Boktor 1963: 66).

2 See www.iht.com/articles/1994/02/16/egyptduc.php? page=1).

3 Currently schools are divided into: 1) public governmental; 2) government language; 3) Arabic private; 4) private language; 5) experimental Arabic; 6) schools that prepare for foreign certificates; 7) cooperative schools; 8) foreign language schools (Ammar 2005: 163).

4 Supreme Council of Universities in Egypt, www.scu.eun.eg/wps/portal.

5 Al Azhar is Egypt's oldest mosque and university and the second oldest in the Islamic world for the study of Sunni theology and Islamic law. Its pre-university education system runs in parallel with the public educational system. It consists of four years of primary stage, a three-year preparatory stage and three years of secondary stage. The Al Azhar education system is supervised by the Supreme Council of the Al Azhar Institution.

6 Industrial education is the most prestigious, followed by agricultural then commercial.

7 In recent years, higher institutes have fallen into disfavour (Helal 2007).

8 'Affiliation and Open University: the universities' means of developing resources', Rose El Youssef, 658, 20 September 2007, p. 6.

9 Informality is used here to describe employment activities linked to industrial and service work in settings in which the job holders are not 'recognized, supported, or regulated by the government and even when they are registered' (Mokhtar and Wahba 2002: 133).

References

Abdel-Fadil, M. (1980) *The Political Economy of Nasserism*, Cambridge: Cambridge University Press.

— (1982) 'Educational expansion and income distribution in Egypt', in G. Abdel-Khalek and R. Tignor (eds), *The Political Economy of Income Distribution in Egypt*, New York and London: Holmes and Meier.

Abou-Zeid, H. (1970) *The Education of Women in the UAR*, Cairo: Cairo University Press.

Amer, M. (2009) 'The Egyptian youth labour market school to work transition: 1988–2006', in R. Assaad (ed.), *The Egyptian Labour Market Revisited*, Cairo: American University in Cairo, pp. 177–218.

Ammar, H. (2005) *Derassat fil Tarbiya Wal Thaqafa: Al Siyak Al Tarikhy Letatweer Al Ta'leem el Massry – Mashahed men Al Mady Wal Hader Wal Mustaqbal* [Studies in education and culture: the historic context of the development of Egyptian education], Cairo: Al Dar Al Arabiya Lil Kitab (in Arabic).

Angliker, H. W. (1935) *Industrial and Commercial Education in Egypt*, Cairo.

Antoninis, M. (2001) *The Vocational School Fallacy Revisited: Technical secondary schools in Egypt*, Mediterranean Programme Series, Robert Schuman Centre, European University Institute.

Assaad, R. (2006) *Unemployment and Youth Insertion in the Labour Market in Egypt*, Cairo: Egyptian Centre for Economic Studies.

— (2009) 'Labour supply, employment, and unemployment in the Egyptian economy 1988–2006', in R. Assaad (ed.), *The Egyptian Labour Market Revisited*, Cairo: American University in Cairo Press, pp. 1–52.

— (2010) *Human Development and the Labour Market*, Cairo: Human Development Project, Institute of National Planning.

Assaad, R. and M. Arntz (2005) 'Constrained geographical mobility and gendered labour market outcomes under structural adjustment: evidence from Egypt', *World Development*, 33(3): 431–54.

Assaad, R. and G. Barsoum (2007) *Youth Exclusion in Egypt: In Search of 'Second Chances'*, Wolfensohn Centre for Development and Dubai School of Government.

Assaad, R. and A. Elbadawy (2007) *Private and Group Tutoring in Egypt: Where is the Gender Inequality?*, Paper presented at the workshop on 'Gender, work and family in the Middle East and North Africa', Mahdia, Tunisia, 7–11 June.

Assaad, R. et al. (2009) 'Women in the Egyptian labour market: an analysis of developments, 1988–2006', in R. Assaad (ed.), *The Egyptian Labour Market Revisited*, Cairo: American University in Cairo, pp. 219–59.

— (2010) 'The effect of domestic work on girls' schooling: evidence from Egypt', *Feminist Economics*, 16(1): 79–128.

Ayubi, N. (1980) *Bureaucracy and Politics in Contemporary Egypt*, St Anthony's College/Ithaca Press.

Becker, R. and A. E. Hecken (2009) 'Why are working class children diverted from university? An empirical assessment of the diversion thesis', *European Sociological Review*, 25(2): 233–50.

Bertaux, D. and I. Bertaux-Wiame

(1981) 'Life stories in the baker's trade', in *Biography and Society: The life history approach in the social sciences*, Beverly Hills, CA: Sage, pp. 169–89.

Birdsall, N. and L. O'Connell (1999) *Putting Education to Work in Egypt*, Working Paper no. 5, Washington, DC: Carnegie Endowment for International Peace.

Boktor, A. (1963) *The Development and Expansion of Education in the United Arab Republic*, Cairo: American University in Cairo Press.

Boudon, R. (1974) *Education, Opportunity, and Social Inequality: Changing Prospects in Western Society*, New York: John Wiley & Sons.

Bourdieu, P. (1977) *Outline of a Theory of Practice*, trans. R. Nice, Cambridge: Cambridge University Press.

CAPMAS (Central Agency for Public Mobilisation and Statistics) (2000) *Statistical Yearbook, Egypt's Population*, Cairo: CAPMAS.

Cochran, J. (1986) *Education in Egypt*, London: Croom Helm.

El-Tawila, S. et al. (1999) *Transitions to Adulthood: A National Survey of Egyptian Adolescents*, Cairo: Population Council.

— (2001) *The School Environment in Egypt: A Situation Analysis of Public Preparatory Schools*, Cairo: Population Council.

Elbadawy, A. and R. Assaad (2009) *Analysis of Educational Gender Inequalities in Egypt*, Cairo: GERPA.

ETF (European Training Foundation) and World Bank (2005) *Integrating TVET into the Knowledge Economy: Reform and Challenges in the Middle East and North Africa*, Washington, DC.

Faksh, M. A. (1976) 'An historical survey of the educational system in Egypt', *International Review of Education*, 22: 234–44.

Fathi, S. E. S. (1991) *Ektessadiat al Tawazof Al Hokoumy fi Misr* [Economics of government employment in Egypt], in E. S. A.-M. Ghanem (ed.), *Al Tawazof Al Hokoumy fi Misr: Al Hader wa E'dad al Mustaqbal* [Government employment in Egypt: the present and the future], Cairo: Centre for Political and Strategic Studies (in Arabic), pp. 111–68.

Galal, A. (2002) *The Paradox of Education and Employment in Egypt*, Egyptian Centre for Economic Studies.

Gill, I. S. and S. P. Heynemann (2000) 'Arab Republic of Egypt', in I. S. Gill et al. (eds), *Vocational Education and Training Reform*, Oxford: Oxford University Press, pp. 401–29.

Heggy, A. I. (1991) *Nizam Al Ta'leem fi Misr* [The education system in Egypt], Cairo: Dar Al Nahda Al Arabiya (in Arabic).

Helal, H. (2007) *Strategic Planning in Higher Education*, www.cairo. daad.de/imperia/md/content/ kairo/tempus/saad_sharaf_-_ higher_education_enhancement_strategy_in_egypt.pdf, accessed 5 June 2008.

Hinnebusch, R. (2003) 'Conclusion', in R. El-Ghonemy (ed.), *Egypt in the Twenty First Century: Challenges for Development*, London and New York: Routledge Curzon, pp. 221–51.

Hopwood, D. (1982) *Egypt: Politics and Society 1945–1981*, London: George Allen and Unwin.

Hozayin, R. (2007) 'Higher education in Egypt – basic statistics', Personal communication.

Hyde, G. D. M. (1978) *Education in Modern Egypt: Ideals and Realities*, London, Henley and Boston, MA: Routledge and Kegan Paul.

Ibrahim, B. L. and H. Wassef (2000) 'Caught between two worlds: youth in the Egyptian hinterland', in R. Meijer (ed.), *Youth and Culture in the Arab World*, London: Curzon.

Ibrahim, S. E. (1982) 'Social mobility and income distribution in Egypt, 1952–1977', in G. A.-K. and R. Tignor (eds), *The Political Economy of Income Distribution in Egypt*, New York and London: Holmes and Meier, pp. 375–435.

Imam, S. S. (1985) *The Social Origins of the Infitah Elite in Egyptian Society: 1974–1980*, MA thesis, Cairo University.

Institute of National Planning (1963) *Research Project on Employment and Unemployment among the Educated*, Cairo: Author.

Langsten, R. and T. Hassan (2009) *Education Transitions in Egypt*, Paper presented at the annual meeting of the Population Association of America.

Lloyd, C. et al. (2003) 'The impact of educational quality on school exit in Egypt', *Comparative Education Review*, 47(4): 444–67.

Megahed, N. (2002) *Secondary Education Reforms in Egypt: Rectifying Inequality of Educational and Employment Opportunities*, American Institute of Research and the Academy for Educational Development.

Mensch, B. et al. (2003) *Gender-role Attitudes among Egyptian Adolescents*, www.popcouncil. org/pdfs/councilarticles/sfp/ SFP341Mensch.pdf, accessed 1 May 2010.

Metwalli, F. B. (1989) *Al Ta'leem El Fanni: Tarikho, Tashri'ato, Eslaho wa Mostaqbalahu* [Technical education: its history, legislation, reform and future], Alexandria: Dar El Ma'aref Al Game'ia (in Arabic).

Ministry of Education (2006) *National Strategic Plan for Pre-University Education Reform in Egypt 2007/08–2011/12*, knowledge.moe.gov.eg/arabicabout/ strategicplan, accessed 12 June 2010.

Mokhtar, M. and J. Wahba (2002) 'Informalization of labour in Egypt', in R. Assaad (ed.), *The Egyptian Labour Market in an Era of Reform*, Cairo: American University in Cairo Press, pp. 131–57.

NCERD (National Council for Education Research and Development) (2001) *Education Development: National Report of Arab Republic of Egypt from 1990 to 2000*, Cairo: Author.

Population Council (2011) *Survey of Young People in Egypt (SYPE)*, Cairo: Author.

Radwan, S. (2007) 'Good jobs, bad jobs and economic performance: the view from the Middle East and North Africa', in P. Paci and P. M. Serneels (eds), *Employment and Shared Growth*, Washington, DC: World Bank, pp. 37–52.

Richards, A. (1992) *Higher Education in Egypt*, World Bank.

Richards, A. and J. Waterbury (1996) *A Political Economy of the Middle East*, Boulder, CO: Westview Press.

Sanyal, B. C. et al. (1982) *University Education and the Labour Market in the Arab Republic of Egypt*, Oxford: Unesco International Institute for Educational Planning/ Pergamon Press.

Specialized National Councils (1980) *Al Ta'leem Al Fani Wa Dawro Fi E'dad al Qowa Al Amla* [Technical education and its role in preparing manpower], vol. 9: *Egypt till the Year 2000* (in Arabic).

Suliman, E. and S. El-Kogali (2001) *Poverty, Human Capital and Gender: A Comparative Study of Yemen and Egypt*, Economic Research Forum Working Paper Series.

Sultana, R. G. (2008) *The Girls' Education Initiative in Egypt*, Amman: UNICEF.

Szyliowicz, J. (1973) *Education and Modernization in the Middle East*, Ithaca, NY, and London: Cornell University Press.

Waterbury, J. (1983) *The Egypt of Nasser and Sadat: The political economy of two regimes*, Princeton, NJ: Princeton University Press.

Williamson, B. (1987) *Education and Social Change in Egypt and Turkey*, London: Macmillan Press.

World Bank (2002) *Education Sector Review: Progress and Priorities for the Future* (no. 24905-EGT), Human Development Group Middle East and North Africa.

— (2003) *Unlocking the Employment Potential in the Middle East and North Africa: Toward a new social contract*, Washington, DC: World Bank.

— (2007) *Improving Quality, Equality, and Efficiency in the Education Sector: Fostering a Competent Generation of Youth*, Washington, DC: World Bank.

12 | Disability in transition in Egypt: between marginalization and rights

HEBA HAGRASS

Egypt was among the very first of the few countries to have signed and ratified the Convention on the Rights of Persons with Disabilities (CRPD). This was signed in April 2007 and ratified one year later. The ratification raised many hopes for dramatic positive changes in disability policy and practice. The spirit of the 25 January revolution has affected everyone and informs my desire to now address the necessary steps to meet the demands and aspirations of disabled people in Egypt, a group that has long been marginalized.

This chapter deals with three major dimensions to the problems of both understanding and then transforming the lives of disabled people in Egypt. The first dimension is the magnitude of the problem and trying to understand its scale. The evidential base for accounting for the numbers of disabled in Egypt is riddled with inconsistencies, and the government of Egypt (GoE) has always attempted to minimize the numbers. The second dimension is the attempt to describe the situation of disabled people and the services provided for them. This reveals how very marginalized and neglected they are. The third dimension is the need to review existing legislation that deals with disability and reveal how poorly it is implemented – how policy is formulated around a concept of charity and how CRPD should be used to instigate a paradigm shift towards a more rights-based approach to disability. Such an approach would help provide disabled people with their rights to healthcare, education and employment. Finally, I will shed light on the standpoint disabled people took during the 25 January revolution and how the 'revolution's spirit' has affected the way many disabled people think, and how their aspirations have increased.

Reveal or conceal?: disability figures in Egypt

A game of hide and seek has long been played between GoE and Egyptians with regard to the numbers of people who are disabled and the types of disability they may have. One of the reasons for this has been to minimize the 'problem' of disability, not only in

Egypt but more generally in the Arab world. The UN estimates that 20–25 per cent of the populations of developing countries are disabled (DESA 2000; Baylies 2002). However, most developing countries report differently, and this is also the case in Egypt. In 1976 the Central Agency for Mobilization and Statistics (CAPMAS) used a six-category 'disability' typology in its population census to estimate the numbers of disabled people in Egypt. The categories were: blind, had the use of only one eye, deaf and dumb, had lost one or both upper limbs, had lost one or both lower limbs, or suffered mild mental retardation. Based on these criteria the data showed that 111,324 people could be categorized as disabled out of a total population of 36,626,204; three people per thousand (El-Messiri 1995; Fahmy 1995). Surprisingly, in 1976 the United Nations Statistics Division agreed with these figures, which led to the belief that they were using CAPMAS statistics and did not conduct any investigations of their own. In 1981, the UN reported 1.6 per cent as the total number of disabled people in Egypt (United Nations Statistics Division 1981; Bonnel 2004). By 1986, the census was estimating the population at 48.2 million, of whom 191,235 – or four per thousand – were disabled (Emam 1994; El-Messiri 1995). One year later the Polio Institute declared the proportion of disabled people to be 11 per cent (El-Messiri 1995; Shukrallah et al. 1997). In 1989, the ILO announced that Egypt had a total population of 55 million, of whom 5 million suffered from mental retardation, deafness, blindness and/or physical impairment (El-Messiri 1995). In the same year, the Pan-Arab Project for Child Development estimated the proportion of disabled people as only 1.54 per cent of the population studied (Magdi and Shukrallah 1993; El-Messiri 1995).

The CAPMAS census of 1996 expanded its 'disability' categories to eleven. They included people described as 'deaf', 'dumb', suffering from 'polio', experiencing 'total or partial paralysis', and/or suffering 'other impairments'. The survey concluded that 284,188 people out of a population of 59,273,082, or 4.8 per thousand, should be classified as disabled (CAPMAS 1996; JICA 2002). It is also worth noting that the CAPMAS data showed that the number of disabled men far exceeds that of disabled women: 64.4 per cent as against 35.6 per cent. This might be due to the numerous armed conflicts that have plagued Arab countries over recent years (Ahmed 1997) or the fact that impairment among women is less likely to be reported (Hagrass 1998). The 1996 UN estimate for Egypt is 4.4 per cent (DESA 2000; Bonnel 2004). In 2006 the latest CAPMAS census reported that out of a population of 72,798,031 a total of 475,576 were disabled, 305,216 males, 170,360 females, i.e. 6.5 per thousand.

The wide discrepancies among estimates of the incidences of impairment may be attributed to several factors. First, the criteria according to which 'impairment' may be reported are vague. Secondly, in most of these studies, the reporting of impairment is left to disabled people themselves or, in most cases, family members. Hence, there is reliance on subjective understandings of what constitutes impairment or a 'disability'. Thirdly, in each of these studies, the criteria pertaining to impairment are usually considered of minor importance. This led to them being taken lightly or ignored (Fahmy 1995, 2000; Ahmed 1997; Shukrallah et al. 1997). Finally, the categories in the various censuses are not the same. Even the CAPMAS categorizations mentioned above are very limited and do not include all types of impairment. International estimates suggest that around 10 per cent of the population in most nation-states may be considered 'disabled'; these figures have only limited reliability (Fahmy 2000). What is certain is that the number of disabled people in Egypt is not small. So if I use this modest estimate and add to it the number of the immediate family members of the disabled person, given an average family of five, this means that disability has a direct impact on 30 per cent of the Egyptian population. Another major problem with such low figures is that they camouflage the real size of the problem, and government allocation of resources to any problem depends on its size. If the statistics for the disability problem are as low as they appear, government spending and provision of services to disabled people will remain minimal, as it is at present. Therefore, it is extremely important to set the record straight concerning the size of the problem in Egypt to enable us to demand that the government ensure the rights of disabled people through proper service provision, adequate allocation of resources and the enactment of appropriate laws and policies.

The services provided by governmental and non-governmental institutions

The second important dimension that I want to explore to facilitate an understanding of the marginalization of disabled people in Egypt is how disability is catered for and dealt with in Egypt. In doing this I want to discuss the different institutional roles and the services these institutions provide, as well as the coverage and quality of provision. This examination also contributes to an understanding of the formulation of the 'problem' of disabled people – whether disability should be addressed by charity or a compensatory or rights-based approach.

The Egyptian government addresses the issue of impairment by providing services for its disabled citizens. There are different types of services, ranging from purely medical to social care. Although disability and disabled people are supposed to be the responsibility of the state there is usually cooperation between governmental and non-governmental institutions in a number of areas. Here I will discuss the role of both types of institution to highlight their contributions in helping to alleviate the problem of disability. Although all the ministries in Egypt are involved in providing services for disabled people, varying in the type of service they offer and its value in the lives of disabled people, I discuss only those major ministries that deeply affect their lives. The major ministries are the Ministry of Education (MoE), the Ministry of Higher Education (MoHE), the Ministry of Transportation (MoT), the Ministry of Management Development (MoMD), the Ministry of Social Affairs (MoSA), and the Ministry of Manpower and Migration (MMM). MoSA is considered the main body responsible for disabled people. Under its umbrella, the relationships among the various ministries are synchronized and regulated.

Governmental institutions

First, the Ministry of Education (MoE) plays a major part in the care of disabled children. It provides special education programmes for various types of impairment. Its Special Education Programme was established by Ministerial Decree no. 156/1969, by which all rules of admission, curricula and examinations and other regulations are controlled (El-Banna 1989). It states that disabled children are those who have sensory, mental or physical impairments, based on a medical examination, and are unable to pursue their education in regular schools. Thus, it is a completely medical approach which controls the inclusion of people in these special schools. By the same token these criteria serve as the guidelines for the exclusion of disabled children from mainstream schooling (Hak 2000).

There are three types of special schools. The first are the Schools of Light, which accept blind children from the age of six to eight and educate them until they reach university level. There are eighty-eight schools in total, mainly in big cities like Cairo, Alexandria, and so on (El-Messiri 1995; MoE 2007). Secondly, there are the Hope Schools for deaf children. There are about 232 of these schools (MoE 2007). Deaf children are given three years of vocational training after they finish their primary schooling. They are not allowed to access other educational alternatives. This is an added discrimination against deaf people. Thirdly, the Intellectual Development Schools accept children with mild mental impairments. Their schooling lasts for seven years, followed by vocational training. In 1994, the number of these schools reached 691, plus thirty-five classes in non-governmental institutions (El-Messiri 1995). NGOs and institutions that have boarding schools fall under the supervision of both MoSA and MoE (El-Banna 1989; El-Messiri 1995). There has been a significant increase in the number of public schools dealing with special education, operating on a full-board basis (El-Messiri 1995).

Lastly, physically impaired people are expected to join regular schools. No special schools are provided for them. On the other hand, there are no special accessibility measures undertaken for their comfort. Only the Poliomyelitis Institute has a school affiliated to it. Children with physical impairments, who manage to use school premises as they are, survive and stay in school. If they cannot manage to cope with schools that are not built to assist the mobility of the physically impaired, they drop out (El-Banna 1989). However, there are other impairments that are totally excluded from the educational process in both special and regular schools, such as psychosocial differences, autism, multiple impairments, specific hearing difficulties, and dyslexia and communication disorders (Hak 2002; MoE 2007). It is noteworthy when examining the education of disabled children that both the medical and compensatory approaches to understanding disability shape the ideas behind the way in which they are allowed to enter education. With this limited capacity of special education schools and the increasing numbers of disabled children, the overwhelming majority of disabled children of school age are unable to access educational services.

Most of the schools I have mentioned are in urban areas, which force disabled children to leave their families at an early age to live in institutions in order to gain access to education, as these schools are mainly affiliated to care institutions. In total, there are 804 state-owned special education schools catering for only 36,808 children, meaning that fewer than 1.8 per cent of disabled children receive appropriate educational services (MoE 2007).

Although inclusive education is very limited in Egypt, in 2007 Egypt started to consider the inclusion of disabled children in public schools, and planned its educational five-year strategy accordingly. This strategy aims 'to include an additional 10 percent, or a total of 152,800, of the estimated number of children with mild impairments in mainstream basic education gradually over the five year plan period, distributed to schools in all districts' (ibid.). This is a major paradigm shift from the compensatory to a rights-based approach in education. However, all experts are eagerly awaiting the evaluation of the strategy, which is not expected to be favourable.

Secondly, the Ministry of Higher Education (MoHE) offers its educational services to all students who have obtained an accredited or recognized secondary school certificate. Disabled students can apply like anyone else, or resort to special concessions made for disabled students. One of the major concessions is that disabled students can join art universities if they attain only a minimum grade of 50 per cent in their secondary certificate (MoHE 2006). However, some schools and departments are allowed to deny a disabled student her/his right to enter a certain school under their departmental regulations. Thus, a disabled student could be allowed to join Cairo University's Arts School English Department while another might not be admitted to Ain Shams University (Elarabi 2009). In 2007, the number of disabled students in higher education was approximately 1.9 million. Thus, the figures show that the number of disabled students enrolled in higher education is very limited. Disabled services in all universities are minimal and are allocated to students only if they ask for them (ibid.).

Thirdly, the Ministry of Transportation (MoT) grants free public transport to disabled people in government-owned vehicles. However, with increasing privatization, 80 per cent of the means of transportation is now excluded from this deal. Thus, disabled people have to wait for hours to be able to ride on one of these state-owned buses. It is important to note that no modifications have been made to public means of transportation to cater for the various needs of different impairments. Physical barriers have not been removed to facilitate easy access to means of transportation. A disabled person who can use the facilities is at an advantage; but the large number of others who cannot still have the unsolved problem of moving from one place to another. This inaccessibility of government transportation services costs the disabled person and her/his family a lot of money. Furthermore, lack of accessibility to streets and various buildings makes it extremely difficult to move around (Michailakis 1997). Hence, the disabled person who needs certain types of accessibility endures social isolation and marginalization. We can see, therefore, that while the ministry has given concessions to disabled people on some services, it has not tackled the problem of accessibility at all. Physically disabled people are also granted a certain amount of tax exemption on modified cars for their private transport (El-Banna 1989). Thus, an individual compensatory approach is very evident in the type of services the

MoT provides. Either the disabled person can use the services as they are and accept the compensation of a free ride, or s/he is left to his or her own devices. It is (partial and rather insignificant) financial assistance or nothing.

Fourthly, recently the Ministry of Management Development (MoMD) has played a modest role in the recruitment of disabled people since the withdrawal of the government from the 'guaranteed employment scheme' initiated by President Nasser during the 1952 revolution. MoMD took up the role of providing the public sector with its employees as needed. This is usually done through advertisements placed in the major newspapers outlining the job specifications. Twenty years ago, this used to be done twice a year; with the coming of the new millennium, it is happening every few years. The intervals between the advertisements are getting larger. Disabled as well as non-disabled people are allowed to apply. A 5 per cent quota is observed in recruitment, but this does not mean that the public sector has filled its quota at every different level. Also, *wasta*, a form of nepotism depending on influential friends, is another major source of recruitment in the public sector.

> Employment is a constitutional right given to all Egyptian citizens.
> Work is a right, a duty and an honour guaranteed by the state ...
>
> (Egypt [Arab Republic] 1999: Article 13, p. 3; my translation)

The Ministry of Manpower and Migration (MMM) was the ministry responsible for the 'general employment scheme' mentioned above. The MMM's role diminished during the 1980s, to one of catering only for the employment of disabled people in the private sector through its numerous Manpower offices, covering the entire country. It is the Manpower offices which perform the executive role, implementing the ministry's policies. Placement and employment are on a 'first come first served' basis. Each type of degree or skill has its own registry (Qandil 1989; Gad 2002). For example, there is a registry for intermediate educational degrees, another for higher degrees. Some people get placed in a few months while others have to wait for a number of years. It all depends on supply and demand. However, if the disabled person gets the job her/himself, they simply need to go to the Manpower office to obtain a nomination letter, thus bypassing the queues.

Lastly and most importantly there is the Ministry of Social Affairs (MoSA). MoSA was established in 1939, since when it has been responsible for groups in need of special care, including disabled people, as part of its concept of social development (El-Messiri 1995). Since the 23 July revolution this ministry has had three names: Ministry of Insurance and Social Affairs (MISA), Ministry of Social Affairs (MoSA) and Ministry of Social Solidarity (MoSS) respectively. I have used the title MoSA throughout this research in order not to cause confusion, although it is not the latest name. I use it because it has remained the one most commonly in use, and because it was during the period when it was so named that major disability laws were formulated. In 1950, Social Welfare Law no. 116/1950 included a special chapter dealing with the rehabilitation and vocational training of disabled people (Fahmy 1995, 2000). In 1962, a General Department for Social Rehabilitation was established. Its major task was to draw up policies and plan for the rehabilitation of disabled people at the national level. In 1980, the department grew to become part of the Secretariat of Social Development (El-Messiri 1995).

MoSA provides its services through a variety of outlets. First, rehabilitation centres at the provincial level. MoSA has ninety-six rehabilitation centres throughout Egypt and provides services to more than 25,000 people, supposedly in different age categories, to prepare them for employment. However, these centres offer their services mainly to disabled adults. The vast majority of disabled children do not have access to these services. It also provides its clients with basic mobility aids, physiotherapy and financial assistance for the duration of their training. It is important to mention that the available services are limited to traditional vocational training such as basketry, carpet-making and the like. Furthermore, the vocational rehabilitation personnel are mostly unqualified (El-Banna 1989; El-Messiri 1995). There are other rehabilitation centres which offer services for the severely disabled as well as boarding facilities. There are only seven centres catering to 200 persons. Their services and their boarding facilities are extremely poor. Disabled people living in these places have nowhere else to turn. Secondly, the provision of sheltered vocational training workshops is limited. There are only seventeen such centres in the various governorates, which offer services to 10,000 disabled people per year (El-Banna 1989; Nosseir 1990).

Non-governmental institutions

Non-governmental institutions and trade unions are an important element in the provision of assistance to meet the needs of disabled people. Although the new Egypt Association Law 84/2002 was passed to restrict the formation of new NGOs, the number of organizations working in disability all over the country has reached 1,500. The services they provide vary, from rehabilitation to education, training and employment (Nosseir 1990). Most of these organizations are care providers for, rather than organizations of, disabled people. The only organizations considered to be specifically of disabled people are those controlled by parents of 'intellectually' disabled children, and a very few for visually impaired and blind people.

Officially, MoSA is responsible for the rehabilitation and training of disabled people. Nevertheless, it has mostly delegated this role to NGOs concerned with disability. This is because it could not on its own perform the necessary tasks. Yet the ministry is still responsible for providing NGOs with trainers and specialists to carry out the training programmes needed by disabled people within these organizations. Thus, the type and quality of training depends on the organization's financial capacity, which is usually very modest. The training programmes are usually very traditional, including basketry, carpet weaving and knitting and suchlike. This type of training is not based on any assessment of employment market needs but only on what is available and what is possible in organizations. Thus, the training provided for disabled people is often insensitive to employment market needs. The result is that disabled people are unable to compete in the labour market on their own.

From 1900 to 1980 the trend in dealing with disabled people was one of segregation and removal from society by placing them in special schools, residential institutions, separate vocational training courses and sheltered workshops (El-Messiri 1995). This clearly exemplifies the individualistic and compensatory approaches to disability. From the start of the 1980s, new forms of rehabilitation programmes were developed, such as Community-Based Rehabilitation programmes (CBR). These programmes have been funded by UN agencies and various international organizations for training trainers in CBR and other outreach programmes. However, the unsustainable funding these organizations receive creates only short-term programmes. Very few have provided a consistent model for training. Although offering such services to a number of disabled people represents a change, there has been no concomitant shift in concepts of or approaches to dealing with disability. Disability is still dealt with from the medical therapeutic perspective (Kabbara 1997; Shukrallah et al. 1997).

Following the 1952 revolution, trade unions were tamed. They played only a minimal role in the lives of their members (Posusney 1997); their contribution was virtually nil to the lives of their disabled members.

Little or no power was permitted to be in the hands of any people's organizations; trade unions had no influence or effective power. However, the revolution of 25 January, the rise in the number of demonstrations and their demands, and the increased independence of trades unions raise the possibility of establishing a new agenda for action and a commitment to delivering an effective disability policy (Hagrass 2010).

My review of service provision for the disabled indicates how poor it is and how it follows an individual materialist model where the blame falls on the disabled person's bodily deficiency. In addition, a charity approach is dominant among NGOs, making use of the Islamic culture that prevails and encouraging faithful people to give charity to less fortunate people as a way of pleasing the Creator. Despite the limitations and poor quality of these services, disabled people who have access to them are considered lucky. This is because 80 per cent of the rehabilitation services are based in Cairo while only 20 per cent of disabled people live there. There is thus an enormous gap between the demand and the accessibility of services (Nosseir 1989; El-Banna 1989).

Legislation

The third dimension is related to government intervention through legislation and policies to protect the rights of certain groups such as disabled people. Egypt has a long history of this that dates back to even before the 1952 revolution (Fahmy 1995, 2000). It is evident that greater emphasis was placed on disability after the 1952 revolution, when the government issued several legislative measures intended to secure 'care' and security for disabled individuals. There is a variety of articles and clauses in various laws. Among these were Labour Law no. 91/1959, Rehabilitation Law no. 14/1959, Social Welfare Law 133/1964, Health Insurance Law 75/1964 and Law 62/1964, which regulates NGOs' activities (MoSA 1987; El-Messiri 1995).

In the seventies, during Sadat's reign, MoSA gathered the previously scattered rights of disabled people prescribed under various laws under Rehabilitation Law 39/1975 and its amendment, Law 49/1982 (MoSA 1987). Nevertheless, the most recent amendment dates back to 1982, almost three decades ago. Although the Rehabilitation Law is a MoSA law, most of it deals with employment of disabled people and its implementation falls to MMM. According to this law:

> All private employers who employ 50 employees or more and fall under
> Law no. 137/1981 for employment [MMM 1981], whether they operate in
> one area or one country or in dispersed places, are required to employ

disabled people nominated to them by Manpower offices according to their registers. This is done on the basis of five per cent of the number of employees working in that unit. This rule applies to all branches of the company. However, employers can fill the quota without the nomination of Manpower offices on one condition, which is to register their disabled employees in the Manpower office register. In all cases, any firm which employs a disabled person must send a notification letter to their Manpower office [Art. 9]. Disabled people who have received a rehabilitation certificate are required to constitute five per cent of the total number of employees in each of the civil service units of the state, its public organizations, and public sector ... [Art. 10] (MoSA 1987: 5; my translation)

Some sections of the law specify that certain jobs – low-grade and menial jobs – be reserved for the employment of disabled people. This shows that there is inherent discrimination even in the law that is expected to protect them. Penalties are applied to whoever violates the law. Fines and, in extreme cases, imprisonment are specified (Art. 10) (ibid.; Qandil 1989). The fine, which is a maximum of LE100 (approximately £10 sterling) (Art. 16), is a very small amount of money that no employer would have difficulty in paying, and although imprisonment is mentioned, no literature has recorded its actual use. Even the public sector does not abide by the quota (Gad 2002). In this way even the one piece of legislation loses credibility. Furthermore, some sections of the disabled population are treated more favourably under the law than others. For example, Article 3 specifies that disabled citizens on a 'low income' are entitled to free rehabilitation. Those on higher incomes are not included, thus emphasizing the concepts of discrimination and 'otherness' which are the root of disabled people's oppression. The law mainly addresses the needs of disabled people who are looking for an occupation and nothing else (El-Messiri 1995).

The initial site of oppression in this law starts with the definition of disability adopted in it. The disabled person is defined as:

Any individual who becomes unable to depend on him/herself when performing his/her work or another [type of work] or remain in it, his/her inability to do so being the result of physical, mental, sensory or congenital impairment. (MoSA 1987: 1; my translation)

Furthermore, rehabilitation is described as:

Providing social, psychological, medical, educational, and professional assistance to all disabled people and their families to enable them to overcome the negative consequences resulting from impairment. (Ibid.: 1; my translation)

Both definitions focus exclusively on the functional limitations of the individual and their assumed diminished job performance and inability to function without professional support. Thus, the major concern is that impairment is the sole cause of the problems associated with disability, with no reference whatsoever to environmental and cultural barriers. The underlying assumptions are that disabled people's experiences and life chances are determined exclusively by their impairments. At the societal level, the individualization, medicalization and objectification of disabled people's lives remain in force. By continually enforcing and reinforcing the orthodox, essentially negative views of disability and, by implication, of people with impairments, the interpretations of both disability and rehabilitation in Egyptian law inadvertently perpetuate discriminatory attitudes and prejudices towards people with impairments, even though it is supposed to defend their rights. Significantly, there is no reference to disability issues in any other Egyptian legislation. This absence makes policy-makers generally forget and/or ignore disability issues, as they are viewed as someone else's problem. As a result the powerlessness that characterizes the experience of many disabled people's lives goes unchallenged.

In conclusion, it is clear from a review of the institutions, governmental as well as non-governmental, laws and policies relating to disability that they follow a deeply entrenched individual medical model of disability. The disabled person is perceived through her/his impairment and has a 'take it or leave it' choice: adapt to the system or be on your own. However, modest glimpses of an alternative social model are emerging through the influence of the international community in both rehabilitation and education. The role of local and international NGOs has been important in the emerging shift in thinking about disability in Egypt. The chances of disabled people accessing services are very limited. They stand in line with many other disadvantaged groups. No proper, well-developed policies are devised for disabled people. Thus, disabled people are left uncared for, with very little concern shown by the government. The cost of such neglect is borne by disabled people and their families. Therefore, there is an urgent need for new strategies to pressure the new government to fulfil its duties and obligations towards 10 per cent of its citizens. As Greve (2009: 7) puts it: 'much work remains to convert legal rights into genuine social and economic rights for disabled people'.

The boiling point: pre-revolutionary and revolutionary times

Egypt has always been among the first countries to acknowledge any international obligations, agreements, declarations and/or conventions. Although the CRPD entered into force in May 2008, as I am a member of the monitoring committee following up the Convention's implementation in the Arab region, I can say that its impact is not yet felt in the disability field in Egypt. Furthermore, the GoE has not yet provided its first disability state report, which was supposed to be presented by 2010 to the CRPD monitoring committee. However, after the ratification many NGOs dealing with disability started extensive awareness-raising campaigns. The focus was to disseminate the Convention's paradigm shift from a charity-based approach to disability to a rights-based approach. These campaigns were geared towards disabled people, professionals working with disabled people and society in general. They covered many governorates in Egypt. Thus, raising awareness of the many rights and levels of support given to disabled people by CRPD acted as an eye-opener for all parties involved, highlighting the role that needs to be played.

At the beginning of 2010, and as a result of the ratification of the Convention, the minister of state for family and population (MoSFP) decided to revive the idea of drafting a new law for disability and disabled people based on the new concepts of the Convention, instead of the obsolete existing law. As a result, a committee of experts was formed, of which I was a member. A new law was drafted. Although the work of the committee was undertaken *in camera*, news spread, so that by February a large number of disabled people were protesting in front of the People's Assembly. They slept for days in the streets to demonstrate the inhumane conditions under which disabled people were living in Egypt. Entrenched poverty, soaring unemployment and indecent conditions of living were their main motivation (Abdel-Baky 2010; Hassan 2010): 'We've been totally marginalized by the government for decades now [...] All laws stating disabled people's rights are inefficient, and unfortunately the government considers us as second-grade citizens' (Hassan 2010).

This was the first time in history that disabled people spoke loudly for themselves about their needs and unattained rights. As a result the MoSFP made public the work of the committee to raise hopes for the implementation of new changes. The committee members were interviewed in several TV programmes to talk about the new law. Furthermore, a number of meetings were organized by the ministry for the committee to talk to the protesters about the new changes and future prospects to calm their anger and to convince them to end their sit-in protest. These tactics succeeded in dispersing the protesters, but the demonstrations were a landmark: the first open protest of disabled people in Egyptian history.

At the first glimmers of the 25 January revolution long-neglected disabled people were to be found in Tahrir Square. They lined up with frustrated youth, poor workers, government clerks, peasants, poor housewives, pensioners, Muslims and Christians and the rest of the suffering population to demand change (Omar 2011). The first main slogan of the revolution was *'Taghyer, Horreya, 'Adala Egtema'eya'* ('change, liberty, social justice'). This slogan eloquently summarized most of the needs of the Egyptian people. Disabled people had had enough of being second-grade citizens, and now they demanded social justice with the rest of the population. On 10 February 2011, Day 16 of the revolution, a number of disabled youths affiliated to an NGO called the 7 Million Disabled proclaimed the message: 'under the slogan of "Egypt for all" we have decided [...] to join forces with the youth of the revolution against the existing regime to fulfil the dream of dignity for each Egyptian which has been long stolen along with freedom; as a partner and not as a burden'. Furthermore, disabled people were among the first groups to meet with the Supreme Council of the Armed Forces (SCAF) after Mubarak had been deposed. They laid down a number of clear-cut demands. This time they were not asking for but demanding their rights. Among their major demands were quality health insurance, suitable rehabilitation and training, proper implementation of the law governing their employment, a solid welfare system, representation in parliament, and the formation of a high council for disabled people (Elewah 2011; Elmeshad 2011). The demands were followed up by a demonstration exclusively of disabled people in front of the People's Assembly, where they carried handwritten and printed signs listing their demands. One of the banners said: 'Handicapped youth were part of the revolution – so where are our rights?' (Mohsen and Afify 2011). In this way it is clear that disabled people intend to be part of the 'change' and 'social justice' agenda demanded by the revolution.

References

Abdel-Baky, M. (2010) 'Pavement of discontent: the spot in front of the People's Assembly is becoming a favoured meeting point for airing grievances', *Al-Ahram Weekly*, 994, 15–21 April, weekly.

ahram.org.eg/2010/994/eg7.htm, accessed 6 April 2011.

Ahmed, M. (1997) *Al-Khidmah Al-Ijtimaᶜiyah fe Majal Reᶜayat Al-Mucakin* [Social service in the area of care for disabled people],

Alexandria: Dar El-Me^crefah Al-Jami^cayah.

Baylies, C. (2002) 'Disability and the notion of human development: questions of rights and capabilities', *Disability and Society*, 17(7): 725–39.

Bonnel, R. (2004) 'Poverty reduction strategies: their importance for disability', digitalcommons.ilr. cornell.edu/gladnetcollect/442, accessed 6 September 2009.

CAPMAS (Central Agency for Mobilization and Statistics) (1996) *The Distribution of the Disabled Persons in Egypt according to Age Categories, Disability, and Gender in the Republic Governorates according to the Final Results of Population Count 1996*, Arab Republic of Egypt: General Agency and Statistics (in Arabic)

DESA (Department of Economic and Social Affairs Development) (2000) *The United Nations and Disabled Persons: the first 50 years*, www.un.org/esa/socdev/ enable/dis50yoo.htm, accessed 28 November 2009.

Egypt (Arab Republic) (1999) *The Constitution of the Egyptian Arab Republic*, 8th edn, Cairo: Al-Amireya Printing (in Arabic).

— (2002) *Law no. 84 of 2002 on Non-Governmental Societies and Organizations with Its Executive Regulations*, www.egyptlaws.com/ comprehensive01.html, accessed 12 December 2009.

Elarabi, N. (2009) *Higher Education of Students with Special Needs and Challenges in Egyptian Universities*, Council for International Exchange of Scholars, Africa Higher Education Collaborative (AHEC), Improving Equity and Access to Higher Education in Africa.

El-Banna, A. (1989) 'The situation of the disabled in Egypt', in *The Capabilities and Needs of Disabled Persons*, November, Amman.

Elewah, A. (2011) 'Saba Melione Mu'ak Mansiyoun wa Ya'eshoun Hayat Gheair Insaneya' [Seven million disabled persons forgotten and living inhumane lives], *Moheet*, 8 March, www. moheet.com/show_news.aspx? nid=453644&pg=1, accessed 2 April 2011.

Elmeshad, M. (2011) 'Revolution realization: the deaf and mute protest', *Al-Masry Al-Youm*, 13 March, www.almasryalyoum. com/en/node/351235, accessed 2 April 2011.

El-Messiri, S. (1995) *The Status of Social Policy towards Disability in Egypt*, Unpublished research funded by IDRC.

Emam, Y. H. (1994) *A Guidebook of Organizations for the Care and Rehabilitation of the Disabled in Egypt*, Cairo: Union of Organizations for the Care of People with Special Needs.

Fahmy, M. (1995) *Al-Selouk Al-Ijtema^ci Lil Mu^cakin* [The social behaviour of the disabled], Alexandria: Dar El-Me^crefah Al-Jami^cayah.

— (2000) *Waki^c Re^cayat Al- Mu^cakin fe Al-Wattan Al-^carabi* [The situation of care for disabled persons in the Arab homeland], Alexandria: Al-Maktab Al-Jame^ci Al-Hadith.

Gad, H. (2002) 'Dawr Wizarat Al-Kowah Al-^cAmilah wa Al-Hijra fi Damj Zawi Al-Ehteyagat Al-Kassah fi Souk Al-^cAma' [The Role of the Ministry of Manpower and Migration in integrating people with special needs in the labour market], in *Integrating People with Special Needs in Economic and Social Life*, October, Cairo.

Greve, B. (2009) *The Labour*

Market Situation of Disabled People in European Countries and Implementation of Employment Policies: A Summary of Evidence from Country Reports and Research Studies, Report prepared for the Academic Network of European Disability experts (ANED), www.disability-europe.net/content/pdf/ANED%20Task%206%20final%20report%20-%20final%20version%2017-04-09.pdf, accessed 21 October 2009.

Hagrass, H. (1998) Gender, Disability and Marriage, Master's degree thesis, American University in Cairo.

— (2010) Re-Marketing the Unmarketables: A Critical Examination of Disabled People's Experience in Egypt's Labour Market, PhD thesis, University of Leeds.

Hak, H. (2000) Inclusion without Support or Differentiation – a Case Study of Five Children with Severe Learning Difficulties, International Special Education Congress, 24–28 July, Manchester, www.isec2000.org.uk/abstracts/papers_h/hak_1.htm, accessed 14 October 2009.

Hassan, A. (2010) 'Egypt: the disabled protest for more rights, better jobs', Los Angeles Times World, 6 April, latimesblogs.latimes.com/babylonbeyond/2010/04/egypt-disabled-rights-protest.html, accessed 6 April 2011.

JICA (Japan International Cooperation Agency) (2002) Country Profile on Disability: Arab Republic of Egypt, digitalcommons.ilr.cornell.edu/gladnetcollect/233, accessed 21 August 2009.

Kabbara, N. (1997) 'Lebanon', in J. Hodges-Aeberhard and C. Raskin (eds), Affirmative Action in the Employment of Ethic Minorities and Persons with Disabilities, Geneva: ILO, pp. 45–53.

Magdi, S. and A. Shukrallah (1993) Childhood Disability in Egypt, Plan of Operation 1994–2000, Egypt: UNICEF.

Michailakis, D. (1997) Government Action on Disability Policy: A Global Survey, digitalcommons.ilr.cornell.edu/gladnetcollect/231, accessed 6 September 2009.

MMM (Ministry of Manpower and Migration) (1981) Law 137of 1981 for Issuing Employment Law according to the latest Amendments, 23rd edn, Cairo: Al-Amireya Printing (in Arabic).

MoE (Ministry of Education) (2007) Chapter 12, in National Strategic Plan for Pre-University Education Reform in Egypt (2007–2012).

MoHE (Ministry of Higher Education) (2006) Law Regulating Universities and Its Executing Regulations according to the Latest Amendments, 24th edn, www.scu.eun.eg/wps/wcm/connect/7aa3cf804f25256bb9abf9ebc94876d6/tanzeem.pdf?MOD=AJPERES&CACHEID=7aa3cf804f25256bb9abf9ebc94876d6, Cairo: Al-Amiriya (in Arabic).

Mohsen, A. and H. Afify (2011) 'Disabled people's protests block Qasr al-Aini', Al-Masry Al-Youm, 3 March, www.almasryalyoum.com/en/node/337875, accessed 2 April 2011.

MoSA (Ministry of Social Affairs) (1987) Law 39 of 1975 for the Rehabilitation of the Disabled, Cairo: Al-Amireya Printing (in Arabic).

Nosseir, N. (1989) 'Women and disability', in The Capabilities and Needs of Disabled Persons, November, Amman.

— (1990) 'Disabled females: Egypt', in Disabled Women, Vienna.

Omar, M. (2011) 'The spring of the Egyptian revolution', *Al-Masry Al-Youm*, 30 March, www.almasryalyoum.com/en/node/351235, accessed 2 April 2011.

Posusney, M. (1997) *Labor and the State in Egypt: Workers, Unions, and Economic Restructuring*, New York: Columbia University Press.

Qandil, A. (1989) 'Social aspects of the disabled in the western Asia region and the importance of their modification', Paper presented to conference on 'The capabilities and needs of disabled persons' for ESCWA, Amman.

Shukrallah, A., H. Mostafa and S. Magdi (1997) *The Current State of the Disability Question in Egypt: Preliminary National Study*, Presented to the North–South Inserm Network.

UNDP (United Nations Development Programme) (2008) *The Egypt Human Development Report 2008*, www.undp.org.eg/Portals/0/2008%20Egypt%20Human%20Development%20Report%20Complete.pdf, accessed 18 May 2008.

United Nations Statistics Division (1981) *Demographic and Social Statistics*, unstats.un.org/unsd/Demographic/sconcerns/disability/disform.asp?studyid=177., accessed 28 November 2007.

— (2011) 'Shabab Masry mu'ak Youkarreroun Al-nezoul Ela Midan El-Tahrir Lel Musharakah' [Disabled Egyptian youth decide to get down to Tahrir Square for participation], Afra7algomhoor, 2 February, afra7algomhoor.blogspot.com/2011/02/7.html, accessed 2 April 2011.

Contributors

Asef Bayat is professor of sociology and Middle East studies at the University of Illinois, Urbana-Champaign. He was previously the director of the International Institute for the Study of Islam in the Modern World (ISIM), and held the chair of Society and Culture of the Modern Middle East at Leiden University, Netherlands. His research includes social movements and non-movements, Islam and the modern world and international development. His recent books include *Making Islam Democratic: Social Movements and the Post-Islamist Turn* (2007); (with Linda Herrera) *Being Young and Muslim: Cultural Politics in the Global South and North* (2010); and *Life as Politics: How Ordinary People Change the Middle East* (2010).

Moushira Elgeziri is consultant to the Ford Foundation's Higher Education Programme. Before that, she managed the Middle East Research Awards Programme (MEAwards) of the Population Council Regional Office in Cairo for fifteen years. She has also been consultant to, among others, the Woman and Memory Forum, Cairo, the Middle East Research Programme (MERC), Tunis, and the Arab Council for Social Sciences, Beirut. Her publications include two co-edited Arabic volumes on *The State of Social Science in the Arab World* and *The Role of Education in Building Citizenship*.

Rabab el Mahdi is assistant professor of political science at the American University in Cairo. Her publications include (as co-editor, with Philip Marfleet) *Egypt: The Moment of Change* (2009) and *Empowered Participation or Political Manipulation? Civil Society and the State in Egypt and Bolivia* (2011).

Saker el Nour is a sociology research student at the University of Paris Ouest-Nanterre. He is an associate teacher of rural sociology at South Valley University in Upper Egypt. His research interests include social dynamics in rural Egypt, life history and issues of agricultural transformation. He has conducted field research in Egypt, Tunisia and Morocco.

Kamal Fahmi is an assistant professor of sociology at the American University in Cairo. He has a PhD in social work from McGill University, Canada. His professional endeavour aims at making research an integral part of action. In addition to teaching he works as an international consultant in child protection and education and participative action-research methodologies. He has implemented and managed field projects and programmes targeting children at risk in Egypt, Canada and West Africa.

Heba Hagrass is an advocate for the rights of persons with disabilities in Egypt, the Arab region and worldwide. She acted as the women's representative on the former board of the Arab Organization of Disabled People from 1998 to 2008 and was chosen as one of two disabled people to sit on the Higher Council of Rehabilitation in Egypt since 2008. She helped draft Article 6 in the Convention on the Rights of Persons with Disabilities and was lead consultant in drafting the National Strategy of People with Disabilities for Egypt.

Ali Kadri is senior research fellow at the Middle East Institute, the National University of Singapore.

Reem Saad is director of the Middle East Studies Center at the American University in Cairo. She is a social anthropologist with research interests in rural society, historical anthropology, issues of public culture and ethnographic film. Her publications include *Social History of an Agrarian Reform Community in Egypt* (1989) and (as co-editor, with Nicholas Hopkins) *Upper Egypt: Identity and Change* (2004).

Dalia Wahdan is an assistant professor of anthropology and comparative urban studies at the Foundation for Liberal and Management Education in Pune, India. She also instructs trainers for academic and professional capacity-building workshops in Egypt, Saudi Arabia and Afghanistan. Her recent publications include *Governing Livelihoods in Liberalizing States* (2010) and *The Politics of Planning Egypt's New Settlements* (forthcoming). She has recently completed a post-doctoral fellowship at Jawaharlal Nehru University in Delhi.

Index

Economic Reform and Structural Adjustment Programme, 117

education, 28, 115–16; commercial, 191–218 (changing to, 211, 212; elimination of, 208; feminization of, 191; girls in, 203; questioning need for, 205; vulnerability of, 213); costs of, 83–4; drop-out, 83, 198–9, 210 (complexity of reasons for, 199; of disabled children, 223); expansion of university education, 203; gender equality in, 57; general secondary (as site of privilege, 212; associated with sickness, 211); inequality in, 201; of women and girls, 108, 109, 192, 193–4, 198–9, 213; private, 196–7, 198 (universities, 197); related to marginality, 195–203; school admission age reduced, 118; school building programme in Egypt, 193; seen as matter of social justice, 192; shift system in schools in Egypt, 195; special schools for disabled children, 222–3; spending cut, 66; technical, 192–3, 202, 204, 211 (association with poverty, 207–8; choice of the poor, 199–203; problems of, 201, 205–8); university (related to labour market, 212; women's non-identification with, 214); vocational, 191; World Bank's view of, 208 *see also* universities

Egypt, 5, 20, 35, 38, 45; as importer of wheat, 58; as recipient of US aid, 31; economic growth of, 59–61; examples of marginality in, 98–111; food crisis in, 93; growth in, 56; human development index, 61; hydrocarbon exports of, 59; Law 116/1950, 226; Law 14/1959, 228; Law 91/1959, 228; Law 62/1964, 228; Law 75/1964, 228; Law 133/1964, 228; Law 39/1975, 228; Law 137/1981, 228; Law 49/1982, 228; Law 96/1992, 79, 80–4, 86, 162–3; Law 101/1992, 197; Law 84/2002,

226; marginalization of small peasantry in, 72–96; production of poverty in, 55–71; uprising in, 3, 7, 93 (*see also* 25 January revolution); *see also* Upper Egypt

Egyptian Labour Market Panel Survey (ELMPS), 191

Escobar, Arturo, 20

exclusion, 3–13, 62; extreme, 169; from global economy, 19; use of term, 14, 56 (in Egyptian context, 55)

exploitation concept of, 133

Facebook social network, 3–4, 133; role in Egyptian uprising, 143

families, children's moral responsibility towards, 209–11

fatalism, 16

Fathi, Hassan, 99–100; *Architecture for the Poor*, 99

favelas, Brazilian, 25–6; as domain of alternative sociality, 20–1

Fayyoum, Egypt, artists' community in, 25

female-headed households, 65, 84

feudalism, 17, 78

fingernails, long, uses of, 179

fire-eating activity of street children, 185

firewood, collection of, 88

firka, production of, 102–3

Food and Agriculture Organization (FAO), report on rural poverty in Egypt, 163–4

food prices, 58; rise of, 93

food riots, 58

foreign languages, students' fear of, 211

Foucault, Michel, 21

Freire, Paulo: *Education for Critical Consciousness*, 171; *Pedagogy of the Oppressed*, 171

Friedmann, John, 18, 20

Gabes region (Tunisia), 72, 73, 74, 86–9, 89–90, 92

gated communities, 25

gates of cities, lack of, 129

Japan, economic growth of, 22
Jordan, 45, 59; as American protectorate, 31; offensive against Palestinians, 31; poverty in, 60

Kafr El-Sawar factory (Egypt), 141
'Karima', 106–9
Kefaya movement (Egypt), 134
Ketan Tanta factory (Egypt), 141

labour flow in Cairo, 10 *see also* migration, of labour
land: access to, 9; distribution of, 85; fragmentation of holdings, 84–5; 'organized looting' of, 114; reclamation of, 115; scams involving, 117; shift in land-holding categories, 64
land market, liberalization of, 74
land occupations, 9
land reform, 50, 78
landholdings: dispossession of, 86; inequality in, 77
landlessness, 105–6
landowners, beneficiaries of reforms, 64–5
Lenin, V. I., 30
Lewis, Oscar, 16
liberalization, 75, 79–80
Libya, military intervention in, 5
lifestyles, abnormal, 25; choice of, 20
literacy classes for women, 108
'lumpenproletariat', 18

Maghrabi, Ahmed Al-, 155
Mahalla al-Kobra, Egypt, 72; labour protests in, 134, 140
Makhsous road transport, 125
maktab al fanny lil wazeer, el, 138
malnutrition, 55; of children, in Yemen, 31
'Manara' village, 105
Mansour, Mohamed, 121
marginality, 3–13; and capitalism, 17–20; and modernity, 16–17; as catalyst of change, 109; as curse or cure, 14–27; as opportunity, 14; as site of liberation, 20; as space

of opportunity, 25; as terrain of vitality, 21; ascribed, 105–9; chosen, 100; concept of, 6–7 (contradictory character of, 105; definition of, 97–111; efficacy of, 8; extension of, 19–20; in Middle East, 16; trajectory of, 15–16); enjoyment of, 109; extreme, 169, 184; goals of, 22; in education, 195–203; opposed to mainstream, 17; societal, 97–8; spatial, 97–8 (and livelihoods, 127–30); treated negatively, 14; use of term, 56 (in Egyptian context, 55)
marginalization, 97, 133; in Egypt, 76–9; of disabled people, 221; of small farmers, 90–2, 93; of small peasantry, 72–96; opposed to marginality, 18; related to commercial education, 191; resistance to, 133–47; spatial, in Cairo, 112–31
Markaz village (Egypt), 148
marriage, informal, 22
Marx, Karl, 17, 18, 22
Mazny, Nabil El-, 121
Megawir, Husayn, 142
Memmi, Albert, 21
Mer Villager Unit (Egypt), 156–8, 159–60, 161, 162
Mervat, girl from the street, 185–6
methodology, of street work, 174–5; challenges of, 173–7
microbuses, 129; management of, 127–8
middle class, expansion of, 195
migration: of labour, 78, 130 (Asian, 32–3); of Muslims, in Europe, 16, 23 (first-generation, 23); of oasis peasantry, 92; rural to urban, 15, 115, 195
militarism, 29–30, 38, 47
militarization, 7
military, in Egypt, role of, 11
military courts, 12
military expenditure, 68
millennium development goals (MDG), 57, 61

About Zed Books

Zed Books is a critical and dynamic publisher, committed to increasing awareness of important international issues and to promoting diversity, alternative voices and progressive social change. We publish on politics, development, gender, the environment and economics for a global audience of students, academics, activists and general readers. Run as a co-operative, Zed Books aims to operate in an ethical and environmentally sustainable way.

Find out more at:

www.zedbooks.co.uk

For up-to-date news, articles, reviews and events information visit:

http://zed-books.blogspot.com

To subscribe to the monthly Zed Books e-newsletter, send an email headed 'subscribe' to:

marketing@zedbooks.net

We can also be found on **Facebook**, **ZNet**, **Twitter** and **Library Thing**.